Arab American Biography

ARAB AMERICAN BIOGRAPHY

Volume I: A-J

Loretta Hall and Bridget K. Hall

AN IMPRINT OF THE GALE GROUP

DETROIT · SAN FRANCISCO · LONDON
BOSTON · WOODBRIDGE, CT

ARAB AMERICAN BIOGRAPHY

by Loretta Hall and Bridget K. Hall

Staff

Christine Slovey, *U•X•L Editor*
Carol DeKane Nagel, *U•X•L Managing Editor*
Thomas L. Romig, *U•X•L Publisher*

Mary Beth Trimper, *Production Director*
Evi Seoud, *Assistant Production Manager*
Cindy Range, *Production Assistant*

Cynthia Baldwin, *Product Design Manager*
Barbara Yarrow, *Graphic Services Director*
Michelle DiMercurio, *Art Director*

Shalice Shah-Caldwell, *Permissions Associate*

The Graphix Group, *Typesetter*

Library of Congress Cataloging-in-Publication Data

Hall, Loretta.
    Arab American Biography / Loretta Hall and Bridget K. Hall.
      p. cm.
    Includes bibliographical references and index.
    Contents: v. 1. A-J—v. 2. K-Z.
    ISBN 0-7876-2953-7 (set).—ISBN 0-7876-2954-5 (vol. 1).—ISBN 0-7876-2955-3 (vol. 2)
    1. Arab Americans—Biography—Juvenile literature. [1. Arab Americans—Biography.] I. Hall, Bridget K. II. Title
    E184.A65H35 1999
    920'.0092927073--dc21
    [B]

                      98-54466
                          CIP
                          AC

Contents

VOLUME 1: A–J

Entries by Field of Endeavor ix
Entries by Ethnicity. xv
Reader's Guide. xix
Words to Know xxi
Timeline of Arab American Events
   and Accomplishments. xxix

Abboud, Joseph. 1
Abdul, Paula 6
Abinader, Elmaz 12
Abourezk, James 18
Abraham, F. Murray 26
Abraham, Spencer. 33
Addes, George F. 39

Joseph Jamail Jr. Reproduced by permission of the Corbis Corporation.

Anka, Paul 48

Assali, Nicholas S. 55

Atiyeh, Victor 63

Bishallany, Antonio 68

Blatty, William Peter 75

Bourjaily, Vance 82

Chaib, Elie 90

Corey, Elias James 95

Dale, Dick 102

DeBakey, Michael Ellis 110

El-Baz, Farouk 117

El Guindi, Fadwa 126

Elias, Rosalind 134

Farah, Mansour 141

Farr, Jamie 146

Flutie, Doug 152

Gibran, Kahlil. 162

Habib, Philip 171

Haggar, Joseph Marion. 178

Haje, Khrystyne 184

Halaby, Najeeb 189

Hamid, George A., Jr. 197

Hanania, Raymond G. 204

Hazo, Samuel John. 212

Howar, A. Joseph. 219

Jabara, Abdeen. 228

Jabara, James 234

Jacobs, Joseph J. 242

Jamail, Joseph, Jr.. 250

Johns, Ralph 257

Index . . . . **xxxv**

VOLUME 2: K-Z

Entries by Field of Endeavor ix
Entries by Ethnicity. xv
Reader's Guide. xix
Words to Know xxi
Timeline of Arab American Events
    and Accomplishments. xxix

Kamali, Norma. 265
Kasem, Casey 271
Kassar, Mario. 277
Lightner, Candy 284
Maloof, Sam 290
McAuliffe, Christa 296
McNichol, Kristy 305
Mitchell, George John 311
Nader, Ralph 317
Naff, Alixa 324
Najimy, Kathy 329
Nye, Naomi Shihab 334
Orfalea, Gregory Michael 342
Orfalea, Paul 348
Rahal, Bobby. 355
Rahall, Nick Joe, II 363
Rihani, Ameen Ferris 368
Rizk, Salom. 374
Robbie, Joseph 382
Roosevelt, Selwa 390
Said, Edward W. 399
Salhany, Lucie 407
Sarofim, Fayez Shalaby. 411
Seirawan, Yasser 417
Shadid, Michael A. 424

Shalala, Donna 433

Shalhoub, Tony 440

Shammas, Anton 444

Sununu, John Henry 451

Tayback, Vic 458

Thomas, Danny 463

Thomas, Helen A. 472

Thomas, Marlo 478

Thomas, Tony 485

Tiffany 491

Tiny Tim 498

Yokich, Stephen P. 504

Zappa, Frank 510

Index xxxv

Entries by Field of Endeavor

Bold numerals indicate volume numbers.

Anthropology

El Guindi, Fadwa **1:**126

Naff, Alixa **2:**324

Art

Gibran, Kahlil **1:**162

Maloof, Sam **2:**290

Business

Farah, Mansour **1:**141

Haggar, Joseph Marion **1:**178

Halaby, Najeeb **1:**189

Hamid, George A., Jr. **1:**197

Howar, A. Joseph **1:**219

Norma Kamali. Reproduced by permission of AP/Wide World Photos.

Orfalea, Paul **2:**348

Salhany, Lucie **2:**407

Sarofim, Fayez Shalaby **2:**411

Dance
Abdul, Paula **1:**6

Chaib, Elie **1:**90

Education and Academia
Abinader, Elmaz **1:**12

Bourjaily, Vance **1:**82

McAuliffe, Christa **2:**296

Said, Edward W. **2:**399

Shalala, Donna **2:**433

Shammas, Anton **2:**444

Fashion
Abboud, Joseph **1:**1

Kamali, Norma **2:**265

Film and Theater
Abraham, F. Murray **1:**26

Blatty, William Peter **1:**75

El Guindi, Fadwa **1:**126

Elias, Rosalind **1:**134

Farr, Jamie **1:**146

Haje, Khrystyne **1:**184

Kassar, Mario **2:**277

McNichol, Kristy **2:**305

Najimy, Kathy **2:**329

Shalhoub, Tony **2:**440

Tayback, Vic **2:**458

Thomas, Danny **2:**463

Thomas, Tony **2:**485

Government and Politics

Abourezk, James **1:**18

Abraham, Spencer **1:**33

Atiyeh, Victor **1:**63

Habib, Philip **1:**171

Halaby, Najeeb **1:**189

Mitchell, George John **2:**311

Rahall, Nick Joe, II **2:**363

Roosevelt, Selwa **2:**390

Shalala, Donna **2:**433

Sununu, John Henry **2:**451

History

Naff, Alixa **2:**324

Orfalea, Gregory Michael **2:**342

Journalism and Communications

Hanania, Raymond G. **1:**204

Rihani, Ameen Ferris **2:**368

Roosevelt, Selwa **2:**390

Said, Edward W. **2:**399

Sununu, John Henry **2:**451

Thomas, Helen A. **2:**472

Labor Unions

Addes, George F. **1:**39

Yokich, Stephen **2:**504

Law

Jabara, Abdeen **1:**228

Jamail, Joseph, Jr. **1:**250

Literature

Abinader, Elmaz **1:**12

Blatty, William Peter **1:**75

Bourjaily, Vance **1**:82

Gibran, Kahlil **1**:162

Hanania, Raymond G. **1**:204

Hazo, Samuel John. **1**:212

Nye, Naomi Shihab **2**:334

Orfalea, Gregory Michael **2**:342

Rihani, Ameen Ferris **2**:368

Rizk, Salom. **2**:374

Said, Edward W. **2**:399

Shammas, Anton **2**:444

Medicine
Asssali, Nicholas S. **1**:55

DeBakey, Michael Ellis **1**:110

Shadid, Michael A.. . . . . **2**:424

Military
Jabara, James. **1**:234

Music
Abdul, Paula **1**:6

Anka, Paul. **1**:48

Dale, Dick **1**:102

Elias, Rosalind **1**:134

Tiffany **2**:491

Tiny Tim **2**:489

Zappa, Frank. **2**:510

Philanthropy
Flutie, Doug **1**:152

Haggar, Joseph Marion **1**:178

Jacobs, Joseph J. **1**:242

Jamail, Joseph, Jr.. . . . . **1**:250

Rahal, Bobby. **2**:355

Thomas, Danny **2**:463

Political and Social Activism

Abourezk, James **1**:18

Addes, George F. **1**:39

Jabara, Abdeen. **1**:228

Johns, Ralph **1**:257

Kasem, Casey **2**:271

Lightner, Candy **2**:284

Nader, Ralph. **2**:317

Rihani, Ameen Ferris **2**:368

Said, Edward W. **2**:399

Shadid, Michael A.. . . . . **2**:424

Shammas, Anton **2**:444

Thomas, Marlo. **2**:478

Radio

Kasem, Casey **2**:271

Religion

Bishallany, Antonio **1**:68

Science and Technology

Corey, Elias James **1**:95

El-Baz, Farouk **1**:117

Jacobs, Joseph J. **1**:242

Sports

Flutie, Doug **1**:152

Rahal, Bobby. **2**:355

Robbie, Joe. **2**:382

Seirawan, Yasser **2**:417

Television

Farr, Jamie **1**:146

Haje, Khrystyne **1**:184

McNichol, Kristy **2**:305

Najimy, Kathy **2**:329

Salhany, Lucie **2**:407

Shalhoub, Tony **2**:440

Tayback, Vic **2**:458

Thomas, Danny **2**:463

Thomas, Marlo. **2**:478

Thomas, Tony **2**:485

Entries by Ethnicity

Marlo Thomas. Reproduced by permission of Archive Photos, Inc.

Bold numerals indicate volume numbers.

Assyrian-American

Hazo, Samuel John **1**:212

Egyptian-American

El-Baz, Farouk **1**:117

El Guindi, Fadwa. **1**:126

Sarofim, Fayez Shalaby **2**:411

Jordanian-American

Salhany, Lucie **2**:407

Lebanese-American

Abboud, Joseph **1**:1

Abinader, Elmaz. **1**:12

Abourezk, James. **1**:18

Abraham, Spencer **1:**33

Addes, George F. **1:**39

Assali, Nicholas S. **1:**55

Blatty, William Peter **1:**75

Bourjaily, Vance **1:**82

Chaib, Elie **1:**90

Corey, Elias James **1:**95

Dale, Dick **1:**102

DeBakey, Michael Ellis **1:**110

Elias, Rosalind **1:**134

Farah, Mansour **1:**141

Farr, Jamie **1:**146

Flutie, Doug **1:**152

Gibran, Kahlil **1:**162

Habib, Philip **1:**171

Haggar, Joseph Marion **1:**178

Hazo, Samuel John **1:**212

Jabara, Abdeen **1:**228

Jabara, James **1:**234

Jacobs, Joseph J. **1:**242

Jamail, Joseph, Jr. **1:**250

Kamali, Norma **2:**265

Kasem, Casey **2:**271

Kassar, Mario **2:**277

Lightner, Candy **2:**284

Maloof, Sam **2:**290

McAuliffe, Christa **2:**296

Mitchell, George John **2:**311

Nader, Ralph **2:**317

Naff, Alixa **2:**324

Najimy, Kathy **2:**329

Orfalea, Gregory Michael **2:**342

Orfalea, Paul **2**:348

Rahal, Bobby **2**:355

Rahall, Nick Joe, II **2**:363

Rihani, Ameen Ferris **2**:368

Robbie, Joseph **2**:382

Roosevelt, Selwa **2**:390

Salhany, Lucie **2**:407

Shalala, Donna **2**:433

Shalhoub, Tony **2**:440

Shammas, Anton **2**:444

Sununu, John Henry **2**:451

Tayback, Vic **2**:458

Thomas, Danny **2**:463

Thomas, Helen A. **2**:472

Thomas, Marlo **2**:478

Thomas, Tony **2**:485

Tiffany **2**:491

Tiny Tim **2**:498

Yokich, Stephen **2**:504

Palestinian-American

Hanania, Raymond G. **1**:204

Howar, A. Joseph **1**:219

Nye, Naomi Shihab **2**:334

Said, Edward W. **2**:399

Shammas, Anton **2**:444

Syrian-American

Abdul, Paula **1**: 6

Abraham, F. Murray **1**:26

Anka, Paul **1**:48

Atiyeh, Victor **1**:63

Bishallany, Antonio **1**:68

Halaby, Najeeb. **1:**189

Hamid, George A., Jr. **1:**197

Johns, Ralph **1:**257

Naff, Alixa **2:**324

Orfalea, Gregory Michael **2:**342

Rizk, Salom. **2:**374

Seirawan, Yasser **2:**417

Shadid, Michael A.. . . . . **2:**424

Tayback, Vic **2:**458

Reader's Guide

*A*rab American Biography profiles seventy-five noteworthy Americans who trace their ancestry to one or more nations belonging to the League of Arab States. Included are prominent men and women of Egyptian, Jordanian, Lebanese, Palestinian, and Syrian descent, both living and deceased. Profilees are notable for their achievements in fields ranging from social activism to sports, academia to politics, entertainment to science, and religion to the military. Early immigrants as well as contemporary figures are among those included. Black-and-white photographs accompany most entries.

In *Arab American Biography* readers will find:

- Seventy-five alphabetically arranged biographical entries, each focusing on the childhood and formative experiences of the subject as well as his or her career; the background and traditions held by the subject; and how events in the Middle East affected the subject.

Doug Flutie. Reproduced by permission of Archive Photos, Inc.

- Sidebars that provide information on people, events, historical background, and other fascinating facts related to the entry.

- Cross references to individuals covered elsewhere in the volumes noted by "(see entry)" references following the person's name.

- Sources for further reading or research at the end of each entry.

Each volume of *Arab American Biography* begins with a standard table of contents as well as listings of biographical entries by ethnicity and by field of endeavor; a timeline of important events in Arab American history and major achievements of profilees; and a glossary of terms used in the text. Volumes conclude with a subject index so students can easily find the people, places, and events discussed throughout the set.

Related Reference Sources

Arab American Almanac explores the history and culture of the major ethnic groups comprising Arab America. The *Almanac* is organized into eighteen subject chapters covering work, education, family, religion, language, politics, and performing arts. The volume contains more than sixty black-and-white photographs and maps, a glossary, and a cumulative subject index.

Arab American Voices presents twenty full or excerpted speeches, diary entries, newspaper accounts, novels, poems, memoirs, and other materials by and about Arab Americans. Each entry is accompanied by an introduction and boxes explaining some of the terms and events to which the speech refers. The volume is illustrated with black-and-white photographs and drawings and features a cumulative subject index.

Comments and Suggestions

We welcome your comments on *Arab American Biography* as well as your suggestions for persons to be featured in future editions. Please write, Editors, *Arab American Biography*, U•X•L, 27500 Drake Rd., Farmington Hills, Michigan 48331-3535; call toll-free: 1-800-877-4253; fax to (248) 699-8066; or send e-mail via http://www.galegroup.gale.com.

Words to Know

Kahlil Gibran. Reproduced by permission of the Corbis Corporation (New York).

A

Abscam: Short for Abdul Scam; a Federal Bureau of Investigation (FBI) sting operation in which an undercover agent dressed as an Arab tried to bribe several members of the U.S. congress.

American-Arab Anti-Discrimination Committee (ADC): A group started by Senator James Abourezk in 1980 to improve the image of Arab Americans in the United States, to fight racism against Arab Americans, and to reunite the Arab American community.

Arab: A person born in Arabia, or in one of the countries belonging to the League of Arab States; a person whose primary language is Arabic.

Arab-Israeli conflict: Arabs and Jews have been fighting in the Middle East since the early part of the twentieth century when European Jews began settling in the region of Palestine, hoping to establish an independent Jewish state there. The movement for such a state gained the support of the United States, the Soviet Union, and other Western countries after the Holocaust of World War II (1939–45), during which German Nazis killed millions of Jews. But a group of neighboring Arab countries including Egypt, Iraq, Jordan, Lebanon, and Syria opposed the creation of Israel because they saw the Jews as outsiders who were taking Arab land. The region remains in a constant state of struggle as both sides use military force to protect their interests in the area. Major contested areas include the Old City of Jerusalem, the West Bank of the Jordan River, and the Gaza Strip along Israel's southwest Mediterranean coast.

C

Christianity: Religion that believes Jesus was the son of God. The Christian religion is based on Jesus' teachings and the teachings of the Bible.

Civil Rights: The nonpolitical rights of a citizen, as in the rights of personal liberty guaranteed to U.S. citizens: equal treatment and equal access to housing, free speech, employment, and education.

Communism: An economic theory in which there is no private property—all goods are owned by the community, not by individuals. During the twentieth century, many countries (e.g., the Soviet Union and the Peoples Republic of China) were controlled by governments based on the communist ideas of German philosopher Karl Marx (1818–1883). In practice, the governments were harsh dictatorships that outlawed churches and repressed personal freedoms.

Coptic Church: Based in Egypt, the Coptic Church is a Christian denomination that separated from the Roman Catholic Church in the fifth century; Roman Catholics believe that Jesus was both human and divine, while Copts believe that Jesus was exclusively divine. Its services are conducted in Arabic, Greek, and the Coptic language, an otherwise dead language based on ancient Egyptian.

D

Democrat: A member of one of the two major political parties in the United States. Democrats advocate a strong federal government and more spending for programs and agencies to help improve the lives of citizens.

Discrimination: Treatment of people based on their belonging to a certain race, ethnicity, or class rather than on personal merit.

Druse: The Druse (also spelled Druze) is a Muslim sect that differs from other Muslim sects in several ways: it does not use mosques (church buildings) or imams (a mosque's prayer leader), and its members believe in reincarnation.

E

Embargo: To ban all trade or trading of certain goods with another country.

Exile: Removal from one's native country, often forced but sometimes voluntary.

F

Famine: An extreme shortage of food, causing starvation within a certain area.

G

Gaza Strip: A strip of land along Israel's southwest Mediterranean coast occupied by Egypt from 1948 until 1956, when Israel occupied the territory for a year. Israel pulled out in 1957, then annexed the strip again during the 1967 Six Day War. Violence between the Palestinians and Israelis continued in the region. In May 1994 the two groups signed an accord giving the Palestinians self-rule in some sections of the Gaza Strip.

Golan Heights: An area along the border of Israel and Syria that originally belonged to Syria and was annexed by Israel in the 1967 Six Day War.

Guerilla war: Nontraditional warfare in which the enemy is harassed with surprise raids. Guerilla warfare is fought by small bands of soldiers operating within territory held by the enemy; the guerillas usually try to frighten enemies with surprise raids, disrupt their communications, and destroy their supplies.

Gulf War: A 1990–91 war in the Persian Gulf region in which Iraq invaded Kuwait; when Iraqi leader Saddam Hussein refused to withdraw his troops, the United Nations (UN) authorized military action. UN forces (largely American) drove the Iraqi invaders out of Kuwait in 1991.

H

Holy Land: A place of religious pilgrimage. The region occupied by Israel and Palestine is called the Holy Land by Jews, Christians, and Muslims.

Homeland: One's birthplace, or the country one regards as home.

I

Indigenous: Originating, being made, or growing naturally in a particular environment.

Iran-Contra Affair: A covert scheme exposed in 1986 in which money from secret U.S. arms sales to Iran was channeled to support the Contra rebels who were trying to overthrow the Communist Sandinistan government in Nicaragua. Both the sale of arms to Iran in exchange for hostages and the sending of money to the Contras violated U.S. public policy.

Iran Hostage Crisis: On November 4, 1979, Islamic militants seized the U.S. embassy in Tehran, Iran, capturing sixty-six staff members. The hostages were taken in retaliation for the United States allowing the unpopular and deposed Shah of Iran to come to America for medical treatment and to avoid trial in his own country. The militants quickly released thirteen hostages, promising to release the rest if the United States would send the Shah back to Iran. President Jimmy Carter refused. Although the Shah died in Egypt in July 1980, the hostages were not released until January 20, 1981—the day Carter left the presidency.

Islam: The Muslim religion, based on belief in Muhammad as the chief and last prophet of God. Islam follows the teachings of the Qur'an (also spelled Koran). The word "Islam" is sometimes used to mean the worldwide Muslim community.

Israel: A Jewish state established in the Palestine region in 1948. Until the late 1980s, neighboring Arab countries had refused to recognize Israel as a legal state (with the exception of Egypt, which recognized it in 1979). The region remains in a state of constant struggle over the territory.

J

Jerusalem: One of the world's oldest cities, known to have been inhabited as early as 4000 B.C. The city is considered holy by Jews, Christians, and Muslims. At the start of the Arab-Israeli wars in 1948 Jerusalem was divided into the Old City and the New City. Israel's capital was the New City while the Old City was under Jordanian control. During the Six Day War of 1967, Israel annexed the Old City as well.

Judaism: The Jewish religion, based on the teachings of the Old Testament of the Bible and Talmud.

K

Kismet: Meaning fate or destiny, "kismet" comes from the Arabic word *qismah* (portion or lot).

L

League of Arab States (Arab League): Formed in 1945, this group of Arab countries opposed the creation of Israel in the Palestinian region, and used military action to try to force Israelis out of the area. The first countries to join the League were Egypt, Iraq, Lebanon, Saudi Arabia, Syria, Trans-Jordan (which became Jordan), and Yemen. Countries that joined later include Algeria, Bahrain, Kuwait, Libya, Morocco, Oman, Qatar, the Sudan, Tunisia, the Union of Arab Emirates, the Yemen Arab Republic, Mauritania, Somalia, and Djibouti, and the Palestine Liberation Organization. The countries of the League have agreed to work together on issues such as education, law, finance, trade, and foreign policy.

Lobby: To attempt to persuade public officials to take action or vote a particular way on an issue.

M

Middle East: Term used mostly by Westerners to describe the area of southwest Asia and northeast Africa. The Middle East includes the countries of the League of Arab States plus Cyprus, Israel, part of Turkey, and Iran (which is Persian, not Arab).

Mizwiz: A bagpipe-like Lebanese instrument.

Mosque: A building where Muslims go for public worship.

Muslim: A person who practices the Islamic religion (see Islam).

O

Operation Boulder: The Federal Bureau of Investigation (FBI) and several other government agencies closely monitored the activities of Arab immigrants and Arab Americans to battle Middle Eastern terrorism in the early 1970s.

Ottoman Empire: A Turkish Empire that dominated large portions of Asia Minor and southern Europe from about 1300 until the late 1500s. The Ottoman rule of Turkey ended in 1922.

P

Palestine: Region on the eastern shore of the Mediterranean Sea now comprised of Israel and parts of Jordan and Egypt. It is a very ancient region that was called Canaan in the Bible. Jews consider Palestine the Holy Land because it is the land God promised them in the Bible; it is also the Holy Land for Christians because it is where Jesus lived and preached; and for Muslims it is holy because they consider themselves the heirs of both Judaism and Christianity. Palestine was under Turkish Ottoman rule until 1920. After the Turks were on the losing side of World War I (1914–18) Palestine was under British control until 1948, when most of it was turned into the independent Jewish state of Israel.

Palestine National Council (PNC): A legislative body that functions as a Palestinian government with citizens but no physical country.

Palestine Liberation Organization (PLO): A coalition of several Palestinian organizations that acts under the supervision of the Palestine National Council (PNC). For many years after its founding in 1964, the PLO used guerilla war tactics to try to force Israel out of Palestine. The PLO wanted an independent Palestinian state to be created in parts occupied by Israel. In the late 1980s, the PLO and the PNC recognized the existence of Israel and asserted that a Palestinian state could coexist with Israel. Between 1993 and 1995, the head of the PLO, Yasser Arafat, and the leader of Israel, Prime Minister Yitzhak Rabin, reached agreements that would allow Palestinian self-rule in the areas of the Gaza Strip and the West Bank. As of 1999 the agreements had not been fully implemented. Israel continues to consider the PLO a violent threat to its existence and have not pulled out of the West Bank.

Party platform: A statement of that party's political philosophy.

Philanthropist: A person who gives large amounts of money to help other people. The word comes from a Greek word meaning "loving mankind."

Political Action Committee (PAC): Groups that raise money and give at least $1,000 in contributions to candidates running for government office. PACs must register with the Federal Elections Commission (FEC), listing the sources of its income and the size of donations given to each candidate.

R

Radius of Arab-American Writers (RAWI): A network of writers that puts on workshops for youths and helps authors get their work published.

Republican: A member of one of the two major political parties in the United States. Republicans endorse less regulation of business and lower taxes by offering fewer public programs.

S

Six Day War: A conflict that started between Egypt and Israel on June 5, 1967, and lasted until June 10, 1967. Egypt's leader Gamal Abdel Nasser (1918-1970) blocked Israeli ships from passing through the Gulf of Aqaba (Israel's major access to trade with other countries) and began massing troops on the Israeli border. Concerned that it was about to be attacked, Israel moved first and invaded Egypt, taking possession of the Gaza Strip and the Sinai Peninsula as well as the Golan Heights of Syria and part of Jordan.

Stereotype: An oversimplified image of a person based on generalizations.

Suez War: In 1956 Egypt took control of the Suez Canal and was consequently invaded by Israel, Britain, and France.

T

Terrorist: A person who uses violence or threats to accomplish goals, which are usually political.

W

West Bank: An area formerly known as Judea and Samaria, the West Bank of the Jordan River was occupied by Jordan from 1948 until 1967, when it was captured by Israel. It contains several important cities, including Bethlehem and the Old City of Jerusalem.

Z

Zionist: A person who supports the existence of Israel as a Jewish nation in Palestine.

A Timeline of Arab American Events and Accomplishments

1854: Antonio Bishallany becomes the first publicly recognized Syrian immigrant to the United States.

1911: Ameen Rihani publishes *The Book of Khalid.*

1920: Mansour Farah begins manufacturing men's clothing.

1923: Kahlil Gibran publishes *The Prophet.*

1926: J. M. Haggar begins manufacturing men's clothing.

1929: Dr. Michael Shadid founds the first cooperative medical association in the United States.

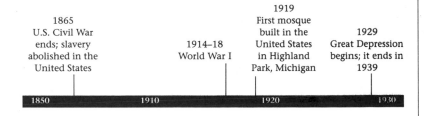

| 1865 U.S. Civil War ends; slavery abolished in the United States | 1914–18 World War I | 1919 First mosque built in the United States in Highland Park, Michigan | 1929 Great Depression begins; it ends in 1939 |

| 1850 | 1910 | 1920 | 1930 |

Tony Shalhoub. Reproduced by permission of Archive Photos, Inc.

Kahlil Gibran

1936: George Addes is elected the first secretary-treasurer of the United Automobile Workers union.

1943: Joseph J. Jacobs develops a process for mass-producing penicillin.

1943: Salom Rizk publishes *Syrian Yankee*.

1947: Vance Bourjaily publishes his first novel, *The End of My Life*.

1948: Sam Maloof begins making furniture.

1951: James Jabara becomes the first jet-to-jet ace in military combat.

1952: Dr. Michael DeBakey performs the first successful surgical repair of an aortic aneurysm in the United States.

1953: Dr. Nicholas Assali becomes a research faculty member of the new medical school at the University of California at Los Angeles (UCLA).

1953: Danny Thomas stars in *Make Room for Daddy* (the name was later changed to *The Danny Thomas Show*), a television series that continues until 1964.

1954: A. Joseph Howar completes construction of the Islamic Center in Washington, D.C.

1957: Paul Anka becomes an overnight singing sensation with his single "Diana."

1958: Dick Dale records his first album, *Surfer's Choice*.

1958: Rosalind Elias plays Erika in the first performance of the opera *Vanessa*.

1959: Samuel John Hazo publishes his first book, *Discovery and Other Poems*.

1960: George Hamid begins booking entertainers for the Steel Pier.

Rosalind Elias in costume for Vanessa. Reproduced by permission of AP/Wide World Photos.

1939–45 World War II	1945 Cold War between the United States and Soviet Union begins	1948 State of Israel proclaimed in Palestine; neighboring Arab countries invade Israel	1956 Gamal Abdel Nasser establishes a republic in Egypt.
1935	1945	1955	1960

1960: Ralph Johns organizes the first "sit-in" of the U.S. civil rights movement.

1961: Najeeb Halaby is appointed Federal Aviation Administrator (head of the FAA).

1963: Fayez Sarofim gets his first major institutional client when he begins managing part of Rice University's endowment fund.

1965: Ralph Nader writes *Unsafe at Any Speed.*

1965: Joe Robbie starts the Miami Dolphins football team.

1966: Marlo Thomas begins playing a single, working woman on the television comedy *That Girl,* a role she plays until 1971.

1966: Frank Zappa's musical group the Mothers of Invention releases its debut album, *Freak Out!*

1967: Farouk El-Baz begins working on lunar projects for the National Aeronautics and Space Administration (NASA).

1969: Tiny Tim marries Miss Vicky on television's *The Tonight Show with Johnny Carson.*

1970: Casey Kasem's radio show, *American Top 40,* debuts on seven stations.

1970: Paul Orfalea opens the first Kinko's copy shop.

1971: William Peter Blatty writes *The Exorcist.*

1972: Jamie Farr begins playing Corporal Klinger on the television series *M*A*S*H.*

1974: Helen Thomas becomes the first female White House bureau chief for a wire service (UPI).

1976: Kristy McNichol begins playing Buddy on *Family,* a television series that runs until 1980.

Marlo Thomas. Reproduced by permission of AP/Wide World Photos.

William Peter Blatty. Reproduced by permission of AP/Wide World Photos.

1965
U.S. troops become involved in the Vietnam War

1967
Six Day War; Israel annexes the Old City of Jerusalem

1969
Neil Armstrong walks on the moon

1973
First Arab-Israeli peace conference held in Geneva

| 1960 | 1965 | 1970 | 1975 |

The Camp David Accords. Reproduced by permission of AP/Wide World Photos.

1976: Nick Joe Rahall II is first elected to the U.S. House of Representatives.

1976: Vic Tayback first appears as Mel Sharples in the television series *Alice,* a role he plays until 1985.

1977: Edward Said begins serving on the Palestine National Council, a position he holds until 1991.

1978: Victor Atiyeh is elected governor of Oregon.

1978: Philip Habib helps Israel and Egypt negotiate a peace treaty known as the Camp David Accords.

1978: Norma Kamali opens her first OMO (On My Own) store.

1980: James Abourezk founds the American-Arab Anti-Discrimination Committee (ADC).

1980: Candy Lightner founds Mothers Against Drunk Driving (MADD).

1982: Mario Kassar produces *First Blood,* the first Rambo movie.

1982: Selwa Roosevelt becomes chief of protocol for President Ronald Reagan, a post she holds for seven years.

1984: F. Murray Abraham wins an Oscar (Academy Award) as best actor for his role as Antonio Salieri in *Amadeus.*

1984: Doug Flutie wins the Heisman Trophy as college football's most outstanding football player of the year.

1984: Abdeen Jabara wins a harassment and illegal surveillance lawsuit against the Federal Bureau of Investigation (FBI).

1984: Alixa Naff donates the Naff Arab American Collection to the Smithsonian Institution and begins serving as its volunteer curator, a job she continues for twelve years.

1985: Joseph Jamail Jr. wins the largest civil judgment in U.S. history ($10.53 billion).

Selwa Roosevelt. Reproduced by permission of AP/Wide World Photos.

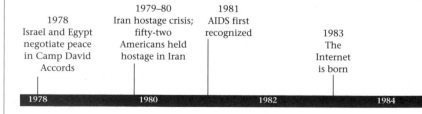

1978 Israel and Egypt negotiate peace in Camp David Accords	1979–80 Iran hostage crisis; fifty-two Americans held hostage in Iran	1981 AIDS first recognized	1983 The Internet is born
1978	1980	1982	1984

1986: Joseph Abboud unveils his first collection of men's fashions.

1986: Fadwa El Guindi releases the award-winning anthropological film *El Sebou'*.

1986: Khrystyne Haje begins playing Simone Foster on *Head of the Class,* a television series that lasts until 1991.

1986: Christa McAuliffe dies as the space shuttle *Challenger* explodes during launch.

1986: Bobby Rahal wins the Indianapolis 500 race.

1986: Anton Shammas publishes *Arabesques*.

1987: Tiffany releases her first album, *Tiffany,* which includes the hit single "I Think We're Alone Now."

1988: Paula Abdul's first album, *Forever Your Girl,* becomes a popular success, selling more than twelve million copies.

1988: George Mitchell becomes U.S. Senate Majority Leader.

1988: Gregory Orfalea publishes *Before the Flames*.

1988: John Sununu is named chief of staff to President George Bush.

1988: Tony Thomas produces *Dead Poets Society,* which wins the Oscar (Academy Award) for best picture the following year.

1990: Elias Corey wins the Nobel Prize for Chemistry.

1991: Elmaz Abinader publishes *Children of the Roojme: A Family's Journey*.

1991: Ray Hanania is nominated for the Pulitzer Prize for a series of newspaper articles about the treatment of Palestinians under Israeli occupation.

1991: Tony Shalhoub first appears as Antonio Scarpacci in the television series *Wings,* a role he plays until 1997.

F. Murray Abraham. Reproduced by permission of AP/Wide World Photos.

Joseph Jamail Jr. Reproduced by permission the Corbis Corporation (Bellevue).

1986
Iran Contra
affair is
revealed

1989
Berlin Wall
comes down

1990–91
Persian
Gulf War

1992
Los Angeles
Riots

1986   1988   1990   1992

Kathy Najimy in Sister Act 2. *Reproduced by permission of The Kobal Collection.*

1992: Elie Chaib is named "Dancer of the Year" by the *New York Times.*

1992: Kathy Najimy plays Sister Mary Patrick in the movie *Sister Act.*

1993: Lucie Salhany is named chairman of Fox Broadcasting, becoming the first woman to head an American television network.

1993: Donna Shalala becomes Secretary of Health and Human Services in the Clinton administration.

1994: Spencer Abraham is elected to the U.S. Senate.

1994: Naomi Shihab Nye publishes *Sitti's Secrets,* a children's picture book inspired by the 1991 Persian Gulf War.

1994: Yasser Seirawan wins an Olympic gold medal for chess.

1995: Stephen Yokich is elected president of the International Union of United Automobile, Aerospace, and Agricultural Implement Workers of America (UAW).

1996: Dr. Michael Ellis DeBakey performs heart surgery on the leader of Russia, Boris Yeltsin.

1998: Race car driver Bobby Rahal retires.

1999: Actor Tony Shalhoub appears in *A Civil Action* with John Travolta.

Dr. Michael Ellis DeBakey. Reproduced by permission of AP/Wide World Photos.

1992 Ethnic warfare erupts in Bosnia and Hercegovina	1993–1995 PLO leader Yasser Arafat and Israeli Prime Minister Yitzhak Rabin engage in peace talks	1995 Prime Minister Yitzak Rabin of Israel is assassinated	1999 King Hussein of Jordan dies
1992	1994	1996	1999

Joseph Abboud

Lebanese-American fashion designer

Born May 5, 1950
Boston, Massachusetts

Inspired by a muted palette—light beiges and grays, warm browns, and the classic black—Joseph Abboud has designed striking men's clothes for his own label since 1986. The preppie influence of his Boston upbringing and his work for designer Ralph Lauren (1939–) still show in his designs and are mixed with his own preference for earthy tones and ethnic patterns. Although his pricey creations account for only 1 percent of all purchases by men's clothing buyers, Abboud is a weighty presence in the fashion world, leading the trend toward softer, more versatile clothes.

Voted "best dressed"

Joseph Abboud was born in Boston's South End to first-generation Lebanese-American parents in 1950. The South End neighborhood was a melting pot—with Armenians, Chinese, Greeks, Irish, and Syrians—that introduced Abboud to a variety of ethnic styles that would later influence his worldly designs. A heavy-lifting accident left his father mostly debilitated, and his mother worked long hours as a nurse, so

"I WANT TO RAISE THE TASTE LEVEL OF THE AMERICAN MAN AND TEACH HIM THAT 'STYLE' AND 'FASHION' ARE NOT DIRTY WORDS."

Abboud had a good deal of freedom as a child. With money he saved from peddling swan boats in the Public Garden he went to the movie theaters every day and soaked in the style of heroic characters like Robin Hood and Don Juan. "I loved clothes when I was a kid," Abboud told *GQ*. "Maybe it was like being a part of these people. All I know is that there was a relationship not with what they wore, but [with] who they were. Cary Grant, Fred Astaire—they're cliches now, but they were so wonderfully dressed."

Abboud carried his love of classically styled clothes to Roslindale High School, where the football and track star was voted "best dressed." He naturally gravitated toward jobs at clothing stores—first at Anderson-Little, an affordable men's store where he worked part-time during high school, then at Louis Boston, an extravagant men's store where he worked while studying comparative literature at the University of Massachusetts.

A fashion education

After graduating from University of Massachusetts in 1972, Abboud won a fellowship to study literature at the Sorbonne, a prestigious university in Paris, France. The year and a half he spent living in Paris' Latin Quarter also proved to be an education in European fashion—the way scarves could be worn, the way suits should hang on men, the way colors should complement and not startle. When he returned to the United States, Abboud passed up opportunities to teach high school and study French literature at Yale's graduate school so he could become a full-time manager at the Louis Boston store. Abboud helped choose the colors, materials, and cuts for the private-label sweaters, shirts, and suits produced by Louis Boston. It was then, he told *New York* magazine, that "I realized that I was *good* at this business."

In 1980, Abboud was hired as an associate director of menswear design for Ralph Lauren, a prestigious fashion house in New York. Although he had been shaped by Boston's preppie fashion scene, Abboud also had a taste for the exotic that he found hard to reconcile with the traditional look he was supposed to produce for the Polo/Ralph Lauren label. "I was always pushing Ralph to do something a little bit different," Abboud told *GQ*. "What he was doing wasn't *wrong*, I

just thought there was room to do more sophisticated stuff."
The first time Abboud tried his hand at a more sophisticated
look, however, the result was disastrous. He credits himself
with designing "one of the worst seasons [Ralph Lauren] ever
had."

During the four years he designed for Ralph Lauren,
Abboud developed a more concrete concept of the colors and
cuts that would later become the foundation of his line—
earthy tones, straight and simple lines, and an oversized fit
for a comfortable look. In 1984, Abboud left Lauren to design
his own label for Freedberg of Boston. Early on he decided to
base his clothes on natural hues of green, blue, red, and
brown. The first line came out in the fall of 1986 and was
called "An American in India," based on exotic geometric
prints and paisleys of the East.

Since the late 1980s Abboud has been designing his own brand of men's clothing using traditional fabrics and earthy tones. Reproduced by permission of the Corbis Corporation.

Subsequent collections mined the patterns and hues of Eskimos, Pueblo Indians, and Latin Americans. An avid collector of *kilims,* turkish woven rugs with eye-catching geometric patterns, Abboud has based other prints on those designs. Although he kept some traditional elements, such as tweed for pants and jackets, he defied the label of "preppie." "Preppie is traditional, button-down, unimaginative, and very confining," he told *Connoisseur.* "My clothes are sensible but hip. They stretch imaginations, but they're believable."

Straddling the Spectrum

With his blending of fashion staples and exotic elements, Abboud has said he strikes just the right balance. "If you put [fashion designer] Giorgio Armani [1934–] over here and Ralph Lauren over there," Abboud told *The Atlantic Monthly,* outstretching his arms to indicate the fashion scale from modern to traditional, "we are right in the middle."

In 1988, Abboud signed with GFT, an Italian clothing company, to expand his line. His big break came that same year when American TV broadcaster Bryant Gumbel (1948–) began wearing Abboud clothing while covering the Winter Olympics for the Columbia Broadcasting System (CBS). Gumbel continued to wear Abboud fashions as the host of the National Broadcasting Company's (NBC) *Today* show (which he left in 1996), giving tremendous exposure to the young designer's look.

After winning the Cutty Stark Award and the Woolmark Award in 1988, Abboud's work was recognized by the Council of Fashion Designers of America (1989 and 1990), the Japanese Government (1993), and the Neckwear Association of America (1994). At $700 for a jacket, $200 for a shirt, $80 for a tie, and more than $1,000 for a suit, Abboud's clothes are only within the buying power of wealthy shoppers. Although relatively few people can buy his clothes, Abboud still sees his goal as improving the confidence with which men dress. "I want to raise the taste level of the American man and teach him that 'style' and 'fashion' are not dirty words," he told *New York*. "And I know that I'm on the right track."

FURTHER READING

Beatty, Jack. "The Transatlantic Look." *The Atlantic Monthly* (December 1995): 48+.

Boehlert, Bart. "All About Abboud." *New York* (August 17, 1988): 14.

Dolce, Joe. "Last of the Updated Traditionals." *Connoisseur* (March 1987): 38+.

Stern, Ellen. "Joseph Abboud, Down to Earth." *GQ* (October 1989): 320+.

Paula Abdul

Syrian-Brazilian-French-Canadian-Jewish-American singer

*Born June 19, 1962
North Hollywood, California*

"I LOVED CHOREOGRAPHY, BUT I WANTED TO BE A PERFORMER. MY IDOLS WERE PEOPLE WHO COULD DO MANY THINGS—SING, DANCE, ACT, CHOREOGRAPH."

Paula Abdul has worn many hats in the entertainment industry: leader of the Los Angeles Lakers' cheerleaders, choreographer for performers including pop singer Janet Jackson (1966–) and actor Tom Hanks (1956–), songwriter, music producer, and actress. But Abdul is best known as the singing and dancing sensation behind 1988's *Forever Your Girl* album, which sold more than 12 million copies and featured four chart-topping singles, including "Straight Up" and "Opposites Attract."

Born to perform

Paula Julie Abdul was born in 1962, the second child of Harry and Lorraine Abdul. The Abdul daughters—Paula and her older sister Wendy—grew up as "valley girls" in a middle-class neighborhood in North Hollywood, California. Abdul's Arab roots came from her father, a cattle trader of mixed Syrian-Brazilian heritage. Her mother, a French-Canadian Jew, enjoyed a brief stint as a concert pianist before becoming an assistant to famed film director Billy Wilder (1906–). Abdul's parents divorced when she was seven, and her father moved more than 200 miles away to northern California, where she visited him on weekends.

When Abdul was six years old, she began watching old movie musicals and idolizing entertainers who could sing, dance, and act, such as American actor and dancer Gene Kelly (1912–1996). She daydreamed about starring in musicals, and even created parts for herself and other make-believe characters. Abdul was introduced to dance lessons two years later almost by accident: "She was supposed to go to a friend's house," Abdul's mother told *People* magazine. "The mother called me and said she forgot her daughter had a dance lesson and wanted to know if she could take Paula. I said sure. I picked them up, and all I heard on the way home was, 'I have to take dancing.'"

Soon Abdul added ballet, tap, and modern dance lessons to her schedule, and she proved to be a talented and hardworking student who picked up new moves the first time she saw them. As she attended Van Nuys High School, Abdul's love of dancing and sports (she and her father have been lifelong fans of the University of California at Los Angeles [UCLA] basketball teams) led her to try out for cheerleading. She made the squad and later became its leader. As head of the squad, Abdul held practices in her backyard for several hours until every move was perfect. Abdul cast aside pompoms and traditional cheers, leading the squad in energetic dance routines set to pop music.

Abdul's drive for perfection carried over into her other high-school activities. While class president, flutist in the school orchestra, member of the speech and debate team, and cheerleader, Abdul earned excellent grades, graduating with a 3.85 grade point average (on a 4.0 scale). After high school, Abdul enrolled at the Northridge branch of California State (Cal-State) University in 1981. She dreamed of becoming a performer, and she took dance, music, and acting classes. At five-feet-two inches, Abdul is not as tall as most professional dancers. This sparked her decision to major in sports broadcasting so she could have another career in case she was not able to work as a performer.

From Laker Girl to choreographer to the stars

During her freshman year at Cal-State, Abdul tried out for the Laker Girls, the cheerleaders who perform at the Los

Angeles Lakers basketball games. More than 700 dancers came out for the auditions, and Abdul had only sixty seconds to impress the selection committee. In one minute, Abdul wowed the judges and was awarded a spot on the squad. Three weeks later, she also added choreography—the art of arranging the steps and movements of dancers—to her responsibilities on the squad.

Her work with the Laker Girls consumed most of her time, and six months after she joined the squad, Abdul left Cal-State. At age twenty, Abdul was working for one of the most high-profile sports franchises of the 1980s, and her squad was setting new trends in cheerleading and dance. Each week Abdul taught the squad new routines, blending together elements from her modern dance classes and the popular breakdancing moves of the streets. Her work was a hit with many Lakers fans, including members of the Jackson Five singing group, who approached Abdul after one of the games and asked if she would choreograph their upcoming "Torture" video. Abdul went on to choreograph their 1984 concert tour—the last Jackson Five tour with pop star Michael Jackson (1958–).

Through her work with the Lakers and the Jacksons, Abdul was offered a job as video choreographer for Janet Jackson, who was getting ready to release her *Control* album. Abdul's athletic and angular dance style proved to be the perfect complement to the pulsing beat of Jackson's music, and the combination propelled Jackson into stardom. Before long, Abdul became the entertainment industry's most-wanted choreographer. She planned all the right moves for entertainers like British pop singer George Michael (1963–), British band Duran Duran, and the soulful American trio The Pointer Sisters. Abdul created the dance sequences in movies such as *Coming to America* (starring American actor and comedian Eddie Murphy [1961–]) and Fox television's *The Tracey Ullman Show*. She even choreographed the 1990 and 1991 Academy Awards ceremonies.

Singing career goes "Straight Up"

Abdul's behind-the-scenes success wasn't enough; she still longed to be an entertainer in her own right. "I loved choreography, but I wanted to be a performer," she told *Peo-*

ple. "My idols were people who could do many things—sing, dance, act, choreograph." Using $35,000 she had saved, Abdul recorded a singing demo tape in 1987 and met with record producers. Although her voice was untrained and had a short range, her dance moves made her highly marketable in a music industry driven by videos and concerts. Seven songwriting teams and six of the industry's most accomplished producers worked with Abdul to polish her pop debut, _Forever Your Girl._ The first two singles from the June 1988 release, "(It's Just) The Way That You Love Me" and "Knocked Out," received lukewarm response. It was only six months later, when MTV began heavy play of the video for Abdul's third single, "Straight Up," that Abdul's career went the same way.

Forever Your Girl enjoyed tremendous popular response: Abdul was the first female vocalist to have four singles from a debut album top the Billboard music charts, and she took home several awards from the MTV Video Music Awards and the American Music Awards in 1990. The album sold more than 12 million copies.

ABDUL'S AWARDS

MTV Video Music Awards
Best Choreography—"Nasty" by Janet Jackson (1986)
Best Female Video—"Straight Up" (1990)
Best Dance Video—"Straight Up" (1990)
Best Choreography in a Video—"Straight Up" (1990)
Best Editing in a Video—"Straight Up" (1990)

American Music Awards
Favorite Dance Artist (1990)
Favorite Pop-Rock Female Artist (1990)
Favorite Pop-Rock Female Artist (1992)

Grammy Awards
Best Music Video, Short Form—"Opposites Attract" (1991)
Best Album Package, Compact (special package)—_Spellbound_ (1993)

People's Choice Awards
Favorite Female Musical Performer (1990)

Emmy Awards
Best choreography of a television series—_The Tracey Ullman Show_ (1989)

American Dance Awards
Choreographer of the Year (1990)

Backup singer challenges Abdul

Abdul's status as one of the queens of pop was challenged in 1991, when Yvette Marine, one of the backup singers on _Forever Your Girl,_ said her singing parts had been electronically blended with Abdul's to give Abdul a stronger voice on the album. Marine sued Abdul's record label, Virgin Records, for $1 million for not naming her as a lead singer on the album. Although Marine lost the lawsuit in 1993, Abdul was greatly upset by the charges. "I do not profess to be any Aretha Franklin," Abdul told the _Los Angeles Times,_ "but that is my voice." Abdul began working with a vocal trainer three to five times a week and immersed herself in preparations for a follow-up album.

For her 1991 release, *Spellbound,* Abdul co-wrote four songs and helped produce eight of the tracks. *Spellbound* enjoyed moderate success, selling more than six million copies and producing two number one hits, "Rush, Rush" and "Promise of a New Day." The following year, Abdul married American actor Emilio Estevez (1962–)—a marriage that would last only two years. Their split stemmed from their differences over children: Abdul wanted them, and Estevez, already a father of two, did not want more children. When the couple divorced in May 1994, Abdul sank into depression.

Battles with bulimia

For more than fifteen years, Abdul had fought a long battle against the serious eating disorder bulimia. Bulimics binge on large amounts of food in a short amount of time and then purge, or rid, their bodies of the food in various ways, such as forcing themselves to throw up or taking laxatives to cause bowel movements. Abdul first saw girls forcing themselves to throw up when she went to a Palm Springs, California, dance camp at age fifteen. When Abdul told her mother what she had seen, her mother warned her, "That's not normal. Don't do that." At first she didn't; but a year later, after seeing many of her friends purge meals to prevent weight gain, Abdul began forcing herself to throw up. "No one thought it was bad," Abdul told *People* magazine. "Once I tried it, I felt it was an amazing way to control my weight."

Her struggle with bulimia continued through her years as a choreographer. On the days that she didn't throw up most of her food, Abdul worked out for up to four hours to burn the calories she had consumed. In 1989 Abdul joined Overeaters Anonymous and began attending meetings three times a week. Troubled by Marine's allegations about her singing and her split with Estevez, Abdul found her eating problems becoming worse. In July 1994, Abdul checked herself into the Laureate Clinic in Tulsa, Oklahoma, to deal with her eating disorder and other emotional problems.

Abdul came out of treatment with a new lease on life. She limits her exercise to one hour a day, she does not skip meals, and she is trying to accept the body shape she was born with. In July 1995, Abdul released her third album, *Head Over Heels,* an album she said is her most honest and personal project so far. The following October she married fashion designer Brad Beckerman in a traditional Jewish ceremony—a marriage that lasted until March 1998. Abdul has made several cameo appearances on television, and in January 1997, she made her acting debut in a television movie, *Touched By Evil.*

"I've experienced some personal growth that has allowed me to really get back to what I enjoy doing best," Abdul said about the release of *Head Over Heels.* "And that's being totally connected to the creative source as a recording artist and a dancer."

FURTHER READING

"Abdul, Paula." *Current Biography Yearbook 1991,* New York: H.W. Wilson, 1991, pp. 1–4.

Hirschberg, Lynn. "On Her Toes." *Vanity Fair* (March 1991): 172–73.

Malkin, Nina. "Paula Abdul's Double Life." *Mademoiselle* (November 1989): 94+.

Park, Jeannie, and Todd Gold. "Straight Up ... And Up and Up." *People Weekly* (March 12, 1990): 65–70.

Schneider, Karen S., and Todd Gold. "A Brave New Song." *People Weekly* (June 19, 1995): 88–94.

Elmaz Abinader

Lebanese-American poet and educator

Born January 19, 1954
Carmichaels, Pennsylvania

Elmaz Abinader (EL-mahz AH-bin-ay-der) grew up in a family of unpublished poets. She has made a career of creative writing, composing both poetry and prose as well as teaching others to put their deepest thoughts and emotions into words. Her first visit to her ancestral homeland at the age of nineteen sparked an urge to explore her Lebanese and American heritages—"fighting the two cultures that were controlling my life," as she described the quest to *Aramco World* magazine in 1990. Through the personal stories of her relatives, she began to understand both her ethnicity and universal human truths.

Backdrop

Elmaz Abinader's father, Jean, had spent his teen and young-adult years with his father in Brazil. His father went there to earn a living while the rest of his family stayed in Abdelli, Lebanon. Abinader's mother, Camille, had gone to America with her parents at the age of six but returned to Lebanon in 1935, about the time her cousin Jean returned to

Lebanon from Brazil. Camille and Jean fell in love, married, and moved to America in 1937.

At first, the growing family moved from town to town in western Pennsylvania as Jean Abinader sold clothing from a rented shop or the back of a truck. By the early 1950s, the family settled in the mining town of Carmichaels and opened a permanent store. In *Before the Flames,* a history of Arab immigration to American, Gregory Orfalea (1949-; see entry) described how a local dentist made it clear that because of their Arab heritage the Abinader family was not welcome in Carmichaels. Refusing to be bullied, Jean Abinader replied, "This now is my town. If you don't like it, you may leave."

A secret life

Elmaz Abinader was one of eight children. Two of her siblings died when they were quite young. Although they were the only Arab family in their town, they found fellowship in Lebanese communities in other cities. They visited Maronite Catholic parishes frequently and participated in festivals and celebrations. This almost secret life was separate from their daily life in Carmichaels, where they tried to blend as well as they could into the non-Arab population.

"We were discriminated against in our hometown, so we experienced questioning and disdain and fear from people around us," Abinader told Loretta Hall in a 1998 interview. "I think that created a kind of aloneness or solitude." Although she described her early childhood as "mildly comfortable" in terms of this discrimination, the atmosphere worsened after the 1967 Six Day War.

Middle East conflict hits home

Abinader was thirteen years old when the Six Day War intruded on her life. This conflict between Egypt and Israel lasted from June 5 to June 10 of 1967. Some people blamed Egypt (an Arab country) for the war because they cut the Israelis off from their only ocean port, thus restricting the Israelis' ability to trade with other countries. Egypt also massed troops on the Israeli border. Believing they were going to be attacked, Israel took the initiative and attacked first. Israel won the war and in six short days took control of some of Egypt's territory (the Gaza Strip and the Sinai Peninsula).

THE IRAN HOSTAGE CRISIS

In a 1998 interview, Elmaz Abinader called the Iran hostage crisis "the most dramatic turn in American culture against Arabs."

Mohammed Reza Pahlavi became shah (king) of Iran in 1941. For nearly thirty years, he ruled Iran with the friendship of the U.S. government. He was, however, not a popular shah. Some of his social and economic reforms angered powerful Iranians; for example, he transferred ownership of land from large landholders (including Islamic religious leaders) to poor people. Yet many Iranians remained terribly poor while the shah's family lived extravagantly. In January 1979, the shah fled Iran. A new Islamic government was formed under the leadership of the Ayatollah Ruhollah Khomeini, an anti-American Muslim who referred to the United States as "the great Satan." The following fall, President Jimmy Carter allowed the shah to enter the United States for medical treatment. On November 4, 1979, a group of militants took over the U.S. embassy in Tehran, Iran, capturing sixty-six staff members. The militants quickly released thirteen hostages, promising to release the rest if the United States would send the shah to Iran to stand trial. Carter refused. Five months later, Carter ordered a military mission to free the hostages, but it failed when two of the aircraft in the mission collided on their way to Tehran. Although the shah died in Egypt in July 1980 the hostages were not released until January 20, 1981—the day Carter left the presidency.

Many Arab Americans felt increased resentment in the United States during this time. "People were looking at our family and asking us to take sides and give an explanation of how Lebanon was involved in this," Abinader told Hall. "When you're confronted that way, you begin to question: Who *am* I, what *do* I think, and where *do* I stand?"

The United States had long supported Israel in conflicts in the Middle East, and the Six Day War was no exception. American support for Israel led some people in this country to have negative attitudes towards Arabs in the Middle East and Arab Americans in this country. According to Abinader, people became "directly abusive" during the 1980 Iran hostage crisis. In November 1980 sixty-five staff members were taken hostage at the U.S. embassy in Tehran, Iran, in retaliation for the United States allowing the unpopular ex-Shah of Iran to come to America for medical treatment and avoid trial in his own country.

Making sense of it

Abinader's family responded to questions about where they stood on such issues by learning all they could about the political situation in the Middle East and trying to explain to their critics the background and meaning of what was happening. "The way we dealt with it was ... we developed a stand and a sense of participation," Abinader told Hall. "Before, we were really trying to integrate and blend and contribute; we kept those things going, but in the meantime, we were saying 'We're Lebanese, we're Arab, this is what we believe, this is what we feel.'"

After finishing high school, Abinader headed for college, intending to prepare for law school. However, she had come from a family of writers (they kept extensive diaries) and poets (while she was growing up, her family ended each day with a friendly competition to see who could create the most beautiful word-images). She couldn't resist taking writing classes, and she finally decided that writing was what she really wanted to do. "Then," she told *Al-Jadid* newspaper, "my life started to make sense." She graduated from the University of Pittsburgh in 1974 with a bachelor's degree in writing. In 1978, she earned a master's degree in poetry writing from the Columbia University School of the Arts. In 1985, she earned a Ph.D. in English fiction and nonfiction writing from the University of Nebraska.

Finding reality

While she was in college Abinader accompanied her parents and a sister on her first trip to Lebanon. She told *Al-Jadid* that while she was growing up, "my parents would talk about Lebanon in such a way that I never understood why they left because it was the perfect place. They talked about their parents and their grandparents as people who were infallible and had no faults whatsoever." Meeting her relatives and seeing where her parents had lived as children helped her to realistically envision their lives in Lebanon.

The trip gave Abinader a chance to read the detailed diaries her grandparents had written. From these diaries, she began to understand their personalities, their struggles, and the reasons some family members left Lebanon for Brazil or the United States. For years, she studied the diaries, trying to understand each person and how each affected the family as a whole. Abinader assembled her grandparents' stories into a book called *Children of the Roojme* (the "roojme" [ROOZHmee] was an ocean overlook where Jean and Camille Abinader had watched the stars while courting).

Cutting through globs

Abinader tried to use her family story to illustrate universal experiences and observations. In all of her poems and stories, including *Children of the Roojme,* Abinader told *Al-Jadid,* "I want the reader to understand through my writing the human situation of larger historical events. I think that part of the problem with the way we perceive the world is that we perceive it in big globs of history, big globs of geography. We do not think that what this war means is no food for this child. I want to tell the story of the child and by telling the story of the child I am telling the story of the war."

Refreshing work

Since 1978, Abinader has taught writing at several colleges in Nebraska, New York, and California. She told Hall she considers herself a natural-born teacher who enjoys watching her students progress from one level of awareness to another. Although her teaching duties take time away from her writing projects, she said teaching is "a wonderful way to have an on-going discussion about the things that are important. It's a wonderful way to constantly regenerate myself in my beliefs, or to stimulate and inspire new ones."

Both, but neither

In 1993, the same year she joined the faculty of Mills College in Oakland, California, Abinader was invited to visit several Middle Eastern countries on a tour sponsored by the United States Information Agency (USIA). She told Hall she came to the USIA's attention because some of her poems were published in a book called *Grape Leaves: A Century of Arab American Poetry.* The purpose of the tour, she explained, was "to show my work and have discussions and teach, but also for me to get a sense of what's going on in those places—both in terms of literature and of life." Of the 1993 tour and a similar one she took in 1996, she said, "I read to people, was on television, was published, met with groups of writers, met with groups of women. It really enriched my sense of my work and a connection with the culture, but also very much defined that territory, for the first-generation person, that you're neither one [nationality] nor the other."

From 1998 to 1999, Abinader plans to do similar tours before and after teaching ethnic American literature for a semester at Helwan University in Cairo, Egypt. She commented, "The whole purpose [of spending a semester in Egypt] is to learn Arabic. I'm dying to learn Arabic. For me, learning a language is an immersion process; it's much easier for me to hear it and see it."

Where's home?

Walking along paths through the Lebanese hills for the first time at the age of nineteen, Abinader sensed what she described as a "fundamental kinship with the land," feeling as though she had been there before. Years later, after having traveled more extensively, she told *Al-Jadid,* "I do not think home is as much a place for me as it is an idea.... Home, I think, for anybody is their own sense of self. I feel so strongly about who I am—I can take that anywhere and make it my home."

FURTHER READING

Abinader, Elmaz. *Children of the Roojme: A Family's Journey.* New York: W. W. Norton & Company, Inc., 1991.

Handal, Nathalie. "Poet Finds Duality and Common Bonds on Mideast Tour." *Al-Jadid* (November-December 1996): 8+.

Orfalea, Gregory, and Sharif Elmusa, eds. *Grape Leaves: A Century of Arab American Poetry.* Salt Lake City: University of Utah Press, 1988.

Simarski, Lynn Teo. "Poetry in the Blood." *Aramco World* (July-August 1990): 52.

James Abourezk

*Lebanese-American U.S. senator and founder
of American-Arab Anti-Discrimination
Committee (ADC)*

*Born February 14, 1931
Wood, South Dakota*

A s a U.S. senator and founder of the American-Arab Anti-Discrimination Committee (ADC), James Abourezk has been one of the most vocal advocates for the Arab quest of establishing an independent Palestinian state in the Middle East. Abourezk has always fought for the causes of the less empowered. He has supported the Democratic Party in a state dominated by Republicans, defended Native Americans' rights, and backed the Arabs when U.S. policy favored Israel.

An Arab on a Sioux Indian reservation

Abourezk was born on a Sioux Indian reservation in South Dakota during the Great Depression (1929–39; a period in U.S. history in which the economy declined sharply and many people could not find jobs). His parents were Charles Abourezk, the owner of two general stores, and Lena Mickel, a homemaker who was twenty years younger than her husband. Both were Lebanese immigrants. Abourezk's father came to South Dakota in 1898, where he farmed, peddled spices and linens, and even sold snow cones to make a living.

Charles returned to Lebanon, where he met and married Lena, and the couple had two children, Helen and Chick. Charles then went back to South Dakota, and Lena and the children joined him there in 1920. While living in South Dakota, Charles and Lena had three more children—Tom, James, and Virginia.

Growing up during the Great Depression, young James and his family did not face the same hardships that many people at that time faced. His father's grocery stores had steady business from Native Americans who redeemed food vouchers there from the U.S. government. The government reimbursed Abourezk for the goods he gave to people with food vouchers, ensuring the Abourezks a reliable source of income. Charles was generous with his good fortune, extending store credit to people he knew could never repay him.

As a young boy, Abourezk spoke only Arabic. Living on the Rosebud Indian Reservation, he had little contact with English-speaking people until he attended elementary school. A favorite tradition in James's family was to gather with the neighboring Abdnor family every Sunday to listen to Arabic music on a wind-up Victrola (a popular brand of record players), enjoy Lebanese meals, and exchange stories into the late hours.

Abourezk was a mischievous student who spent most of his free time behind the bar at the Bloody Bucket saloon in Wood, South Dakota. At age sixteen, Abourezk was expelled from high school for tying his teacher to a radiator. Tired of their son's pranks, Abourezk's parents kicked him out of the house. Abourezk went to live with his older brother Tom in a nearby town and completed high school there in 1948. For years, Abourezk had dreamed of joining the navy. Both of his older brothers fought in World War II (1939–45; when the United States and certain European countries fought to stop Nazi Germany and Japan from conquering the world), and he heard stories of the exotic places and exciting adventures awaiting sailors. As soon as he was seventeen and got his father's permission, Abourezk enlisted.

"The quickest ticket out of town"

After twelve weeks of boot camp, Abourezk enrolled in the Electricians' Mate School. For the next four years,

Abourezk repaired hot water boilers, electric motors, refrigerators, and other machines aboard U.S. ships stationed near Japan. All he learned from the navy, Abourezk wrote in his memoirs, was that it wasn't something he wanted to do. "Aside from giving me a few years of supervision while I continued to grow up, I can say, without fear of contradiction, that the navy taught me little more than how to withstand the routine of military life."

After he returned to South Dakota in 1952, Abourezk eloped with Mary Ann Houlton and began a series of jobs working in bars, where he poured drinks and broke up fights. In 1957, Abourezk's mother and brothers offered to pay for his college education. Because the government was sponsoring the expansion of interstate highways across the country, Abourezk decided a degree in civil engineering would be "the quickest ticket out of town," even though he had no idea what civil engineering entailed or whether he would be good at it. Civil engineers plan and help construct a variety of public works, such as railroads, highways, canals, bridges, dams, and tunnels.

Gets a taste of politics

Despite his difficulty with mathematics, Abourezk earned his civil engineering degree from the South Dakota School of Mines and Technology in 1961. Abourezk also became politically active during his college years, founding a young Democratic group that wrote letters to the conservative local newspapers and helped Democratic candidates run for office in the predominantly Republican state. After working on several small construction projects and, with encouragement from one of his college professors, Abourezk abandoned engineering and enrolled in the University of South Dakota's law school in 1963.

Abourezk earned his law degree in three years and entered private practice in Rapid City, South Dakota, in 1966, representing victims of personal injury and criminal defendants who could not afford a lawyer. Abourezk returned to politics in 1968, helping with Robert F. Kennedy's (1925–1968) presidential campaign and serving as a South Dakota delegate to the Democratic National Convention in Chicago, Illinois. For Abourezk, 1968 was a bitter year: Robert Kennedy was assassinated less than three months before the Chicago convention; people protesting the Vietnam War (1965–73; when the United States sent troops to help South Vietnam fight off its communist neighbor, North Vietnam) clashed violently with police at the convention; and Abourezk lost his bid for state attorney general. These events failed to shake his passion for politics. In 1970, he decided to run for one of South Dakota's two seats in the U.S. House of Representatives.

Abourezk won the Democratic primary for the House seat by a narrow margin. Primaries are elections in which political parties nominate (choose) a candidate to run against the other parties' candidates in the main election. Abourezk thought his candidacy for the House seat was hopeless. South Dakota's Second Congressional District (located in the western half of the state) was the more conservative of the state's two districts, electing only one Democrat in its history (Theo "Dates" Werner in 1932). At this time, Abourezk was broke—having used his personal funds to finance his campaign. He couldn't even buy groceries for his wife and three children. But there were several factors working in Abourezk's favor. He had the support of South Dakota Senator George McGovern (1922–), whom Abourezk supported for the presidency in 1968 after Robert Kennedy's assassination. This along with his pro-agriculture, anti-Vietnam War stance won him support throughout the district. Abourezk slid by his Republican challenger, Fred Brady, winning 51.3 percent of the vote.

An unlikely Senate agenda

Abourezk shouldered most of the responsibility for representing South Dakota in Washington while the two South Dakota senators, Karl Mundt and George McGovern, were unable to meet the responsibilities of their office. Mundt had suffered permanent brain damage from a stroke, and McGovern was preparing for his 1972 presidential campaign. During this time, Abourezk maintained contact with his constituents (the citizens he represented) and fought for programs that would favor the small farmers of his state. Working hard as a representative, Abourezk seemed like the natural candidate to fill Mundt's Senate seat in 1972. He captured it with 57 percent of the vote.

Abourezk's mixed background gave him an unlikely Senate agenda. As a South Dakota native, he was deeply concerned about domestic programs affecting farmers and Native Americans, and as a first-generation Lebanese-American, he also had strong opinions about U.S. foreign policy in the Middle East. As chair of the Indian Affairs Subcommittee, Abourezk supported Native Americans' rights without alienating his constituents who had opposing interests. He demanded that health-care changes guarantee quality and affordable coverage for the elderly, and he opposed big business farming operations that would ruin independent farmers. In its 1974 feature, "200 Faces for the Future," *Time* magazine said Abourezk "knows more about the American Indian than any of his 99 colleagues." The same article also described Abourezk as "the Senate's most forceful spokesman for the Arab cause in the conflict over a Palestinian state."

Experiences the shock of his life

Abourezk was drawn into the conflict in the Middle East as soon as he became a senator. Problems in the Middle East stemmed from the 1948 creation of Israel as an independent Jewish state in what was once Palestine. Arab countries had opposed the creation of an Israeli state in the Middle East, feeling that the Israelis were outsiders who forced their way into Palestine. Both Arabs and Israelis used military force to protect their interests in the area, causing the area to be in a constant state of war. Abourezk was approached almost daily by Jewish lobbyists (professionals who tried to persuade members of Congress to provide more aid for Israel and impose sanctions on its Arab enemies) and Arab Americans who wanted to meet one of America's only Arab American congressmen.

In 1973, the Lebanese embassy invited Abourezk to visit Beirut, Lebanon, a trip that Abourezk later said gave him "the shock of [his] life." He saw families living among the ruins of war, housed in rows of flimsy tin huts separated by lines of open sewers. Bombings had left piles of rubble that served as playgrounds for the children. "I left Lebanon feeling immensely betrayed," Abourezk recounted in his memoirs. "For most of my adult life I had believed that Israel had been picked on by the Arab countries.... To learn in Lebanon that the truth had been stood on its head was an emotional shock for me."

Later in 1973, Abourezk met with Arab leaders in the Middle East and discussed the possibilities for peace. When Abourezk returned to Washington, D.C., he told Congress that Arab leaders would agree to a truce if Israel gave back the Arab land (areas that include the Old City of Jerusalem, the West Bank, and the Gaza Strip) that it had seized in 1967. Israel refused to agree to those terms. Abourezk's support of the Arabs, he said, made him a target of other senators and journalists who sympathized with the Israeli cause. By opposing his candidacy for certain Senate committees and printing unfair stories about him in the press, Israeli sympathizers tried to discredit him, Abourezk stated in his memoirs.

Deconstructing the Arab stereotype

In an interview with Brian Lamb, Abourezk commented on the Arab stereotype in America: "I think the image is either that of a high spending, greedy, spendthrift Arab sheik, or a terrorist—Arab terrorist." That stereotype, he said, made it easier to blame Arabs for American economic problems,

AMERICAN-ARAB ANTI-DISCRIMINATION COMMITTEE (ADC)

The American-Arab Anti-Discrimination Committee (ADC) is a 25,000-member organization that James Abourezk founded in 1980 to draw attention to the unfair stereotyping of Arabs in the media and offer assistance to Arab Americans facing discrimination. Through a network of local chapters, the ADC provides legal advice and lawyer referrals to Arab Americans with immigration problems or civil rights abuses. Its Washington, D.C. headquarters monitors legislation—including foreign aid bills and immigration laws—that is of interest to Arab Americans. The organization calls for "more detailed and accurate accounts" of Middle Eastern history in school textbooks and promotes Arab heritage through chapter activities and national conventions. All of these efforts, according to ADC President Hala Maksoud, go toward "building self-confidence for individuals as well as for all Arab Americans."

How to contact the ADC:
4201 Connecticut Ave. N.W.
Suite 300
Washington, D.C. 20008
Tel: (202) 244-2990

such as the rising price of oil in the late 1970s when Arab countries embargoed (prohibited) oil shipments to the United States in protest of American support of Israel.

Abourezk has also remarked that the Abscam (short for Abdul Scam) scandal, which became public in February 1980, was an example of American prejudice toward Arab peoples. Abscam was a Federal Bureau of Investigation (FBI) sting operation in which an undercover agent dressed as an Arab tried to bribe several members of the U.S. Congress. When asked why the agent wore Arab garb, an FBI spokesperson said it was necessary to dress the agent as a member of an ethnic group that the public would believe to be capable of bribing elected officials. Abourezk felt the FBI's actions demonstrated the widespread prejudice against Arabs in the United States and encouraged negative images of Arabs. "Use of a phony Arab figure in Abscam was the direct result of the seven-year escalation, following the oil embargo, of anti-Arab racism that was projected by the media and cheered on by the Israeli lobby," Abourezk wrote in his memoirs. "It was clear to me that unless something was done about it, the outcome would be disastrous generally for Americans and specifically for every Arab American."

As the senator's six-year term came to a close, Abourezk decided not to run for reelection. He didn't fear he would not win—in fact, polls showed he had enough support to retain his seat. Rather he had grown tired of Washington politics. Abourezk retired to the private sector in 1980 but still found himself very involved in Arab American issues.

In the aftermath of Abscam, Abourezk decided it was time to do something about the "very low image" of Arabs that he believed existed in the United States. In 1980, Abourezk founded the American-Arab Anti-Discrimination Committee (ADC) to fight racism against Arabs. The ADC's "specific purpose," Abourezk said in a 1996 speech, "was to try to reunite the entire Arab American community." The 25,000-member ADC provides legal assistance to Arabs facing immigration or discrimination problems, speaks out against the stereotyping of Arabs in television and movies, rallies for more education about the Middle East in American classrooms, and lobbies for Arab American interests in Washington, D.C. Abourezk remains involved with the ADC as an advisor.

Personal notes

After twenty-nine years of marriage, Abourezk and his wife, Mary Ann, divorced in 1981. Their marriage produced three children: Charlie, Nikki, and Paul. In 1982, Abourezk married Margaret Bethea, a former administrative assistant to House Representative Ken Holland of South Carolina. The couple split after six years. Abourezk and his third wife, Sanaa Dieb, live in Rapid City, South Dakota, where Abourezk continues his private law practice.

FURTHER READING

Abourezk, James G. *Advise & Dissent: Memoirs of South Dakota and the U.S. Senate*. Chicago: Lawrence Hill Books, 1989.

Abourezk, James G., and Hyman Bookbinder. *Through Different Eyes*. Bethesda, MD: Adler & Adler, 1987.

Almanac of American Politics. New York: E.P. Dutton, 1978, pp. 782–86.

Douth, George. *Leaders in Profile: The United States Senate*. New York: Sperr & Douth, Inc., 1975.

F. Murray Abraham

Syrian-Italian actor

Born October 24, 1939
Philadelphia, Pennsylvania

> "ON STAGE I MUST RELY ON MYSELF AND THAT'S WHY I LOVE THE THEATER, AND COMEDY IN PARTICULAR. NO ONE HAS TO TELL ME IF I WAS GOOD OR NOT. EITHER THEY LAUGH OR THEY DON'T."

F. Murray Abraham is best known for his Academy Award-winning role as eighteenth-century Italian composer Antonio Salieri in the 1984 movie *Amadeus.* Despite receiving tremendous critical acclaim for his performance as Salieri, Abraham prefers the New York theater scene over the movie glitz of Hollywood, California. Theater, Abraham told *New York Newsday,* is "my touchstone, my pole star. Here I have many outlets—children's theater, street theater. The theater here exists as a respected entity. In Los Angeles, all it is is a showcase for movies."

In cahoots with Coppola

Farhid Murray Abraham was born in Pittsburgh, Pennsylvania, in 1939, one of fourteen children. He was named after his father, Farhid, a name that means "the one and only," but Abraham has always been called by his middle name. His father was a mechanic who had immigrated to the United States when he was five years old after a swarm of locusts caused famine in his native Syria. Abraham's mother, Josephine, was an American of Italian heritage. When he was still a child, the family moved to El Paso, Texas.

Abraham enjoyed telling jokes and stories, but he was never exposed to theater or acting until high school, when a teacher persuaded him to try out for the school play. Abraham took his teacher's advice and landed the part of a Scottish soldier in the school's production of *The Old Lady Shows Her Medals*. As soon as he came out on stage, Abraham knew that theater was where he belonged.

After high school, Abraham accepted a drama scholarship at the University of Texas at El Paso, where he studied for two years before dropping out in 1961 to look for acting jobs in Los Angeles, California. With little drama experience, Abraham lacked confidence in his abilities. Unable to muster enough courage to show up at auditions, Abraham took a job working backstage for University of California at Los Angeles (UCLA) theater productions. As a stagehand, Abraham met UCLA film student Francis Ford Coppola (1939–), who would later go on to direct the award-winning classics *The Godfather* (1972) and *Apocalypse Now* (1979). When Coppola offered Abraham a part in a small film he was producing, Abraham turned it down—not because he didn't want the role, but because he feared he wasn't good enough.

After several years in Los Angeles, Abraham finally got up the nerve to try out at auditions, and in 1965, he landed the part of Mr. Shumway in *The Wonderful Ice Cream Suit*. When that production finished its run, Abraham decided it was time he *really* learned how to act. He set his sights on Broadway and packed his bags for New York.

Making his Broadway debut

While Abraham studied acting at the HB (Herbert Berghof) Studio in New York City, he picked up small jobs, such as playing Santa Claus at Macy's department store and parking cars, to pay the rent. To neutralize the Texas twang he picked up in El Paso, he listened to tapes of radio announcers. In 1966, Abraham was cast as the Actor in the Off-Broadway production of *The Fantasticks,* and two years later he debuted on Broadway as Rudin in *The Man in the Glass Booth*. Abraham appeared in a steady succession of plays during the

1970s, including his critically acclaimed performance as Chris, in *The Ritz* (1975).

During the 1970s, Abraham also did some voice-overs and commercials (including appearing as a giant leaf in Fruit of the Loom underwear ads) to add to his meager theater income. His wife, Kate Hannan, whom he married in 1962, worked as a secretary so the couple would have enough money to get by. In 1978, however, Abraham gave up doing commercials because he felt that "No one was taking my acting seriously." Kate took a job as an assistant to the head of the Brooklyn Friends School, and Abraham helped out with raising their two children and performing household chores. At times, being a "house husband" was "very rough on my macho idea of life," Abraham told *People* magazine.

Making everything *fine*

Abraham continued to act, picking up leading roles such as Alchonon in the Broadway production of *Teibele and Her Demon* (1979), the title character in a Baltimore performance of *Cyrano de Bergerac* (1980), and Creon in the Public Theater's *Antigone* (1982). Although Abraham was unknown outside of New York's theater circles, he reassured himself that he was blessed with a great talent. "If you think of yourself in any terms less than great, you're never going to achieve greatness," Abraham told the *New York Times*. "It doesn't mean you can only express it in grand parts, it means making whatever you do ... *fine*."

Abraham continued to garner critical praise for his work. *Variety* described Abraham's interpretation of Davies in *The Caretaker* (1982) as "a daring and steadily surprising performance by one of the most gifted actors working regularly in the theatre." His performance as the country doctor Astrov in *Uncle Vanya* (1983) earned him the *Village Voice*'s Obie Award for Off- and Off-Off-Broadway theater achievement. Abraham delivered a "stirring portrait" as the rabbi, who builds a monster to protect the Jews in Prague from their enemies, in *The Golem* (1984). Despite his success on stage, Abraham told the *Washington Post*, "There were times when I was forty and couldn't pay the rent. There were times when I had to borrow money, from my dad, from friends."

Abraham made his debut on the silver screen in the 1970s with the bit part of a deluded judge in *They Might Be Giants*

(1971). He played police detectives in *Serpico* (1974) and *All the President's Men* (1976), and he kept his part as Chris in the movie version of *The Ritz* (1976). He made several other movie appearances, including his part as Omar in *Scarface* (1983), before being chosen for the lead role in *Amadeus* (1984).

Brings Salieri to life

When director Milos Forman began casting for the film version of *Amadeus,* a production about Austrian composer Wolfgang Amadeus Mozart (1756–1791) and his jealous rival Antonio Salieri (1750–1825), well-known Hollywood actors like Jack Nicholson (1937–) and Al Pacino (1940–) lined up for the part of Salieri. Although Abraham really wanted the part, he fully expected it would be given to a foreign or more famous American actor. Abraham was stunned when Forman gave the highly coveted role—a part Abraham called "the best role written in the last three decades"—to him.

Abraham studied for the part by learning to play the piano and to write musical notation. Like Abraham, Salieri felt the calling to perform, but his years of artistic labor had failed to bring him much fame; unlike Abraham, Salieri took his obsession to an extreme, denouncing God for rewarding Mozart's giddy immaturity while ignoring his own hard work. Throughout the movie, Salieri is tormented by his awareness that Mozart is a better composer than him. In his old age, Salieri is left with the realization that his own bitterness has consumed his life.

Ironically, Abraham's performance as the neglected composer brought the actor great critical and popular recognition. Abraham took home best actor honors from the Academy Awards and the Golden Globe Awards for 1984, as well as the Los Angeles Film Critics Award and the Albert Schweitzer Award for classic film acting. *Amadeus* earned seven other Academy Awards that year, including the award for best picture.

A villain even darker than Salieri?

For Abraham, the new-found fame brought some small improvements—the family could afford to eat out more and buy a second television and a second car—but he did not want his celebrity status to interfere with his love of good acting. After receiving the Academy Award, Abraham rejected more than $1.5 million in scripts. He felt he would not be

CAREER HIGHLIGHTS

Major roles

Chris in *The Ritz* (1975)

Alchonon in *Teibele and Her Demon* (1979)

Cyrano de Bergerac in *Cyrano de Bergerac* (1980)

Creon in *Antigone* (1982)

Davies in *The Caretaker* (1982)

Astrov in *Uncle Vanya* (1983)

Rabbi in *The Golem* (1984)

Antonio Salieri in *Amadeus* (1984)

Bernardo Gui in *Name of the Rose* (1986)

Malvolio in *Twelfth Night* (1986)

Roy Cohn in *Angels in America* (1994)

Awards

Obie Award for Off- and Off-Off-Broadway theater achievement, for playing Astrov in *Uncle Vanya* (1983)

Abraham won the following awards for his portrayal of Antonio Salieri in *Amadeus*:

Academy Awards, Best Actor (1984)

Golden Globe Awards, Best Actor (1984)

Los Angeles Film Critics Award (1984)

Albert Schweitzer Award for classical film acting (1984)

taken seriously if he cashed in on his Oscar fame with high-paying but mediocre roles.

Abraham hoped his next acting project would be a comedic role. He prefers comedy for the same reason he favors theater over movies: the thrill of the audience response. "On stage I must rely on myself and that's why I love the theater, and comedy in particular," Abraham told the *New York Times*. "No one has to tell me if I was good or not. Either they laugh or they don't." The next role that intrigued Abraham, however, was that of Grand Inquisitor Bernardo Gui, a character even darker than Salieri. Grand inquisitors were Roman Catholic Church officials in medieval Europe who interrogated non-Catholics. They would often use torture to make Christians confess their sins and execute those they believed to be in opposition to the Church. Despite Abraham's strong sinister performance as Gui in *Name of the Rose* (1986), the movie was a critical and commercial flop.

Abraham has remained very active in the New York theater circuit, playing Malvolio in a Central Park production of Shakespeare's *Twelfth Night* (1986), Roy Cohn in the critically acclaimed *Angels in America* (1994), and assisting with children's and street theater productions. Since 1985, Abraham has also taught acting at New York's Brooklyn College. Abraham offers more than just tips on acting techniques to his students. He prepares his students for the emotional blow that comes with being turned away for parts. "I tell them the thing that's hard is that when you're rejected, it's you that's rejected," he told the *Washington Post*. "You! Your face. The sound of your voice."

Abraham has also appeared in numerous movies since *Amadeus,* including *Bonfire of the Vanities* (1990), *Last Action Hero* (1993), and *Mighty Aphrodite* (1995). Abraham and his wife live in their Greenwich Village apartment in New York

Abraham applies makeup for the stage. Reproduced by permission of AP/Wide World Photos

City, where Abraham continues to work on various acting projects. "Keep working. Drama, comedies, television—I'd do it all," Abraham told *Parade* magazine. "I love to work."

FURTHER READING

"Abraham, F. Murray." *Current Biography Yearbook 1991,* New York: H. W. Wilson, 1991, pp. 4–8.

Bachmann, Gideon. "C.I.A.: Central Intelligence Actor." *Film Comment* (Sept-October 1986): 16–18+.

Berreby, David. "He Hates Mozart, Loves Brooklyn." *New York Newsday* (July 17, 1986).

Brady, James. "In Step with F. Murray Abraham." *Parade Magazine* (October 12, 1986): 22.

Solway, Diane. "An Actor Prepares for Malvolio." *New York Times* (June 29, 1986): section 2, p. 1.

Span, Paula. "F. Murray Abraham, Take 1." *Washington Post* (September 29, 1986): C1.

Stark, John. "His Meanie Role in *Amadeus* Makes Nice Guy F. Murray Abraham the Man to Beat for the Oscar." *People* (March 18, 1985): 55–56.

Spencer Abraham

Lebanese-American politician

Born June 12, 1952
Lansing, Michigan

Spencer Abraham became a U.S. Senator in 1994, but the Michigan Republican has been on the political scene since the early 1980s. Many party insiders credit his leadership as chair of the state Republican Committee for the resurgence of the Republican Party in Michigan. After serving as an aide to Vice President Dan Quayle (1947–), Abraham won his Senate seat, becoming an outspoken supporter of legal immigration and pressing to lift the ban on travel to Lebanon.

The prudent party-builder

Edward Spencer Abraham was born in 1952, the grandson of Lebanese immigrants. His father, Eddie, worked at the Oldsmobile car plant in Lansing, Michigan, and was a member of the United Auto Workers (UAW) union. Upon leaving the plant, Eddie managed and later owned a "mom and pop" retail store with his wife, Jane.

Abraham was raised in a conservative household that valued the traditional family and stressed the importance of hard work. After graduating from Michigan State University

"MY STRATEGY IS TO BUILD THE CASE FOR LEGAL IMMIGRATION. I WANT TO ACCENT THE POSITIVE—WHAT IMMIGRANTS DO FOR THIS COUNTRY—AND MAKE CLEAR THAT YOU'RE GOING TO ADDRESS THE NEGATIVES, ESPECIALLY CRIMINAL ALIENS."

Senator Spencer Abraham (center), with New York Mayor Rudolph Giuliani (left) and Senator Frank Lautenberg (right) arrive at a U.S. Senate Subcommittee on Immigration at Ellis Island, New York. Reproduced by permission of Archive Photos, Inc.

in 1974, he enrolled in law school at Harvard University. Noticing that the school sponsored many liberal law journals (advocating more government involvement in economic affairs but little intervention in personal activities) but no conservative ones (calling for less government involvement in economic affairs but providing a stricter reading of the personal liberties granted by the Constitution), Abraham approached the university for funding for a conservative law journal. Harvard denied his request, so Abraham sought private donations to print the *Harvard Journal of Law and Public Policy.* Although the journal started in the late 1970s with only twenty writers and a handful of subscribers, today it is the second-most widely read law review in the country.

After graduating from Harvard in 1979, Abraham went on to work in politics, getting his first hands-on electoral experience in 1982 as a campaign aide for Richard Headlee, the Republican candidate for governor of Michigan. Although Headlee lost, Abraham gained experience building support for a candidate within the party. Later in 1982, at the age of thirty, he became the youngest chairman of the Michigan Republican Party, inheriting the party's $450,000 debt. Worse than the party's debt was its morale: in Michigan, Democrats controlled both houses of the legislature (the Senate and the House of Representatives) and held every statewide office. Abraham turned the Republican party's fortunes around: in his first year, he not only repaid the party's debt but added $2.5 million to the Republicans' treasury. Republicans capitalized on a special election in 1983 by ousting two state Senate Democrats, thus taking enough seats to control the Senate. In the 1984 elections, Republicans gained a majority of seats on the state's education board, picked up two spots on the state Supreme Court, won a seat in Congress, and filled many county offices. Although the popularity of Republican President Ronald Reagan helped many Republican candidates in Michigan, Abraham's fundraising efforts were a key part of the party's return to power.

Engineers Engler's message

Abraham's last major accomplishment as state party chairman was his role in helping then-state Senate Majority Leader John Engler win the 1990 governor's race. After the election, Vice President Dan Quayle appointed Abraham to be his deputy chief of staff, helping head Quayle's domestic initiatives. He also became cochair of the National Republican Congressional Committee, which helps Republican candidates run for Congress. In the 1992 elections, Abraham headed fundraisers to help Republicans win ten new seats in Congress, but with the defeat of President George Bush and Vice President Quayle, Abraham was out of a job. After making an unsuccessful bid in 1993 for chair of the National Republican Committee, Abraham decided to run for the Senate. Although he had never held his own elected office, Abraham was described by the *National Review* as "very nearly a genius, one of the finest nuts-and-bolts political technicians of his generation."

As a candidate to fill the seat of Michigan's retiring Senator Donald W. Riegle, Jr., Abraham hitched his 1994 campaign to the success of Michigan's Governor Engler, whom

IMMIGRATION

Seen abroad as the land of opportunity, the United States is the final destination for millions of people from other countries seeking a better life. The Immigration and Naturalization Service (INS) reports that in 1996, 915,900 immigrants were allowed into the United States. In October 1996, INS estimated that another 5 million undocumented immigrants (or "illegal aliens") were living in America, with that number growing by 275,000 a year. About half of the illegal aliens are from Mexico, and most of them live in California, Texas, New York, and Florida.

Since 1875, the United States has had policies to determine the number and kind of immigrants that will be allowed into the country. The first law turned away criminals; later laws discriminated on the basis of country of origin (such as the Chinese Exclusion Act of 1882, which temporarily barred the entry of Chinese immigrants). A 1917 act set literacy requirements (in English or another language) for immigrants, and from 1921 to 1965, there were limits on how many people from each country could come to the United States.

A series of reforms beginning in the late 1960s has changed the face of American immigration policy. There are no more limits based on nation of origin, and employers who hire illegal aliens face stiff penalties. Immigrants with special occupational training or close family members in the United States are given preference. Senator Spencer Abraham believes that immigration policies should still allow law-abiding newcomers to come and seek the American Dream. "We should not slam the door shut on people yearning to be free and to build a better life for themselves and their families," he wrote in an article.

Abraham helped get elected only four years earlier. In those four years, Engler had cut taxes, made major changes to the welfare system, and helped bring the state out of debt. Under Engler, Abraham said, "Michigan has proved you can cut taxes and create jobs at the same time, and I want to take that message to Washington."

According to a *New York Times* article, however, Abraham had some trouble connecting with voters. On one occasion Abraham, who is "a bit stiff in manner to begin with," according to the *Times*, visited an inner-city job-training program overdressed in a fancy pinstriped suit, which "immediately set him apart." Voters also reacted negatively when Abraham ran a misleading add about his opponent, Congressional Representative Bob Carr, during the campaign. Abraham pulled the ad, which erroneously stated that Carr would receive millions of dollars, instead of thousands, from his federal pension, but refused to describe the ad as "wrong." Carr, who had trouble raising enough money for a strong campaign or gaining enough media attention, fared even worse.

On election night, Abraham defeated Carr by ten percentage points.

Building the case for legal immigration

Like most of his fellow Republicans, Abraham supports less government involvement in business and social services, lower taxes, free trade with other countries, term limits for elected officials, and bills that make it harder for women to get an abortion. He is a member of the Senate committees on Budget, Commerce, and Judiciary, and he chaired the Immigration Subcommittee. The grandson of Lebanese immigrants, Abraham told the *New York Times* that he is a believer in the American Dream—that the poor but determined people from other countries can come to America to build a new life for themselves and a brighter future for their children. He has opposed legislation that would cut back on the number of legal immigrants allowed into the country, and he has supported bills that deport legal and illegal immigrants who violate American laws. "My strategy is to build the case for legal immigration," he told the *Times*. "I want to accent the positive—what immigrants do for this country—and make clear that you're going to address the negatives, especially criminal aliens."

Some groups, like the Federation for American Immigration Reform (FAIR) have criticized Abraham for allowing loopholes in the immigration laws. In one such case, Abraham allowed an exception to the law forbidding aliens who overstay their visas to reenter the United States for a period of many years. The senator allowed a provision for the offender to pay $1000 fine instead. "He appears captive to pressure from industries that rely on cheap foreign labor," FAIR executive director Dan Stein said. "They're pushing retention of a loophole that effectively guts Abraham's own reform."

Abraham's other accomplishments as a Senator include being the first member of his Congressional "freshman class" to get a bill signed into law—an act preventing the U.S. Sentencing Commission from lowering the penalties for crack cocaine dealers. He also wrote the "Prison Litigation Reform Act," making it harder for prisoners to file unnecessary lawsuits. As part of an effort to shrink the federal government, Abraham is among the Republicans calling for the dismantling of the Department of Commerce, the cabinet agency that promotes business growth and trade. Although many opponents of this initiative say the department plays an important role in promoting business interests, Abraham feels the department is unnecessary and costly to taxpayers.

Along with Senator Bob Graham (1936–), Abraham has called for the White House to lift its official policy of discouraging Americans from going to Lebanon. "Lebanon is now a different place, in which terrorists, including those who committed acts against Americans, are being tried and punished for their crimes," he wrote in a statement issued by his office. The Clinton Administration lifted the policy in July 1997.

Personal notes

Abraham and his wife, Jane, have twin daughters, Betsy and Julie, and a son, Spencer Robert. In addition to his political career, Abraham has taught as an assistant professor at Thomas M. Cooley Law School and worked for the law firm of Miller, Canfield, Paddock and Stone in Detroit, Michigan.

FURTHER READING

Apple, Jr., R.W. "In 2 Bellwether States, Republicans See the Chance to Relive a Landslide." *New York Times* (October 30, 1994): 24.

Polsby, Daniel D. "Go Forth, Abraham." *National Review* (November 7, 1994): 25.

George F. Addes

Lebanese-American union leader

Born August 26, 1910
La Crosse, Wisconsin

Died June 19, 1990
Grosse Pointe, Michigan

As a young man, George Addes left high school and worked as a factory laborer to help his family out financially. His strong sense of right and wrong, instilled in him by his immigrant parents, stirred him to protest the factory's unfair treatment of its employees. He continued pursuing justice for workers and became increasingly active in labor union activities. He helped start the United Automobile Workers (UAW) union, which grew to be one of the United States' most powerful labor organizations. For the first decade of the UAW's existence, Addes was one of its most influential leaders.

Lebanese and American

By the time Addes's father, Nicholas Addes, came to the United States in 1905 at the age of fifteen, he had already been teaching French and Arabic at a school in his hometown of Rachaya al-Fukhar, Lebanon. He came to La Crosse, Wisconsin, where some of his relatives lived, with the intention of making some money and then returning to Lebanon.

GEORGE F. ADDES'S STRONG SENSE OF RIGHT AND WRONG, INSTILLED IN HIM BY HIS IMMIGRANT PARENTS, STIRRED HIM TO PROTEST UNFAIR TREATMENT OF EMPLOYEES.

Reproduced by permission of the Archives of Labor and Urban Affairs at Wayne State University.

Instead, he got married and settled into his new country. The young woman Addes married was also from Rachaya. As many Lebanese immigrants did, he first earned a living by working as a peddler; he carried two heavy suitcases of products as he traveled around Wisconsin, selling kitchen tools and linens door-to-door. As his family grew (he had two sons and three daughters), he took other kinds of jobs that involved less traveling—working as a locomotive fireman on the railroad and then laboring in factories.

George Addes, the younger of the two Addes sons, was born in 1910. During his childhood, he was exposed to a blend of Lebanese and American cultures. His father taught the children Arabic in regular classes in the home for five or six years; besides having a large collection of Arabic books, the father subscribed to *Al-Ahram,* an Arabic-language newspaper from Egypt. Addes told Arab American historian and archivist Alixa Naff (see entry) in a 1980 interview that he remembered his parents spending a lot of time talking with their children, telling them stories, jokes, experiences, and "what is right and what is wrong."

The Addes family had many Lebanese friends, and much of their socializing centered around La Crosse's Eastern Orthodox and Melkite Catholic church communities. Addes, though, recalled having both American and Lebanese friends as he was growing up. Although his father sometimes talked about current events in the Middle East, Addes felt no particular attachment to Lebanon. He told Naff, "That was another country; they had their own problems. We were having our problems here too."

Resisting racism

When Addes was about twelve, his family moved to Toledo, Ohio, so his father could find a better job. To help with the family's finances, young Addes began selling newspapers, and on weekends he shined shoes for ten cents a pair. The factory Addes's father worked for had periodic financial problems and workers were often let go, leaving the family with little or no income. In the mid-1920s the Addes family moved to Flint, Michigan looking for a more stable job situation. They lived there for two years. The social climate in Flint was very different from what they had experienced in La Crosse and Toledo.

THE KU KLUX KLAN

The Ku Klux Klan (KKK or Klan) is a secret terrorist organization that was founded in the mid-1800s and has been disbanded and revived several times since then. The organization's name comes from the Greek word *kuklos* (circle) and the English word *clan* (a group with common ancestry). The Klan arose in the south at the end of the Civil War, organized by whites who were still angry with the United States Government. Their violence was originally aimed at blacks—whom they didn't think should be citizens—and white government leaders who were loyal to the U.S. government and working to reunite the north and the south. During Klan events, members dress in white, wearing robes or sheets, masks, and pointed hoods. Their terrorist tactics have included burning large wooden crosses near the homes of people they wish to frighten, beating victims with whips, cutting them with knives, or murdering them.

The KKK was officially disbanded in 1869, although some local groups continued to function. The organization was then officially revived in 1915; membership was restricted to white, Protestant men who were native-born Americans. Blacks, Roman Catholics, and Jews were specifically excluded from membership and became targets for persecution, along with labor union members and foreigners. In 1944 the parent organization went bankrupt. In the 1960s, the Klan became more active again, and by the 1970s, about fifteen different Klan organizations existed. There was another resurgence in the early 1990s under a new charismatic leader, David Duke of Louisiana. Duke has since attempted to distance himself from the Klan as he attempts to get more involved in government and politics.

Addes remembered feeling a definite atmosphere of prejudice during those two years in Flint—resentment directed not only toward the Lebanese, but "against foreigners in general." He told Naff, "Flint was very bad. I recall the [Ku Klux] Klan movement—burning of the crosses, and so forth." Addes normally went to parochial schools (private schools run by churches), but he attended the public school in Flint. He said that students who supported the Ku Klux Klan wore a cross with a red rhinestone, and they beat up students who didn't wear the emblem. When Naff asked Addes if he wore such a cross to avoid fights, he replied, "No way."

Walking out

To help support his family, Addes dropped out of high school after two years. Like his father, he became a factory worker. Addes had hoped to become an airplane mechanic, but his family couldn't afford to pay for the training. Sending his brother to a mechanics trade school had already overstretched the family's financial limits. The family moved back to Toledo around 1927, and Addes and his brother started working for the Willys-Overland company, an automobile plant that eventually developed the Jeep as a military vehicle for the U.S. Army during World War II (1939–45; when the United States and certain European countries fought to stop aggressions by Nazi Germany and Japan).

It wasn't long before Addes became upset with the factory's treatment of its employees. His first complaint involved abuse of overtime. He told Naff that the company told the workers to "punch out" on the time clock at the end of the regular work day and then expected them to work for another hour or two without being paid for the extra time. "I couldn't see this," he said. He and his brother told the other workers, "When quitting time comes, we punch out and go home. We don't have to work overtime." Out of fear of losing their jobs, none of the other workers joined Addes and his brother when they left. Their fears were justified; both Addes and his brother were fired. However, because of his brother's training as a mechanic and Addes' friendship with a personnel officer, both men were rehired to work in different departments of the company.

Gaining confidence

Addes continued to see injustice in the workplace, and he began to read about the growing movement to organize workers into labor unions (organizations that represent employees in negotiations with an employer about such things as pay, hours, and working conditions). Unions had developed some strength during World War I (1914–18; a war that started in Europe and eventually involved many other countries from all around the world) but were experiencing severe setbacks during the Great Depression (1929–39; a period in U.S. history when the economy declined sharply and many people were out of work). During the Depression, unemployment was very high, so people who had jobs worried about the possibility of losing them. This made it easier for employers to force long hours, low wages, and unfair practices on their workers. When Franklin D. Roosevelt (1882–1945) became U.S. President in 1933, he appointed Frances Perkins, a factory labor activist, as his Secretary of Labor (she was the first female cabinet member). Congress joined the President's efforts to help laborers, quickly passing the National Industrial Recovery Act (NIRA).

In addition to establishing a procedure for setting minimum wage levels and maximum work hours for different industries, the NIRA guaranteed workers the right to join together and bargain as a unit with employers.

The government's actions gave Addes confidence to continue fighting for better treatment for workers. He told Naff he wasn't afraid to actively organize workers because "the law was behind [me]." He started with his own department. The employees were paid only thirty-five cents an hour, which he thought was too low, so he convinced them to join their individual voices into a unified request to increase the wage to sixty-five cents an hour.

Stirring things up

The union local, or chapter, Addes joined in 1933 while working at the Willys-Overland plant was connected with a national union called the American Federation of Labor (AFL). John L. Lewis (1880–1969), one of that era's most powerful union leaders, was president of the United Mine Workers (UMW) and was also a member of the executive council of the AFL. Frustrated with the AFL's hesitancy to organize new locals and actively recruit new members among the mass-production industries (like automobile factories), Lewis left the AFL in 1935. He started a rival union called the Committee for Industrial Organization (CIO). The first industries Lewis sought to organize were the automobile makers and the steel manufacturers.

Meanwhile, Addes's local and others in the automobile industry were becoming more energetic in their demands for better treatment of workers. In 1935, the United Automobile Workers (UAW) union was formed. In addition to organizing new chapters, it attracted some former AFL locals. Addes, who by this time was financial secretary of his local, quit working for the Willys-Overland company and became a full-time union organizer. He had helped organize a 1934 strike (a strike is a temporary work stoppage by a group of employees intended to force the employer to agree to certain changes such as better pay, shorter work days, or better working conditions) against the Auto-Lite plant in Toledo and a 1935 strike against General Motors' Toledo plant. Eldorous Dayton described Addes in a biography of Walter Reuther, another

In 1934, Addes convinced workers at the Auto-Lite plant in Toledo, Ohio to strike for better pay and a forty-hour work week. Reproduced by permission of AP/Wide World Photos.

UAW leader: "Swarthy, young, hard, shrewd, Addes agitated [stirred others to action] ahead of the boiling sitdown strikes." With financial support from the CIO, the strikes spread. By late 1936, the entire automobile industry was shut down. When the strikes were finally settled the following year, the UAW had established itself in 400 companies in the industry. It had won for its members a forty-hour work week and a minimum wage of seventy-five cents an hour.

When the UAW union held its first annual convention in 1936, Addes was a vocal leader who was respected for his actions as well as his words. He was elected the UAW's first secretary-treasurer, a post to which he would be reelected ten times. After he became an officer in the UAW, Addes moved to Detroit, Michigan, with his wife. He had married Victoria Rose Joseph, the daughter of immigrants from Beirut,

Lebanon, in 1933. His parents also moved to Detroit and lived there the rest of their lives. While living in Detroit, Addes took classes at Wayne University Law School (Wayne is now called Wayne State University) for a year.

Showdown

In 1939 Addes made what he later called "the biggest mistake of my life," according to Martin Halpern's article in *Labor History*. At the UAW convention, "Addes was clearly the most popular figure in the union," Halpern wrote. "He was viewed as a person of integrity who put the interests of the union first." Halpern quoted an observer at the convention: "Every time Addes stood up for anything that convention went wild; if he went to the restroom it went wild." In that atmosphere, Addes considered running for president of the UAW.

Addes's decision was a difficult one. Clearly, he had the support of a majority of the members. However, he had recently been involved in a highly publicized dispute with the current UAW president, Homer Martin. Leaders of the powerful CIO, which had helped the UAW endure and prevail during the widespread strikes of 1936, pressured Addes to heal the division within the UAW by allowing the election of a new president who had not been involved with the recent controversy. Reluctantly, Addes agreed not to run for president, choosing instead to run for reelection to the secretary-treasurer position.

Red, pink, or not?

Although he was not the president of the UAW, Addes continued to be an important figure. A 1941 article in *Fortune* magazine referred to him as one of the two most important men in the union, the other being his rival, Walter Reuther. This rivalry became an issue at the UAW's annual convention in 1947. Reuther was running for presidency of the union. Addes was once again running for secretary-treasurer; his presidential running mate was R. J. Thomas, who had been president since 1939 and who was described by Dayton as "little more than a jovial front man for Addes."

For years, Reuther and his supporters had accused Addes of being a communist sympathizer. Communism is the belief that all people should receive an equal share of everything and are not separated by state or class. In the 1940s, communists were called "reds," while communist sympathizers were called "pink-os." Reuther's charge was a serious one at the beginning of the Cold War (1945–89), in which communist countries and democratic countries competed for world dominance. In fact, the Taft-Hartley Act (officially, the Labor-Management Relations Act) passed by Congress in 1947 specifically required union officers to file sworn statements certifying that they were not members of the Communist Party. Interestingly, in the early 1930s, Reuther had lived and worked in an automobile factory in the Communist Soviet Union for two years.

In Naff's interview, Addes emphatically denied that he was sympathetic to communism. He explained that because communism was anti-Catholic, and he was a lifelong Catholic, he was opposed to communism. In fact, Addes said that at the first UAW convention in 1936, he hadn't wanted to "get associated with [Reuther] ... because he just got back from Russia." Addes realized that during his years as a UAW officer, communist members of the union tended to vote for him, but he didn't care about the ideology, politics, or religion of people who joined the union or voted for him. "If he is a delegate, I want his vote," he said.

Out of power

Reuther's strategy succeeded. He was elected UAW president, while Addes and his running mates were defeated. After losing his position with the union, Addes had to find another job. He bought and managed a bar, taking a break from the automobile industry and labor activities. Later, however, he worked for the parts division of Ford Motor Company; he was a district manager when he retired in 1975.

In 1980 Addes spoke at the UAW national convention in Anaheim, California. He was honored to be invited, and he said the experience was a highlight of his life. He died ten years later, at nearly eighty years of age.

FURTHER READING

"Addes, George P." [sic] *Biographical Dictionary of American Labor.* Westport, CT: Greenwood Press, 1984, pp. 85–86.

Dayton, Eldorous L. *Walter Reuther: The Autocrat of the Bargaining Table.* New York: The Devin-Adair Company, 1958.

Halpern, Martin. "The 1939 UAW Convention: Turning Point for Communist Power in the Auto Union?" *Labor History* (Spring 1992): 190–216.

Stieber, Jack. *Governing the UAW.* New York: John Wiley and Sons, 1962.

Paul Anka

*Syrian-American
singer, songwriter, and businessman*

*Born July 30, 1941
Ottawa, Canada*

"I CAN FEEL SOMETHING *MAKING* ME WRITE! IT SCARES ME SOMETIMES, BECAUSE I HAVE A FEELING AND IT'S SOMETHING OUTSIDE OF ME COMING IN AND TAKING OVER."

Paul Anka became an overnight sensation at age fifteen, when his song "Diana" topped the music charts in 1957. Considered by many to be a musical prodigy, Anka developed staying power in the music industry by writing popular songs such as "My Way" and the theme to *The Tonight Show with Johnny Carson.* Often inspired by the Arab melodies he heard growing up, Anka has written hundreds of songs, including eighteen that have sold more than one million copies each. Anka always aspired to be an entertainer, but he has proved to be a savvy businessman as well, getting involved in many aspects of the music industry and shrewdly investing his earnings.

An early street performer

Paul Albert Anka was born in 1941 to Syrian immigrants Andrew Anka and Camilia Tannis Anka. The Ankas owned a sandwich shop and later a popular restaurant, the Locanda, in Ottawa, Canada. Anka is the oldest child; he has a sister Miriam and a brother Andrew.

Anka's knack for performing surfaced at an early age. He would sing for anyone who would listen—family, neighbors, and even city workers. At age six, Anka sang songs for the men laying a sewer pipe near his house. As a student he spent his free time hanging around nightclubs and talking to performers, not studying his schoolwork. His after-school job at a soda shop was short-lived because he spent more time entertaining his customers than serving them.

His musical training was brief—six piano lessons from a private teacher and nine music theory lessons from his Syrian Orthodox church choir instructor—but Anka seemed to have a natural gift for music. By age thirteen he was writing original songs, sometimes drawing inspiration from the winding Arabic melodies and chanting he heard on records his parents played. Anka teamed up with two school buddies to form the Bobbysoxers, a band that played at the Central Canada Exhibition in 1955. The band also played at clubs, earning up to $45 a night.

Anka also performed solo, winning a singing contest at the Fairmount Country Club. He received a standing ovation from a 300-member audience and a week-long gig at the club. Up until that time, his father disapproved of Anka's musical interest, seeing it as a distraction that kept him from taking his studies seriously. After hearing his son play, however, a tearful Andrew Anka decided to help his young son launch his musical career.

Instant fame

In 1955, Anka went to California and recorded a song that sold just enough copies to pay for the recording expense. Discouraged, Anka returned to Ottawa. Seven months later, during the spring of his tenth-grade year, he borrowed $100 from his father and went to New York City. Some musicians he knew there arranged an audition for him with American Broadcasting Company (ABC)-Paramount record executives,

---

ARABIC CHANTS

Arabic chants that influenced Paul Anka's songwriting are rooted in the musical poetry of early Bedouin tribes. Words in such chants had to be carefully arranged to fit within the poetic meter (or rhythm) of the music so that the pronunciation, inflection, and meaning of each word would be correct. Bedouin poet-musicians were important figures: their pieces could irritate enemies, gain respect for the tribe, and provide lasting tribute to tribesmen who died in battle. Like the Bedouin poems on which they were based, Arabic chants were usually performed by one person and contained only one line of melody (monophonic), as opposed to several melodies that would make a harmony. The single melody was enriched using alternating rhythms and changes in pitch (the highness or lowness of a sound). Arabic chants were primarily used to call Muslims to prayer and to recite passages from the Koran, the sacred book of the Muslim faith.

Anka first gained popularity with teenagers in Europe. Here he is surrounded by young fans in Stockholm, Sweden. Reproduced by permission of the Corbis Corporation.

whom Anka immediately impressed with his enthusiasm. "Can you imagine this fifteen-year-old kid bouncing into the office and playing ten of his own songs?" one executive told *Life* magazine. "He leapt at the piano like it was a steak dinner and he hadn't eaten for months." They were especially taken with a love song called "Diana," about Anka's crush on his babysitter who was several years older than him.

ABC-Paramount gave Anka a record deal, and his first single, "Diana" shot up the charts. The song became a hit first in Europe, and eventually sold more than 9 million copies. Anka embarked on international tours and was rushed by fans on every continent. He had to be airlifted out of a San Juan department store where he was signing autographs because the crowd of teenage fans turned into a mob. Crowds were so dense when Anka performed in Algeria that paratroopers had to escort him out of the concert hall. In Japan, Anka was so popular that fans waited outside in a typhoon to buy standing-room-only tickets. Anka's songs were very accessible to teenage audiences. He used upbeat rhythms and simple, honest lyrics that placed him on popular music's middle ground, between the sexually charged Elvis Presley (1935–1977) and squeaky-clean Pat Boone (1934–).

Anka followed up with several more hits, including "Lonely Boy" (1959), "Put Your Head on My Shoulder" (1959), and "Puppy Love" (1960). A prolific songwriter, Anka was churning out more tunes than he could record, so he sold them to other singers. Anka could write up to six songs a day, sometimes penning a song in only twenty minutes, and his most productive period was from 3 a.m. to 6 a.m. "I can feel something *making* me write!" he told *Maclean's.* "It scares me sometimes, because I have a feeling it's something outside of me coming in and taking over. I *have* to sit down and write, and everything falls into place."

SONGWRITING HIGHLIGHTS

"Diana" (1957)

"Lonely Boy" (1959)

"Put Your Head on My Shoulder" (1959)

"Puppy Love" (1960)

Theme song for *The Tonight Show Starring Johnny Carson* (1962)

"My Way" (1968—recorded by Frank Sinatra [1915–98])

"She's a Lady" (1971—recorded by Tom Jones [1940–])

"You're Having My Baby" (1974)

"One Man, One Woman" (1974)

"I Don't Like to Sleep Alone" (1975)

"Times of Your Life" (1975)

Paul Anka, Inc.

Part of Anka's image as a good guy with an edge was crafted by his manager, Irvin Feld. At Feld's suggestion, Anka cut his hair, shed forty pounds and got a nose job. Even Anka's outings with young women, like actress Annette Funicello (1942–), were arranged in part to provide good publicity for him. Anka's image-building was explored in the short movie, *Lonely Boy,* which was chosen as the 1963 Canadian Film of the Year.

With the help of Feld, Anka also made smart business decisions. He bought all the master tapes and rights to his music from ABC-Paramount, ensuring that the royalties for songs played on the air would go to him, not the record company. In the music industry, royalties are a share of the profit paid to the song's owner every time it's played. Anka's 1962 theme for the National Broadcasting Company's (NBC) *The Tonight Show Starring Johnny Carson,* for example, brought him more than $20,000 per year in royalties. Anka also incorporated himself in 1962. For business purposes, Paul Anka the entertainer became a company, able to hire employees (such as managers and band members), take advantage of corporate tax breaks, and pass company property (such as the master tapes of his music) on to successors without paying inheritance tax. By incorporating himself, Anka was able to enjoy the economic and legal benefits that businesses have.

Anka established his Spanka Music Corporation to hold rights to more than 200 of his songs, many of which other singers performed. He also owned a company that managed other budding singers. "Anka's influence extends so far into so many different aspects of the popular-record business that he can fairly be called one of its dictators of trends and tastes," *Maclean's* reported in 1962, when Anka was only twenty-one. At that time, Anka was making about $1.5 million a year, but spent only a small portion of that. Most of it was diverted to other investments, like his Camy Productions record printers, a 300-room apartment tower, a souvenir program printing firm, and sponsorship of National Basketball Association (NBA) games.

Seeing that his popularity among teenagers might be short-lived, Anka engineered his crossover into adult music, playing more sophisticated ballads for nightclubs. He saw his first gig at New York's Copacobana club in 1960 as a rite of passage from his boyhood appeal to his arrival as an established artist. By 1962, he was earning $20,000 to $25,000 per week performing at the Sands Hotel, a famous casino on the Las Vegas strip.

Does it his way

The British invasion of popular music in the mid-1960s, signaled by the arrival of the British band The Beatles, pushed performers like Anka out of the limelight. Anka continued working behind the scenes as a songwriter, writing "My Way" (1968) for Frank Sinatra and "She's a Lady" (1971) for Tom Jones. Anka also helped other singers and songwriters, like Steve Goodman and John Prine, get started in the music business. "Paul never stays still," Las Vegas journalist Joe Delaney told *Saturday Night.* "When he couldn't write for himself, he wrote for others. He sleeps with a tape recorder at his side in case he has an idea for a song."

Lounging Around

During the 1960s and 1970s, Anka firmly established himself on the glitzy Las Vegas strip, where his singing and showmanship made him a favorite among "lounge lizards"—patrons of the extravagant casino bars. Clad in a pressed tuxedo, Anka often entered the lounge from the back door, as the brass orchestra began playing "Diana." During his performances, Anka wandered out into the audience, shook hands with patrons, and even wooed the ladies with lines from his songs. "He was and is the kind of velvet-voiced baritone that Las Vegas' middle-aged audience likes best," *Time* said of Anka in 1975.

You might see him on TV

Anka returned to the studio in 1974 to record his hit song, "You're Having My Baby." Subsequent hits included "One Man, One Woman" (1974), "I Don't Like to Sleep Alone" (1975), and "Times of Your Life" (1975). Anka worked with other performers like Michael McDonald and Kenny Loggins to record his following albums, *Headlines* (1979) and *Walk a Fine Line* (1983). In 1981, Anka was awarded an honorary doctorate in music by St. John's University in New York. As a member of Broadcast Music, Inc., Anka has won twenty-two songwriting awards, four of which are for songs performed more than a million times.

Anka has also appeared in a made-for-TV Perry Mason movie and the 1993 Canadian film, *Ordinary Magic*. Over the span of his lengthy career, Anka has penned more than 800 songs, eighteen of which have sold more than a million singles each. Anka lives in his Beverly Hills, California, home with his wife, former fashion model Anne deZogheb, the daughter of Count and Countess Charles deZogheb of Paris, France and Alexandria, Egypt. Anka married deZogheb on February 16, 1963 in Paris, France. The couple has five daughters: Alexandria, Amanda, Alicia, Anthea, and Amelia. The Ankas are avid art collectors who showcase Oriental porcelains and Andy Warhol prints of Anka.

FURTHER READING

"Anka, Paul." *Current Biography Yearbook 1964*. New York: H.W. Wilson, 1964, pp. 3–6.

"Anka's Aweigh." *Time* (December 8, 1975): p. 61.

Gardner, Paul A. "What it Takes to Crash the Pan Alley at Fifteen." *Maclean's* (January 4, 1958): p. 12+.

Hardy, Phil and Dave Laing. *Encyclopedia of Rock*. New York: Schirmer Books, 1988, p. 18.

Knelman, Martin. "Lounge Wizard." *Saturday Night* (December 1994): 133-36.

Mair, Shirley. "The World's Reigning Juvenile." *Maclean's* (December 1, 1962): 25+.

Prideaux, Tom. "Paul Anka, Kids' Wonder Singer." *Life* (August 29, 1960): 67+.

Nicholas S. Assali

Lebanese-American medical researcher

Born 1916
Rachaya, Lebanon

The son of a political revolutionary, Nicholas Assali has always believed in speaking out on important issues, even when his opinion is not popular. Assali grew up in Lebanon, trained as a medical doctor in Brazil, and then came to the United States to do research that would help doctors prevent and treat complications during pregnancy and birth. His research in this field resulted in a great deal of new information and drastically changed the science of obstetrics (the branch of medicine concerned with pregnancy and childbirth).

Son of a rebel

Assali was nine years old in 1925 when his father, Salem Assali, died trying to overthrow the oppressive French government that had occupied Lebanon since the end of World War I (1914–18; a war that started in Europe and eventually involved many other countries from all around the world). His father had worked in America for five years during the 1890s, and he returned to Lebanon with two things: money

"AS A YOUNG SHEPHERD OR A LATRINE-DIGGER IN THE PRISON CAMP IN LEBANON OR AS A MEDICAL STUDENT IN BRAZIL, I NEVER DREAMED THAT ONE DAY I WOULD BECOME A PROMINENT [SCIENTIST] IN THE UNITED STATES OF AMERICA."

SEEDS OF FREEDOM

In 1925, Nicholas Assali's father, Salem Assali, died leading an unsuccessful revolt against the French. Lebanon had been ruled by the Ottoman Turkish Empire for nearly 400 years, but they lost control of the country to France after they were on the losing side of World War I (1914-18). Salem Assali was inspired to lead his revolt by the freedom he witnessed while working in the United States for five years during the 1890s.

In his autobiography *A Doctor's Life,* Nicholas Assali wrote about his father's experience in the United States: "He saw people, white and black alike, working together freely, without any interference from armed sentries or police. Although he observed differences in the living conditions and treatment of whites and blacks, these never both-

ered him, because they were minor by comparison with the differences between the Turks and Arabs in his own country." He talked to people and read books, trying to understand how the American patriots had managed to break free of British rule.

In 1924, Salem Assali felt it was time for the Lebanese people to free themselves from the harsh French colonialism. "He traveled on foot, mostly at night ... explaining, exhorting, and instilling a love of freedom among his countrymen. He told them how a small band of Americans was able to defeat the powerful British army and navy," Nicholas Assali wrote. "The sentence from his reading that he would repeat time and again to his fellow Lebanese, and with fervor, was Patrick Henry's [1736–1799] famous line, 'Give me liberty or give me death.'"

and a sense of freedom. He used the money to buy farmland, vineyards, goats, and sheep for his family and to repair his parents' home, barn, and butcher shop. He tried to use his knowledge of the freedom America had won in its revolution against England to lead his countrymen on a similar path. Unfortunately, he and his followers could not match the power of the French army, and their revolt failed.

As the hopeless battle ended, Assali's badly wounded father led his mother, his wife (Suraya Assali), and his six children out of their devastated village of Rachaya. Five miles outside the village, his father could go no farther. He said to his family before he died: "Whatever adversity you may encounter in the future, don't fear to fight for what you think is right. Don't be afraid to tell the truth, whatever the consequences. Be compassionate to your fellow men." While trying frantically to bury the man they loved (to protect his body from wild animals), the family was captured by French forces. Assali recalled in his autobiography that a soldier "hit my mother with the butt of his rifle. My brother and I rushed to protect her, but we were beaten badly. I received a cut over my left eye. The scar remains to this day and is a continuing reminder of those terrifying moments."

Not summer camp

The women and children were sent directly to a prison camp in a bug-infested swamp in Lebanon. After a year in the camp, Assali and his older brother were allowed to leave the prison camp each day to go to a nearby school. Eventually, Assali helped his older brother escape (relatives arranged for the boy to flee to Brazil where their uncle lived). For several months afterward, Assali was not allowed to go to school.

When Assali returned to school, he was treated harshly by teachers who were sympathetic to the French government. After repeatedly running away from school, he was expelled when he was twelve years old. He was assigned to hard labor at the camp hospital, which he described as "probably the most unsanitary part of the whole compound.... Bedbugs, flies, mosquitoes, and cockroaches could be seen everywhere." The hospital was used only by prisoners; soldiers who were injured or sick were taken to hospitals in Beirut. Assali's job was digging and covering open pits that were used as latrines (toilets) by the patients.

A step up

After eight months of digging latrines, Assali was assigned to help the camp pharmacist. He learned later that his uncle, who was the Catholic Archbishop of Baalbek, Lebanon, had convinced the camp commander to give him a better job. The pharmacist not only dispensed medicines to both prisoners and soldiers, but he also cleaned and treated infected areas on their bodies. "I decided that my first job was to cultivate his [the pharmacist's] friendship and goodwill," Assali wrote. He learned how to prepare the medicines the pharmacist dispensed, and while pretending to clean the room, he watched to see how the pharmacist treated patients' sores.

When a malaria epidemic broke out in the countryside surrounding the camp, another doctor was sent to the region. The doctor stopped at the camp pharmacy to get a supply of medicine and an assistant to accompany him. Assali was chosen to travel with the doctor throughout the Bekaa Valley for almost three months; he was responsible for giving each patient the right amount of medicine and explaining how it should be taken. "I began to feel a love for medicine and a compassion for the sick and helpless patients," he later wrote.

Sudden freedom

On December 1, 1932, after being imprisoned for nearly eight years, Assali was summoned to the camp commander's office and told that he and his family were to be set free in twenty-four hours. They would have to leave Lebanon within a week. "There were two major obstacles that had to be dealt with immediately: raising money to buy tickets and finding a country that would accept us and give us a visa (official permission from a government allowing a foreigner to enter and reside in that country) on such short notice," he recalled.

Not knowing where else to turn for help, Assali went to see his uncle, the Archbishop. In fact, it was the Archbishop who had arranged the family's release. He loaned the family half of the money they needed and contacted other family members in America and Brazil to ask their help. (Assali's two oldest sisters had married and immigrated to the United States before their father's death, and his two older brothers lived in Brazil with their uncle.) Within days, the money arrived for their tickets. Because they had just been released from a prison camp, the United States denied them permission to enter the country. Brazil, however, agreed to let them come.

As the family set out on a three-week ocean voyage, Assali recalled, "We thought it was the last time we would see our country, a prediction that turned out to be true for everyone except me. I did return in 1962 to search, unsuccessfully, for the place where we buried my father."

Pursuing a dream

Assali arrived in Brazil four months before his seventeenth birthday. His mother was a strong woman who took charge of the family's efforts to build a new life. She told Assali to work with his older brothers at their uncle's clothing store. This job helped support the family, but working in a store was not how Assali wanted to spend the rest of his life. He had enjoyed working at the pharmacy in the prison camp and assisting the doctors there. He decided that he wanted to become a doctor.

Assali knew that his mother would not like his decision, but he was determined. When he announced to the family that he was going to study medicine, "A stunned silence followed," he wrote. "Then my mother exploded. She argued that I was leaving the business in which we were doing well.... She always thought I could make more money in business than in medicine, and in that respect she was right." Despite her objections, he enrolled in night school while continuing to work ten-hour days at the store.

At the beginning of 1936, Assali had to prepare for the entrance and scholarship examinations for medical school. The examinations were difficult—six days of written tests followed by twelve hours of oral exams over a three-week period. Out of 900 or more applicants, only about 70 students would qualify for scholarships, and Assali knew he would be unable to attend school without that financial assistance. He told his mother he was going to quit working at the store so he could prepare for the examinations. She was very upset, but she agreed to let him try. She even brought meals to his room while he studied. He later wrote, "It was a crusade not only to accomplish my own goal and satisfy my ego, but also to conquer my family's opposition, and particularly my mother's. I remained in my room for three months."

Choosing a field

When Assali finally took the exams, he earned the third-highest score of all the applicants. Two months later, he started a six-year program at the State University of São Paulo, Brazil. In his final year he decided he wanted to specialize in obstetrics. Obstetricians care for women during pregnancy, childbirth, and the period just after childbirth. Assali liked the field for several reasons. Partly, he was influenced by a professor he enjoyed working with in that field, Dr. Delascio, who taught him how to conduct research and publish his results. He also liked helping, as he said in his autobiography, "young people who came to the hospital to have a healthy experience and were rewarded with a new life." Assali also felt that this field was challenging and offered many opportunities for innovative medical research.

A short visit extended

After Assali graduated from medical school in 1943, he

ran a government-supported health clinic. In 1945, his cousin, who was a prominent government official, became very ill. Assali was asked to accompany his cousin to Chicago for medical treatment that was not available in Brazil. Unfortunately, the treatment was unsuccessful and his cousin died.

Assali decided to stay in the United States for a year. "I wanted to observe how medicine was practiced there and what was new in obstetrics, particularly in regard to toxemia of pregnancy." Toxemia of pregnancy (also called preeclampsia [pre-i-KLAMP-see-a]) is a complication that fascinated Assali. Assali wrote that he and his professor had "asked ourselves why young women should suffer high blood pressure, protein in the urine, swelling, and convulsions ending in death. Delascio would say, 'This is an area where a man could make a major contribution'—a sentence that was implanted in my mind forever."

After a few months of searching for financial support and the right professional opportunity, Assali began working at Bethesda Hospital in Cincinnati, Ohio. Doctors at the hospital had developed a new treatment for toxemia of pregnancy, and Assali began a research program to figure out why and how the treatment worked. In a separate project, he also devised a way to measure the strength of uterine contractions (the shortening and quickening of muscles in the uterus) during labor. "This had never been done before, but it was essential to our understanding of the mechanisms of labor and delivery," he wrote.

Faces deportation

About two years after Assali began working in Ohio, a problem arose. He had made some changes in hospital procedures that angered some of the other doctors, and he had exposed some colleagues for increasing their profits by doing unnecessary surgeries. Some of these doctors tried to get him fired, blocked his admission to medical societies, and asked the U.S. Immigration and Naturalization Service (INS) to investigate Assali's status as a visitor to the United States. The INS found that he had been admitted on a visitor's visa, which did not allow him to work for pay while in the country—a rule he was breaking by working at the hospital. They told him he would have to return to Brazil.

"Our group was just then on the verge of an important breakthrough in our research on pregnant women," Assali recalled. They were close to figuring out why so many babies died when the mother had toxemia. Because Assali's work was so important, Ohio congressmen appealed to President Harry Truman (1884–1972). The day before Assali was to leave the United States, the INS received an order from Truman to reconsider the case. Months later, Assali was given a permanent visa and told that after five years' residency he would be eligible for U.S. citizenship, which he gained in 1951.

Uncommon family

In 1948, Assali married Pauline Hanna, whom he met in a Lebanese community he visited frequently in Toledo, Ohio. Her parents had come from a town near Rachaya, Lebanon, and had even known Assali's father. In 1950, Assali and his wife visited his family in Brazil. While he was in medical school, Assali had a son, who had remained in Brazil with his mother and was now eight years old. Assali wanted the boy to come live with him and Pauline in the United States. The boy's mother agreed to let him go.

Seven years later, Assali returned to Brazil to attend his younger brother's wedding and to give some medical lectures. The day he gave one of his talks, someone abandoned a three-week-old baby boy at the university hospital where Assali was speaking. Assali and his wife had tried unsuccessfully to adopt a child in the United States, so Assali decided to adopt this abandoned baby. It was difficult to make all the arrangements with the Brazilian and U.S. governments to adopt the baby and bring him into the United States. Fearing that the arrangements might be unsuccessful, Assali didn't tell his wife what he was trying to do. When he arrived home and she met him at the airport, he introduced her to their new child.

UCLA

The research Assali and his group were doing in Ohio received national attention, and he began to receive job offers from other universities around the country. In 1953, he took a position at the newly founded medical school of the University of California at Los Angeles (UCLA). During the years that followed, he continued to develop and conduct creative research projects—projects that uncovered much useful information in preventing and treating problems that arise during pregnancy and birth.

Peaceful rebel

Assali has always been something of a rebel—ready to speak up for causes he believes in. As a teenager, he spent a month in prison for organizing a student protest against Brazil's dictator. After becoming a U.S. citizen, he challenged the powerful American Medical Association (AMA) by publicly supporting President John F. Kennedy's health-care proposal, which the AMA did not want instituted. The plan became known as Medicare when it was later passed under the next president, Lyndon B. Johnson. During the United States' military involvement in Vietnam (1965–73; when the United States sent troops into Vietnam to help South Vietnam fight off its communist neighbor, North Vietnam), Assali was active in the antiwar movement, writing and visiting congressmen, picketing the White House, and supporting the rights of students to protest peacefully on the UCLA campus.

"Looking back on my life, I find little in it that I willed or planned," Assali wrote in his autobiography. "As a young shepherd or a latrine-digger in the prison camp in Lebanon or as a medical student in Brazil, I never dreamed that one day I would become a prominent [scientist] in the United States of America."

FURTHER READING

Assali, Nicholas S. *A Doctor's Life.* New York: Harcourt Brace Jovanovich, 1979.

Victor Atiyeh

Syrian-American governor of Oregon

Born February 20, 1923
Portland, Oregon

For eight years, Republican Victor Atiyeh served as governor of Oregon, a predominantly Democratic state. He was a popular governor, however, because he focused on issues close to the hearts of most Oregonians: education and the environment. He was also a shrewd businessman, able to shrink state government while expanding the market for Oregon's products. At the end of his term in 1987, Atiyeh returned to the private sector, serving on the Board of Directors for the family-owned rug import business started by his Syrian father and uncle.

Climbs the political ladder

Victor George Atiyeh was born in 1923 in Portland, Oregon. His father, George, raised Arabian horses in Amar El Hosn, Syria, before immigrating to the United States in the late 1800s. Around the turn of the century, Atiyeh's father and uncle Aziz Atiyeh opened an Oriental rug import business, named Atiyeh Brothers, in Oregon, mostly bringing in rugs woven in Iran.

"THE BEAUTY OF OUR SYSTEM IS THAT WE ARE RICHER FOR HAVING BOTH EFFECTIVE GOVERNMENT AND AN INDEPENDENT FREE PRESS."

Reproduced by permission of AP/Wide World Photos.

MAGIC CARPET RIDE

In 1929, Vic Atiyeh's uncle Aziz took a trip to Iran to buy rugs for the Atiyeh Brothers business that he and his brother George started in Portland, Oregon. A letter he sent to his brother explained the complications of the trip, the benefits of newer technology, and the Iranians' resistance to foreign ways. "My first task was to inspect the looms and see the course of weaving to ascertain what colors and designs are used, and how soon some will be finished," Aziz wrote. That task was a demanding one, as Aziz had to inspect some 300 looms that were scattered throughout the area. Then he met with the people who designed the patterns for the rugs, the suppliers who provided the right dyes for the yarn, and the contractors who arranged for the sale of the rugs. "None of them seem willing to take any advice or suggestions for they think their methods are the only correct ones," he wrote. "Those who agreed with me on some points and promise to follow them, in second inspection were found still following the old methods and stated mine were not so good. Finally, I gave up in despair for it is impossible to change their minds."

The advent of the automobile made transporting the rugs to shipping ports much easier and faster. Instead of taking thirty-five days by camel caravan, rugs could be sent in twelve days by trucks. However, fighting between Kashgar tribes and the Iranian government made some roads unsafe; the rarity of trucks also complicated the plans. In some areas, donkeys were the only mode of transportation. Aziz's travels did give him the chance to meet new people, and he wrote with excitement about an Arab-speaking man and an English-speaking Iranian he met while in Kerman. "Both are to call on me this afternoon, and we will have a game of bridge," he exclaimed. "What a treat!"

For the full text of the letter, visit the World Wide Web site for Atiyeh International, Ltd., at http://www.atiyeh.com.

Vic Atiyeh attended the first two years of a pre-law program at the University of Oregon in Eugene from 1941 to 1943 before serving two years (1944 to 1945) in the Coast Guard Reserve in Portland. He joined the Atiyeh Brothers rug company, where he served as president of the business until 1979. He also became interested in politics, winning a seat in the Oregon state House of Representatives in 1959. After five years in the House, Atiyeh made a successful bid for a state Senate seat, and he served as a state senator from 1965 to 1978. For three of those Senate sessions (from 1971 to 1978), he was the Senate Republican leader.

Atiyeh served as a delegate for Oregon at three Republican National Conventions (1968, 1972, and 1976), and he helped write the party platform (a statement of the party's political philosophy) for the 1968 and 1972 conventions. As a conservative Republican, Atiyeh was a strong supporter of

cutting taxes and government spending by reducing the services it offers. But on one issue he strayed from the traditional Republican party line. While in the senate, Atiyeh introduced numerous bills to protect air and water quality. While environmental protection is not usually on the Republican agenda, since it requires government spending and regulating industry, Atiyeh knew that this was an important issue for Oregon voters. The state's lumber business and the people's protectiveness of their immense forests made Oregonians especially concerned about environmental issues.

Atiyeh made a failed run for the governor's office in 1974—losing to Democrat Robert Straub. In 1978, Atiyeh ran against Straub again. This time, Atiyeh's emphasis on conserving natural resources and pursuing alternative forms of energy

After a failed attempt in 1974, Atiyeh became Governor of Oregon in 1978. Reproduced by permission of AP/Wide World Photos.

while still cutting taxes and reducing government spending reached the voters and he became Governor of Oregon.

Atiyeh's eco-agenda

As governor, Atiyeh worked to help Oregon's ailing lumber industry. However, he also took measures aimed at making the state's economy less dependent on timber. He worked to develop trade with other states and countries, including Japan and China, actively promoted tourism and supported legislation that made Oregon more attractive to businesses. One of these measures reduced the amount of money companies had to pay for workers compensation insurance. Another law reduced the amount of state taxes a company with overseas business had to pay.

While eager to make Oregon inviting to businesses, Atiyeh also focused on environmental policy, working to control development along the Deschules River and the Columbia River Gorge and to uphold Oregon's standards for clean air and water.

Other highlights of Atiyeh's two terms as governor include the establishment of Oregon Food Share—a first-of-its-kind statewide food bank to help feed the hungry—and the passage of strong laws against racial harassment. His leadership in passing those laws earned him honors from the U.S. Department of Justice and Oregon B'Nai B'rith, an American Jewish service organization.

Accessible leader

In addition to being governor, Atiyeh also held several other key posts. In 1979, he was appointed to head the National Task Force for the Indian Education Project of the Education Commission of the States, which studied how states around the country contributed to the education of Native American children. His pet project was the Boy Scouts of America, and he served as president of the Columbia-Pacific council of Boy Scouts. He also held several leadership spots in governors' organizations: chairman of the Western Governors' Conference, vice chairman of the Republican Governors' Association, and vice chairman of the National Governors' Association committees on international trade and foreign relations, criminal justice, and public protection.

During his years as governor, Atiyeh was known for being very accessible to reporters. Each week, he set aside thirty to ninety minutes to meet with the press for regular interviews, in addition to the last-minute interviews he often granted in response to breaking news. "In scheduling my time, only legislators come ahead of the media," Atiyeh told a 1986 audience, "and media come ahead of my own staff." Governing in the aftermath of Watergate (a scandal, vigorously pursued by the press, in which a failed cover-up of wrong-doings by President Richard M. Nixon and his staff ultimately forced Nixon's resignation), Atiyeh was especially sensitive to the loss of public confidence in elected officials. "The beauty of our system is that we are richer for having both effective government and an independent free press," he said.

In 1986, a two-term limit prevented Atiyeh from running again for governor. He now devotes more time to Atiyeh Brothers rug company, where he still serves on the board of directors. He also works as a consultant for international trade. He married Dolores Hewitt in 1944, and the couple have two children.

FURTHER READING

Mullaney, Marie Marmo. *Biographical Directory of the Governors of the United States, 1983-1988*. Westport, CT: Meckler Corp., 1989, pp. 275–77.

"Oregon." *Almanac of American Politics*. New York: Dutton, 1979, pp. 728-33.

Antonio Bishallany

Syrian theology student

Born August 22, 1827
Salima, Lebanon

Died August 22, 1856
New York, New York

Antonio Bishallany has long been regarded as the first recorded Arab immigrant to the United States. Although recent evidence indicates that there may have been a few others who came before him, he was the first to attain public recognition. He arrived in America in 1854 at the age of twenty-seven, hoping to be educated as a Christian missionary (someone who travels to non-Christian nations in the hope of converting people to Christianity). His studies were hindered by illness, and he died only two years later without completing his missionary training.

A biography titled *Sketch of Antonio Bishallany: A Syrian of Mount Lebanon* was written shortly after Bishallany's death and was distributed in Beirut, Lebanon, by American missionaries. In 1954, the one-hundredth anniversary of his arrival in America, Arabic-language publications in New York City published articles about him. The Lebanese government has designated his family home in Salima a historical site. In *Before the Flames: A Quest for the History of Arab Americans*, Gregory Orfalea (1949–; see entry) wrote, "What pushed

[Bishallany] to notch his name in history was a combination of family tragedy, personal pluck, and a burning desire to expand his learning."

Dangerous childhood

Bishallany was born in 1827, by most accounts in the village of Salima, in what was then Syria but is now part of Lebanon. His family grew olive trees and grapevines, which he helped tend during his childhood. The stone house he grew up in had been in the Bishallany family for more than a hundred years. Charles Whitehead, Bishallany's biographer, wrote that "Antonio's earliest recollections were of hard labor, scanty fare, and constant danger." Syria was under the control of the fierce Ottoman Empire (a vast state founded by Ottoman Turks in the late 1400s; it lasted until the early 1900s), and Whitehead explained, "First the ruling pasha [governor], then his horde of underlings, and lastly the priest had to be paid their dues, legal or illegal."

Bishallany's family belonged to the Maronite church, a branch of the Roman Catholic church. There was a bitter rivalry between the Maronites and the Druse (a Muslim sect). When Bishallany was ten years old, a Druse band attacked his home, destroying it along with the family's olive trees and vineyard. His family fled to the relative safety of a mountain village near Beirut. Adele Younis, author of *The Coming of the Arabic-Speaking People to the United States,* wrote that Salima was in fact the village in which the Bishallany family took refuge, and not the town of Bishallany's birth. Another tragedy hit the family about two years later when Bishallany's father died. Not wanting to be a burden to the family and hoping to help support his mother, Bishallany found whatever jobs he could.

Young explorer

When he was about fourteen, Bishallany went to work for the Italian consul (government representative) in Beirut. As the consul's valet (val-AY), or personal attendant, the young man not only served his employer at home but also on trips to islands and other port cities around the Mediterranean Sea. This experience stirred his curiosity about other cultures and languages. While working for the consul, he became fluent in Italian.

THE BIBLE AND THE REFORMATION

Antonio Bishallany told his American friends that when he bought his first Bible, he knew that "the authorities of the church would not allow him to read it." Although Roman Catholics are now encouraged to read the Bible, that was not always the case.

In the 1500s and 1600s there was a religious revolution, called the Protestant Reformation, in Western Europe which centered around objections to beliefs and practices of the Roman Catholic Church. One of the practices in dispute was that the Roman Catholic Church had discouraged its members from reading the Bible for themselves. In the mid-1500s, the Roman Catholic Church held the Council of Trent to address the problems that had triggered the Reformation.

However, the council reaffirmed that the Bible must be understood within the context of the church's traditions and declared that no Catholic should interpret the Bible in a way that contradicted the church's doctrine. Many bishops and priests thought that the best way to prevent contradictory interpretations of the Bible was to discourage common people from reading it themselves. Thus, although it was not the official intent of the church to restrict access to the Bible, the practice continued to be widespread for many more years. Interestingly, Saint Jerome (Eusebius Hieronymus, c. 347–c. 420), whose Latin translation of the Bible had been used by the Catholic Church for 1,000 years when the Council of Trent reaffirmed it as "authentic," had during his lifetime consistently urged everyone to read the Bible daily.

Reading the forbidden book

In addition to traveling, Bishallany loved reading books. Although his local priest encouraged this activity, Bishallany's reading materials did not include the Bible. A turning point for his entire life came one Sunday morning several years after he started working for the consul. As he was walking through the city, a man offered to sell Bishallany a Bible that was printed in Arabic. At first, he was not interested; he thought the book must not be important because it was priced at fifty cents, whereas his copy of *Arabian Nights* had cost him ten dollars. His curiosity was aroused, however, and he came back later to buy a copy even though, as Whitehead wrote, "He knew it was a prohibited volume; that the authorities of the church would not allow him to read it." Leaders of the Roman Catholic Church at the time were afraid that ordinary church members might misunderstand passages. They only allowed clergy members (ordained church leaders such as priests and bishops) to read the bible who would then explain it to the church members (see box for more information).

Bishallany was fascinated with reading the Bible; in the year after he bought his copy, he read it through twice. The following year, he undertook a systematic study of the entire volume. He thought some of what he read contradicted the practices of the Maronite church. He convinced his priest to loan him a copy of the version of the Bible that had been approved by the Catholic Church. He found it to be basically the same as the version he owned, which left the contradictions unresolved. Finally, he stopped going to church.

One evening, while Bishallany was visiting his mother's village, someone overheard him explaining his interpretations of the Bible to another man. The observer reported Bishallany to church officials. He was arrested and charged with heresy (proclaiming beliefs that contradicted those of the church). At that time, Syria was under the control of the Turkish Ottoman Empire, which entrusted ruling authority to church leaders. This meant that Bishallany faced trial by the government for the religious crime of heresy.

On the advice of a friend, Bishallany refused to say anything at his trial so that his answers could not be twisted and used against him (in this way, Bishallany chose to follow the example of his beloved Jesus who, according to the Bible, refused to answer questions by the governor before he was crucified). Nevertheless, Bishallany was declared a heretic. Although he was spared imprisonment, the villagers treated him as an outcast. He went to his mother's home, but she shut the door in his face and would not allow his brothers to talk to him for fear he would contaminate their minds. He returned to Beirut, taking comfort in scriptural passages about being persecuted for the Lord's sake and being willing to forsake father and mother to follow God.

On tour

In 1850, Bishallany stopped working for the Italian consul and became a dragoman. According to Whitehead's description, "The word *dragoman* properly means an interpreter. But someone serving in this capacity ... provides horses, or mules, or camels, for the conveyance of travelers, furnishes tents and provision for their accommodation on the journey, selects the best route, and adopts every means to secure the safety and comfort of those by whom he is employed." Bishallany was a friendly and outgoing person who not only informed his customers about historical sites; he also cooked for them and entertained them around the campfire when they rested for the night. He took travelers on trips up the Nile River in Egypt, through Syria, and to the Holy Land (Palestine—a region on the eastern shore of the Mediterranean Sea that is a place of pilgrimage for several religions).

Through his conversations with his customers, Bishallany learned English. He already knew and admired some Protestant missionaries from America, and now he met a number of friendly and interesting American tourists. He became increasingly curious about the United States. After working four years as a dragoman, he had saved enough money to travel to America.

On August 22, 1854, his twenty-seventh birthday, Bishallany left Beirut on a ship bound for Boston. He managed to talk to his brothers before he left, but his mother still refused to see him. In October, he arrived in Boston, carrying letters of introduction from American missionaries he knew in Syria. He also had addresses of some of his tour customers with whom he had become friendly.

After a brief stay in Boston, Bishallany went to New York City. He dressed himself in his best clothes—wide–legged trousers, a vest with an elegant braided border, and a fez (brimless hat) with a large tassel. Then he went to the office of a businessman who had been in one of his tour groups. The man had no idea Bishallany was coming, and later recalled (as quoted in by Younis in *The Coming of the Arabic-Speaking People to the United States*), "I was astonished by the entrance of Antonio into my office.... He has since told me, when I asked him what he knew of America, and what reason he had to expect a favorable reception from Americans, that he knew the country only as the end of the world, having no idea of its geographical position; and that he judged of his reception of what he had observed of the American character in his own country."

Younis goes on to explain, "Antonio's impression of Americans was not unique to him. Countless subsequent arrivals, later in the century, made the same statement upon reaching the shores of the United States. To them, Americans were kind and hospitable, as they so observed in Syria." Bishallany's trust was rewarded. With the help of a friend, he found work as a butler for a wealthy family. Living in the family's home, he was able to improve his English and learn American customs while supporting himself.

Thanks to his outgoing nature, Bishallany made many friends. Orfalea wrote, "Bishallany amazed his [employer and friend], who knew his butler was impoverished, with his ability to move naturally through the homes of the New York patricians [aristocrats]. Soon, he was a much-invited guest to Manhattan drawing-room receptions. However, many who were attracted to the olive-skinned stranger with pot-shaped hat and gold tassel, were more interested in his reaction to their ways than in discovering the peculiar troubles of his homeland."

The self-absorption of these Americans may have contributed to some of the disillusionment Bishallany eventually felt. Whitehead wrote that, before leaving Syria, Bishallany "thought also of this country from which the missionaries had come, and he wished to see the land where the 'Spirit of Christ' so prevailed." Later in the biography, Whitehead reported that a friend of Bishallany's said, "He expressed himself astonished that there should be in this enlightened country, so favored with religious privileges, any who did not serve God. He said he did not expect to find so many wicked people in America, and was grieved that so few should embrace the religion of Jesus; and felt sure that as soon as he became more familiar with the language, he should be able, God helping him, to bring many to the Saviour."

Interrupted studies

Bishallany continued to study the Bible and was eager to share his interpretations with others. He was delighted when he received an invitation to study at the Amenia Seminary School in rural New York; he would earn his tuition by teaching a class in Arabic for missionary students. By the time he enrolled in the fall of 1855, however, he was suffering from violent coughing episodes. He returned to the relatively warmer climate of New York City after the first semester. His health improved somewhat, and he returned to the seminary from April through June of 1856. He tried to continue his studies despite increasing pains in his chest, but he finally had to return to New York City, where his friends cared for him.

Bishallany died of tuberculosis on August 22, 1856. Several months earlier, a friend in Beirut had written him that his mother was inquiring about him. Bishallany was buried in Greenwood Cemetery in Brooklyn, with an open Bible on his chest.

FURTHER READING

Orfalea, Gregory. *Before the Flames: A Quest for the History of Arab Americans.* Austin: University of Texas Press, 1988.

Whitehead, Rev. Charles. *Sketch of Antonio Bishallany, A Syrian of Mount Lebanon.* New York: American Tract Society, 1856.

Younis, Adele L. *The Coming of the Arabic-Speaking People to the United States.* Staten Island, NY: Center for Migration Studies, 1995, pp. 79–106.

William Peter Blatty

Lebanese-American author

Born January 7, 1928
New York, New York

Although he has written more than a dozen books and scripts, William Blatty is best known for his best-selling book and Academy Award-winning screenplay *The Exorcist,* about a twelve-year-old girl who is possessed by the devil. Always intrigued by the spiritual aspects of existence, Blatty saw cases of demonic possession as the closest proof yet of life beyond death.

Life on the run and in the darkness

William Peter Blatty was born in January 1928 in New York City, the youngest of five children. His parents, Peter and Mary Mouakad Blatty, were Lebanese immigrants. A carpenter in Lebanon, Peter Blatty could only find a job picking up trash in the New York subways for $6 a week. Later he took a job cutting fabric into the right shapes to be sewn into clothes. When Blatty was six, his father moved out, leaving his mother to raise her four sons and one daughter by selling homemade jars of jelly.

"OUR NEIGHBORS SUSPECTED WE WERE 'INTO' THE OCCULT, AS THE SIGHT OF US ALL PLAYING RUMMY IN THE DARKNESS MUST HAVE LOOKED, TO A WINDOW-WATCHER, SOMETHING LIKE A SÉANCE."

Reproduced by permission of Archive Photos.

Mary Blatty was a lively and resourceful woman, but her unpredictable nature contributed to Blatty's unusual youth. In a period of ten years, Blatty recalled, he lived at twenty-eight different addresses. Often the Blattys were evicted for not being able to pay their rent, or they would have to live in darkness because they could not afford their electric bill. Some neighbors thought because the Blattys often lived in the dark, there was something supernatural about them. These accusations aroused Blatty's lifelong interest in the occult, a variety of supernatural practices including astrology, witchcraft, and foretelling the future.

"Our neighbors suspected we were 'into' the occult, as the sight of us all playing rummy in the darkness must have looked, to a window-watcher, something like a séance [meeting to communicate with spirits]," Blatty recalled in his 1973 book *I'll Tell Them I Remember You*. "Dinner, I take it, resembled Black Mass [a ceremony that mocks a Christian mass and worships Satan] and the sight of me writing compositions by candlelight, needless to suggest, was a pact with the Devil."

Since the Blattys moved so frequently, William Blatty found himself moving from one school to another. Once it was time for him to go to high school, his mother decided he would go to one she believed was the best: Brooklyn Prep, a Jesuit boys school. His mother was even able to arrange for her son to attend the school on full scholarship, which was necessary because the school was very expensive. Blatty's love of writing was already becoming apparent, as he wrote short stories and essays that he submitted for publication. One of his pieces, "A Day at Coney Island," appeared in an issue of *Dental News*.

Inspiration for *The Exorcist*

When it was time for Blatty to attend college, his mother decided he would go to Georgetown University, a Jesuit school in Washington, D.C. Again, Blatty earned a full scholarship, this time by earning a high score on the College Boards examinations. While studying at Georgetown in 1949, Blatty saw an article in the *Washington Post* about a fourteen-year-old boy in nearby Mt. Rainer, Maryland, who was supposedly possessed by the Devil. The front-page piece also described the efforts of a Jesuit priest to cure the boy by performing exorcisms. An exorcism is a ritual used to expel a demon from a person who is supposedly possessed. Then a junior in college, Blatty was considering the priesthood but found himself sometimes doubting his Catholic faith. He became fascinated with the case of the possessed boy because to him it was the first solid evidence of spiritual forces at work.

While Blatty was serious about his work, he also liked practical jokes. During the fall of his senior year, he dressed up as a priest to kidnap the ram mascot of Fordham University. Later, while working for the publicity department at the University of Southern California, he used his Arab looks to masquerade as Prince Khair-allah-el-Aswad el Xeer, the son of Saudi Arabian King Saud. He used material from his eight-month escapade as the prince for an article in the *Saturday Evening Post*.

After graduating from Georgetown in 1950, Blatty took some temporary jobs while he searched fruitlessly for a teaching position. He even applied, unsuccessfully, for a job with the Federal Bureau of Investigation (FBI). He joined the air force in 1951, eventually becoming policy chief for the Psychological Warfare Division while the United States fought in the Korean War (1950-53; when the United States helped South Korea repel invasions by communist North Korea.)

Once the war was over, Blatty returned his attention to becoming a writer. He picked up his master's degree in English Literature in 1954 from George Washington University in Washington, D.C. and began writing articles for the *Saturday Evening Post*. He joined the U.S. Foreign Service in 1955 and was stationed in Beirut, Lebanon, where his writing skills were put to use as editor of a U.S. magazine called the *News Review*. He held several public relations jobs and even tried his hand at acting in the 1958 film *No Place to Land* before quitting all other work and devoting himself entirely to his writing.

John Goldfarb and the Notre Dame controversy

It would still be another eleven years before Blatty's writing would earn him widespread recognition, but he did gain national attention in 1963 over his second book, *John Goldfarb, Please Come Home!* The book was about an American pilot who tried to coach a group of Arabs to beat the University of Notre Dame football team because an influential Arab sheik is upset that the university cut his son from the football

THE DEVIL INSIDE

When a person appears to be possessed by a demon, he may speak in several languages or cause objects around him to move without touching them. In the real-life case of "Robbie," the fourteen-year-old boy who inspired William Blatty's book *The Exorcist,* words like "spite" and "hell" emerged and then disappeared in his flesh. When "Robbie" sat in his desk at school or laid in his bed at home, the piece of furniture would levitate. After medical doctors and psychiatrists exhausted every attempt to cure him, his parents asked the Catholic Church to perform an exorcism.

Exorcism, the practice of expelling evil spirits from people or places, has been part of the Jewish and Christian religious traditions for thousands of years. According to the Bible, Jesus expelled demons by calling them out, and his followers later did the same "in God's name." During the early years of the Catholic Church, exorcism was considered to be a special power that anyone might have, but by the third century A.D., a special class of exorcists became the only ones allowed to perform the rite.

In cases where a person is thought to be possessed, a Catholic bishop must first evaluate the case and give permission before a priest can perform the exorcism. The exorcism itself is a very structured ceremony consisting of specific prayers and blessing with holy water. The exorcism can last hours or even days.

The causes of possession are still a mystery. Some psychologists think a possessed person is simply someone who has multiple personality disorder, a mental condition in which the person copes with a traumatic experience by developing several competing personalities. Priests who have worked with people believed to be possessed note that often the victim lives in the midst of violent or abusive people. "Robbie" lived in an area charged by racial hatred, and Blatty set his possessed character in *The Exorcist* in a family where the parents fought bitterly. "We often see that ... the victim is innocent, but there is intense hate or some other powerful evil all around the victim," one priest told author Thomas B. Allen.

The documented cases of possession challenge most people's rational understanding of the world, but for those who have witnessed the afflictions of a possessed person, seeing is believing. "I can assure you of one thing," wrote one of the priests involved with "Robbie." "The case in which I was involved was the real thing. I had no doubt about it then and I have no doubt about it now."

squad. The book was also turned into a screenplay, but it would not be made into a movie without a fight from the University of Notre Dame. Concerned that the story would smear the good name of the university, Notre Dame trustees asked a judge to ban the book and the movie. While the circuit judge ruled in favor of the university, a higher court reversed the ruling and allowed the 1963 release of the book. The movie, which came out the following year, was a critical and commercial flop.

Other works from this time included the novel *Which way to Mecca, Jack?* (1960); the film *The Man from the Diner's Club* (1963) starring comedian Danny Kaye; the book *I, Billy Shakespeare!* (1965) about the ghost of William Shakespeare; the Inspector Clouseau movie *A Shot in the Dark* (1966); the novel *Twinkle, Twinkle, Killer Kane!* (1967); and the musical *Darling Lili* (1970) starring Julie Andrews. None of these works garnered much praise from the critics or the public.

Expelling the demons

Crushed by his string of professional failures and the death of his mother in 1967, Blatty retreated to a cabin in Lake Tahoe, California, and decided to pursue the subject that had interested him some twenty years earlier: exorcism. The book that resulted in 1971, *The Exorcist,* drew its inspiration from the 1949 case Blatty had read about in the papers, but he used his research on demonic possession to create a new story. "[The 1949 case] gave me the idea, nothing more," he told the *Washington Post.* "The rest—except for the possession syndrome which is the same all the way to ancient Egyptian records on exorcism—came entirely out of my head. Everything is made up."

In *The Exorcist,* a twelve-year-old girl named Regan baffles medical and psychiatric experts by speaking several foreign languages she had never learned, spinning her head all the way around, and causing pieces of furniture to float. Having exhausted all conventional forms of treatment, the girl's mother asks a priest to perform an exorcism on Regan. The priest succeeds in drawing the demon out of the girl and into himself, throwing himself out the window to keep Regan safe. The death of the priest does not mean victory for the demon, Blatty told the *Washington Post.* "Mortal death is not defeat; only death of the spirit is a true loss," he said.

The book was on the best-seller lists for fifty-five weeks, and the movie made $165 million in its opening weekend, making it one of the fifty most money-making pictures of all time. Blatty also won an Academy Award for best screenplay for *The Exorcist.*

The Exorcist caused widespread controversy when it was released. Although it contained no sex, nudity, or graphic violence, it showed the possessed girl spewing vomit and jabbing herself with a crucifix. In some places, the "R" rating wasn't considered severe enough—Washington, D.C. was among several cities that imposed an "X" rating on the movie. In England, the movie was banned and still cannot be rented on video. Some critics rendered harsh verdicts on the film, calling it "tiresomely moralistic" or simply an "elaborate freak show." Blatty defended his work, calling it "an apostolic work" that provided viewers with a feeling of release from the evil forces in the world.

Later works

Blatty followed the success of *The Exorcist* with *Mastermind,* a 1976 movie that was not nearly as popular. He penned several more novels, including *I'll Tell Them I Remember You,* a 1973 autobiography and tribute to his mother. Adding "movie director" to his list of titles, Blatty directed his screenplay *The Ninth Configuration* in 1980. While not a box office hit, the movie was very popular in some circles and garnered Blatty a Golden Globe Award.

Blatty reexamined the topic of exorcism in 1983, with his book *Legion,* a detective novel about murders committed as Satanic sacrifices. He reworked the best-selling book into a movie script called *The Exorcist 1990* (there was a 1977 sequel, *Exorcist II: The Heretic,* a flop with which Blatty was not involved). The 1990 movie enjoyed moderate success. Blatty also continued with his writing, publishing *Demons Five, Exorcists Nothing,* in 1996. The book drew on some of his personal experience, telling the story of a Hollywood scriptwriter who had produced several flops and was better known as the husband of his famous wife.

Personal notes

Blatty has been married four times and has seven children. In 1950, during the middle of his senior year at Georgetown University, he married Mary Margaret Rigard, with whom he had three children: Christine Ann, Michael Peter, and Mary JoAnne. His second wife was Elizabeth Gilman. He had two children with his third wife, Linda Tuero, and two more with his fourth wife, Julie. He lives in Montecito, California.

FURTHER READING

"Blatty, William Peter." *Current Biography Yearbook 1974.* New York: H.W. Wilson, 1974, pp. 36–39.

Blatty, William. *I'll Tell Them I Remember You.* New York: W. W. Norton, 1973.

Slovick, Matt. "William Peter Blatty: Author, Screenwriter, Director." Available http://www.washingtonpost.com/wp-srv/style/longterm/movies/features/dcmovies/blattytalk.htm (February 16, 1999).

Vance Bourjaily

Lebanese-American novelist

Born September 17, 1922
Cleveland, Ohio

"I AM NEITHER WEALTHY NOR WELL KNOWN. PERHAPS FULFILLED."

With ten novels, several plays, two dozen television scripts, and an opera libretto (the text of an opera) to his credit, Vance Bourjaily has established a solid reputation as a skillful and innovative author. He has also written numerous nonfiction articles about outdoor activities, some of which have been published in collections like his 1997 book *Fishing by Mail: An Outdoor Life of a Father and Son.* "Vance Bourjaily is the only serious American novelist of Lebanese heritage to make a name for himself in fiction," wrote Gregory Orfalea (1949–; see entry) in *Before the Flames.* Although, he added, "William Peter Blatty [1928–; see entry] has made far more money with demonic potboilers," books of inferior quality written chiefly for profit. Bourjaily has achieved a certain level of professional recognition; his novel *Brill Among the Ruins* was nominated for the National Book Award for fiction in 1971, and he received an Academy Award in Literature from the American Academy of Arts and Letters in 1993. However, his success has been limited. This is what prompted him to say to Orfalea, "I am neither wealthy nor well known. Perhaps fulfilled."

Family influences

Vance Bourjaily was born in Ohio in 1922, but his family moved a year later. He told interviewer Matthew Bruccoli that he grew up "up and down the East Coast." Even though Bourjaily's family moved often, he found stability through his relationships with the people in his family. He credits his parents and his grandmother as being important influences on his life and career.

When Bourjaily's grandmother, Terkman Bourjaily, was a young woman, she ran away from an abusive husband. She and her young son, Mansour, sneaked out of Kabb Elias, the village that was their home in Lebanon's Bekaa Valley. Mother and son hid in a cave as her husband rode past, searching for them. They traveled first to France, where an immigration officer gave their Arabic name a French spelling. Then, in 1894, Terkman and her five-year-old son came to the United States. She supported her family by working as a housekeeper and a cook in a Massachusetts boarding house. After Mansour was grown, Terkman lived with him and his family, which included young Vance Bourjaily. Bourjaily told Orfalea that his grandmother was "the total strength in my life."

Bourjaily's father, Mansour "Monte" Bourjaily, was sensitive about being an Arab. In fact, as an adult, he downplayed his heritage. "Whatever it was in the Lebanese boyhood and adolescence which Irish kids teased [my father] about—being dark, big nose, not speaking English very good, poverty—he didn't want to be tarred with it," Bourjaily told Orfalea. After working as a newspaper reporter and editor, Bourjaily's father became the manager of United Features Syndicate, where he sold columns and comic strips to newspapers around the world. Among the people he convinced to write newspaper columns for the syndicate were Italian dictator Benito Mussolini (1883–1945) and Eleanor Roosevelt (1884–1962), the wife of U.S. President Franklin D. Roosevelt.

Bourjaily's mother, Barbara (Webb) Bourjaily, was also a journalist; in fact, she met and married her husband when they were both working for a Cleveland, Ohio, newspaper. After her three sons were born (Bourjaily was the middle one), she quit her newspaper job and worked out of her home as a freelance writer. Among the things she wrote were a cookbook, a book of fairy tales, and novels that were serialized (published in installments at regular intervals) in women's magazines. She read to her sons every night throughout their childhood, teaching them to appreciate good novels and poetry. "She was absolutely determined that one of her sons be a writer," Bourjaily told interviewer Matthew Bruccoli. "I was the one with whom it took."

From poetry to ads for shaving cream

Bourjaily wrote a poem, "The Dance of the Fireflies," at the age of seven. It was his first original work. He told Bruccoli, "By the time I was eight or nine it was perfectly evident to me that I was going to be a writer." In an article for *Contemporary Authors Autobiography Series,* he wrote, "I played shortstop for the fourth grade team, hit singles, stole bases, and hollered a lot. I had a big voice, was extroverted and mischievous." When he turned eleven, Bourjaily took some acting lessons; this made him decide that he wanted to become a playwright.

During his childhood, Bourjaily's mother left her husband several times, taking her sons with her on each occasion. The couple finally separated and divorced when Bourjaily was about twelve. Soon after, he and his brothers were sent to a military-style boarding school. The boys went on to attend a public school in Virginia and a private school in New Jersey. Bourjaily enrolled in prep school (a private school that prepares students for college) in Pennsylvania, but he was expelled at the end of his sophomore (second) year of high school. "I wasn't a flamboyant violator of school rules," he told Bruccoli, "but I had a hard time persuading myself that they applied to me." In 1939, he graduated from a public high school in Virginia, where he was living with his mother and stepfather.

"I was sixteen when I had graduated from high school, and I decided that the thing for me to do before I went off to college was to write a book," Bourjaily told Bruccoli. The resulting 100 typewritten pages amounted to what Bourjaily says was "a terrible book." In his autobiographical essay, he described the book as "a teenage analysis of life and of the

way I meant to live it, called *Not to Confound My Elders*."
When Bourjaily finished writing the book, he went to New
York City to live with his father. There, he worked for an
advertising agency, writing advertisements for products such
as hair tonic and shaving cream.

Lucky assignment during the war

One year later, with his first book written and some work
experience under his belt, Bourjaily headed off to Bowdoin
College in Brunswick, Maine. In 1942, after two years of college, he joined the American Field Service (AFS) so that he
could work as an ambulance driver during World War II
(1939–45; when the United States and certain European
countries fought to stop Nazi Germany and Japan from conquering the world). Bourjaily was stationed in Lebanon,
Egypt, Libya, and Italy. In 1944, he returned to the United
States to recover from a severe case of jaundice (an illness
related to liver functions) and was promptly drafted into the
U.S. Army. His army division was assigned to defend the
Hawaiian Islands where, he told Bruccoli, "I nearly expired
from boredom.... By the time I left Hawaii I had written a volume of poetry and a fairly ambitious three-act play."

Bourjaily sent the poetry and the play to a literary agent
who had helped his mother sell her work to book publishers.
The agent showed them to Maxwell Perkins (1884–1947), an
editor at Charles Scribner's Sons publishing company. Perkins
was editor to a number of famous authors including several
of Bourjaily's idols, such as Ernest Hemingway (1899–1961)
and F. Scott Fitzgerald (1896–1940). Perkins offered Bourjaily
an advance of $750 "if I'd agree to cut out the poetry-and-
drama nonsense and try to write a novel," Bourjaily wrote.
"When the [offer] arrived, Poet and Playwright were sent off
hand-in-hand into the sunset and there was one, lean, tough,
smallish, blue-eyed, thin-haired, grinning Pfc. [army private
first class] of a novelist, waving them goodbye."

The End of My Life

Bourjaily decided to build this new novel around a short
story he had written while he was in the AFS—a story based
on a personal experience. He had met an attractive, young
female officer who had just arrived in her first combat zone.
When she expressed interest in what the front (battle line)

Vance Bourjaily | **85**

looked like, he offered to take her out to see it in his ambulance when he was off duty. While there, the pair heard impacts of long-range artillery shells and watched British soldiers firing twenty-five-pound shells back toward the enemy. Bourjaily and the woman stopped and chatted with the soldiers before driving back to town. The next morning, he realized what a terrible chance he had taken. "Across the cavern walls of my skull, bitter images flickered of my blonde friend, dead: shell-fire, strafing, a deadly box mine. I may even have seen her impaled on a German bayonet," he wrote in his autobiographical essay. "I just felt terrible and irresponsible and awful, so I did what writers do. I got up and I put all of my guilt into a story about somebody else doing the same thing and the whole thing going wrong," he told Bruccoli.

This short story became the next-to-last chapter in Bourjaily's first novel. He started working backward in time from the short story. Bourjaily tried to figure out what had made the man in his story take such an irresponsible risk. "I started just writing about him and his friends to discover what they were like and what their educations were like and what sort of relationships they had with their girls and that kind of thing," he told Bruccoli. Bourjaily chose Syria and Lebanon for the setting of his novel, making it the only World War II novel set in the Middle East, according to Orfalea. It took Bourjaily about five months to write the novel; however, he spent several more months revising it. Perkins, the editor, liked it but told Bourjaily to fix a few details and write an introductory chapter and a final chapter (the young author had thought it would be "artistic" to leave things hanging, or unresolved, at the end of the book).

In January 1947, after Bourjaily turned in the revised version of the book, which was titled *The End of My Life,* he went back to Bowdoin College to finish his degree. He took his new bride, Bettina "Tina" Yensen, with him. He graduated with a bachelor's degree in literature in late 1947, shortly after the novel was published.

Limping along

Bourjaily and his wife moved to San Francisco, where he got a job as a newspaper reporter and wrote his second novel. In his autobiographical essay, he recalled that the novel's first draft was good enough, but things fell apart during the revision process: "[I was] unable to keep up with the changes in attitude and understanding that were going on in myself. When you're in your twenties, you'd better write fast." His first editor, Perkins, had died, and his new editor was not as helpful. Scribner's rejected the book.

Bourjaily's wife moved back to New York to work for *Woman's Day* magazine, while he went to Mexico to concentrate on writing another novel. He ended up writing a play instead. Joining his wife in New York, Bourjaily found work as a television scriptwriter, and he edited a twice-a-year literary magazine called *discovery*. His second novel, *The Hound of Earth,* was published in 1955. The book earned some good reviews but not many copies were sold.

His next novel, *The Violated,* published in 1958, received good reviews and the book sold well. Bourjaily fondly recalled in his essay that a review in the *New York Times* compared him to famous Russian author Fyodor Dostoevski (1821–1881), who wrote *Crime and Punishment.* "Even better, [it] said that I could write funny."

Practicality

From 1958 until 1980, Bourjaily was an instructor at The Writers Workshop at the University of Iowa in Iowa City. Later, he taught at the University of Arizona before becoming a literature professor at Louisiana State University in Baton Rouge in 1985. "Financially, I guess I have never been a novelist for more than a few giddy weeks at a time," he wrote. "Financially, I'm some kind of editor or journalist or scriptwriter or teacher or migrant [a person who moves regularly in order to find work], and it's teaching which has had the best hours-per-pound ratio to bacon on the table."

Even though he would rather write than teach, he does enjoy the teaching, especially being around the energy and enthusiasm of young people and being able to learn along with his students.

Glimpses of other novels

The Man Who Knew Kennedy (1967) was Bourjaily's first commercial success. The book became a selection of the Literary Guild (a book club) and it made some best-seller lists. "I

WRITING IN DIFFERENT VOICES

"I never do the same thing twice. Having solved one set of technical and mechanical problems I don't want to do them again," Vance Bourjaily told interviewer Matthew Bruccoli. "In Hemingway's phrase, one way that you will know a really fine piece of work is that it won't resemble any other really fine piece of work."

One of the problems he has to solve for every novel is the voice in which he tells the story. In his autobiographical essay, he explained that for his 1958 novel, *The Violated,* he "wanted to produce ... prose like perfect glass, windowpane prose, which would never call attention to itself, or distort the view a reader had of people and action." In his next novel, the autobiographical *Confessions of a Spent Youth,* he wrote, "To avoid the plainness of realistic prose, since the book was to be realistic, and to give it some texture, I set aside my windowpane theory and was working ... in an idiosyncratic [peculiar to one individual], first-person voice." For his ambitious 1976 book *Now Playing at Canterbury,* "I tried to display in the stories all the different modes of narrative I knew about—epic, Gothic, farce, fantasy, and the rest." And when he wrote *A Game Men Play* (1980), he used "careful, simple prose; after all the fancy varieties I'd needed to use for the different voices in *Canterbury,* I went back to the windowpane theory."

Even though Bourjaily pays careful attention to the use of language when establishing each novel's voice, he wrote, "Many writers and critics feel that language is the heart of the novel. I disagree. Language is only skin, to me, and the heart is story."

felt very strongly that there had been a kind of rebirth of hope in the country with [President John F.] Kennedy," he told Orfalea. "There was a tremendous identification on the part of guys my age. He was the best of us. So when he was killed it was like—they got us." The book tries to deal with what happened to the country when Kennedy (1917–63) was assassinated.

When Bourjaily wrote his novel about Mexican archaeology, he titled it *Tell Rain Goodbye.* His publisher wanted to call it *Brill Among the Ruins* (Bob Brill is the main character). Bourjaily finally agreed, but he wrote, "Whether they were right or not, I was wrong to give in. It's like letting a stranger call up on the telephone and name your kid."

It took Bourjaily ten years to write *Now Playing at Canterbury.* The novel is long and complex and is set up in a way similar to the *Arabian Nights* (in which a woman avoids her death sentence by telling the king a story each night, without saying how the story ends so that he will wish to hear the ending the following night). In Bourjaily's novel, there is an overall story about seventeen people involved in producing an opera (for example, singers, director, conductor, composer, and set designer). As they prepare for opening night, each of the characters tells a different story in a different style. The idea, Bourjaily wrote, was that "the stories would advance the book, if they were set in order properly, would comment on each other and on the frame as well, narratives begetting narrative."

Disillusioned supporter of Israel

Bourjaily told Orfalea that his emotions about the Middle East are "enormously complicated." Originally, he felt great sympathy for the Jews. He said, "A lot of the reason I went to the Second World War was because of what [Nazi leader Adolph Hitler (1889–1945)] was doing to the Jews. I got to what was then Palestine. I had family feeling for the people I was seeing in Lebanon, but I also was very enthusiastic about what the Jews were doing on the kibbutzim [communal farms]." When he had some time off duty, he even went to help them harvest wheat on a kibbutz. "I took the naive view, I suppose, that we were all so much together. If you were anti-Semitic, it meant you were anti-Jewish and anti-Arab too."

Over time, Bourjaily grew disillusioned with the terrorist tactics of the Irgun, an armed Jewish underground organization led by Menachem Begin (1913–93) during the mid-1940s (Begin later became the prime minister of Israel). Then Israel invaded Lebanon in 1982. "When that happened, they lost me."

FURTHER READING

Bourjaily, Vance. "Vance Bourjaily." *Contemporary Authors Autobiography Series,* vol. 1. Detroit: Gale Research, 1984, pp. 63-79.

Bruccoli, Matthew J. "Vance Bourjaily." *Conversations with Writers.* Detroit: Gale Research, 1977, pp. 2-23.

Orfalea, Gregory. *Before the Flames: A Quest for the History of Arab Americans.* Austin: University of Texas Press, 1988.

Elie Chaib

Lebanese-American dancer

Born July 1950
Deir al-Qamar, Lebanon

"IT WAS VERY NATURAL FOR ME [TO WANT TO DANCE] BECAUSE I'M A REBEL. EVEN NOW—THE MINUTE I'M NOT SUPPOSED TO DO SOMETHING IT INTERESTS ME EVEN MORE."

Elie Chaib (pronounced El-EE Cha-eeb) has been the youngest and the oldest performer with the famous Paul Taylor dance company based in New York City. He joined the company at the age of twenty-three; twenty years later, he was still performing with the company when he was named "Dancer of the Year" by the *New York Times*. He was featured in a 1993 Taylor production called *Speaking in Tongues* that was filmed by the Public Broadcasting Service (PBS) and televised on its *Great Performances* series; the film won several awards, including an Emmy.

On-screen action

Although his family was from the town of Deir al-Qamar in the Chouf Mountains of southeastern Lebanon, Elie Khalil Chaib grew up in the large city of Beirut, on the country's Mediterranean coast. He liked going to the movies—"seeing the world," as he described it. America seemed to be where the "action" was.

West Side Story

Romeo and Juliet were writer William Shakespeare's (1564–1616) famous teenage characters whose love was forbidden because of a feud between their families. Author Arthur Laurents wrote a similar story of modern teenagers whose love was forbidden because they came from rival gangs in New York City (Tony was Anglo, and Maria was Puerto Rican). The story was created as a Broadway-style musical with songs composed by Leonard Bernstein (1918–1990) and lyrics written by Stephen Sondheim (1930–). The new story closely followed Shakespeare's *Romeo and Juliet,* but it took place in modern times; for example, where Juliet stood on a balcony while Romeo declared his love for her, Maria stood on a tenement fire escape while Tony sang of his feelings. The play was unusual because its dances, choreographed by Jerome Robbins (1918–), formed part of the story's action, rather than being just an entertaining extra element.

Bernstein and Robbins actually came up with the idea for the modern interpretation of Shakespeare's classic tale and asked Laurents and Sondheim to help with the project. They wanted to create a work that would draw attention to the problem of gang violence. According to the West Side Story web site, the movements Robbins created for the show "became a finger-snapping, fist-thrusting, energetic series of dances, which integrated the music, lyrics, and book [spoken dialogue] as never seen before in musical theater."

As a teenager Chaib was interested in physical activities, especially individual sports like bicycling and skiing. He also enjoyed martial arts. "That was a good start to controlling my body," he later told Barbara Newman of *Ballet Review* magazine.

Next, Chaib discovered dancing. He spent his evenings at Beirut's dance clubs. "I felt limited with my steps, so I wanted to learn more dance steps," he told *Ballet Review*. Then he saw a movie that impressed him strongly—*West Side Story*. It used modern dance as a central part of the story's action. Chaib's first reaction was that he could improve his recreational dance using movements like those in the film.

Dancing rebel

His interest in music and dance drew Chaib to the Baalbek International Festival in eastern Lebanon. In addition to featuring Lebanese performers, the festival attracted companies and troups from around the world to present plays, concerts, and dance productions ranging from traditional ballet to innovative modern dance. Chaib was fascinated by the dancing he saw. Chaib felt some pressure from his mother to start a career as a doctor or an engineer, but he was drawn to dance. "It was very natural for me [to want to dance] because I'm a rebel. Even now—the minute I'm not supposed to do something it interests me even more."

When he learned there was a modern dance teacher in Beirut, Chaib decided to take lessons. He didn't think he could make a career out of dancing because he had started later than most professional dancers. He wanted to learn new steps to use when he and his girlfriend went dancing. Despite his lack of experience with modern dance, Chaib found great opportunities. There were very few male dancers in Lebanon, so the school offered Chaib a scholarship and used him almost immediately on the stage.

Learning by doing

When he was twenty years old, Chaib decided to go to the United States. He needed more advanced dance instruction than was available in Lebanon, and he was still interested in American culture. From information in *Dance Magazine,* he made a list of all the dance schools in New York City, and he sent them letters and photographs. The only one he heard back from was one he wasn't particularly interested in, but he accepted their offer of admission to get his student visa. After arriving in New York, he was able to leave that school and study at others that were closer to his taste.

Chaib took lessons at three famous schools at the same time—the Joffrey, Martha Graham, and Merce Cunningham schools. Besides taking five classes a day, he worked from six in the evening until three in the morning selling pastries in a bakery. He explains that this wasn't as exhausting as it sounds because the two days he had off from dance classes were different than the two he had off from work, so there were only three days a week when he had to do both.

"Things didn't work out well the first three years," Chaib told *Ballet Review* in 1991. "In classroom situations, I was terrible, and I still am. In rehearsal, I'm not a quicker-picker-up-er kind of whiz kid. I just like performing and dancing and telling stories through dancing." He auditioned for jobs with several companies without finding steady work.

Wins his dream job

In 1973 Chaib appeared in a two-person show called *After the Ball*. It was a theater production that involved acting and singing as well as dancing. (Because it was a comedy, he didn't have to be particularly good at singing.) He got good reviews in several papers, including one in *Show Business* that ran right next to an announcement that the Paul Taylor Dance Company was holding auditions for a male dancer. Ever since he had seen the Paul Taylor Company perform at Baalbek, Chaib had wanted to join it so he went to the audition.

"I had auditioned a lot, but when I went to audition for Paul I felt really like I was going to make it. I don't know why," he told *Ballet Review*. "I guess it was one of those days where you feel good about yourself." This unexplained burst of confidence helped him perform well at the audition, where he competed against more than a hundred other dancers. He was asked to return the next day as one of five finalists. After the second round of tryouts, he was accepted; at the age of twenty-three he became the youngest dancer ever to join the famous Taylor company.

"It *was* like winning the lottery ticket—I just went bananas," Chaib recalls. "I can't imagine dancing for anybody else." He felt very comfortable with the Taylor company because it didn't have classes like many of the other troups did. He learned through rehearsals and performances.

Loving it, doing it

Most of the time, Chaib loves his work. He explained to *Ballet Review* that he feels like a conductor who interprets music with his whole body rather than just his arms. When he is performing, he doesn't count with the music; he actually sings the music. When he's first learning a piece, he does count the beats, but once he's learned it, he doesn't think about such mechanics. He said in *Ballet Review*, "If you ask me 'Is it left or right? Which leg do you do this on?,' I can't tell you any more. It's not in my head. It's all in the muscles."

The down side

Like all physical activities, dance can lead to injuries. Chaib has had many, including a knee injury that required surgery. He's had to learn to dance in a way that will not only avoid aggravating previous injuries, but will also help heal and strengthen them. Injuries have taught him the importance of staying focused on moving correctly during workouts, rehearsals, and performances.

Atop the Ferris wheel

In 1991, a Taylor Company performance featuring Chaib was recorded by PBS for its *Great Performances* series. The film, *Speaking in Tongues,* won an Emmy Award, a gold medal for performance programs at the International Film & TV Festival of New York, and a gold plaque award in the variety/entertainment category at the Chicago International Film Festival. In 1992, at the age of forty-two, Chaib was named "Dancer of the Year" by the *New York Times.* Despite his other successes, his long-held dream of dancing at the Baalbek Festival remains unfulfilled.

Nevertheless, during his twentieth season with the Taylor Company Chaib told *Aramco World* magazine, "I feel like I'm at the top of the Ferris wheel." With a laugh, he added, "But the future, is obviously, clearly, downhill."

FURTHER READING

Azar, George Baramki. "Master of 20 Seasons." *Aramco World* (July 1993): 18–19.

"A Luminous Collaboration." *West Side Story* Home Page. http://alphabase.com/westside/collaboration.html (April 1998).

Newman, Barbara. "A Conversation with Elie Chaib." *Ballet Review* (Summer 1991): 81–90.

Elias James Corey

Lebanese-American chemist

Born July 12, 1928
Methuen, Massachusetts

D r. Elias Corey won the Nobel Prize in Chemistry in 1990 for developing a logical process that changed the face of synthetic organic chemistry. This is a field of chemistry (the science that studies the composition, structure, and activity of substances) that creates organic chemicals in a laboratory by combining, or synthesizing, other simpler compounds and elements. Organic chemicals are materials whose molecules (the basic unit of a substance) contain carbon, an element found in all living things. By creating organic chemicals in the lab, chemists learn more about how they work. Also, organic chemicals are often key ingredients in medicines. Synthesizing them in a laboratory allows manufacturers to produce large quantities of the chemicals at reasonable prices, making the medicines they are in more accessible and affordable. Before Corey developed this logical process, chemists in the synthetic organic chemistry field worked mostly by trial and error. Now chemists use his system like a road map that leads them directly to their goal.

SYNTHETIC CHEMISTS ARE PEOPLE WHO CAN GET "SOMETHING VALUABLE FROM ALMOST NOTHING" BY TURNING CHEAP MATERIALS "INTO NEW MATERIALS OR SUBSTANCES OF RELATIVELY GREAT, OR EVEN LIFESAVING, VALUE."

A three-parent family

When Corey was born in 1928, his parents named him William. Eighteen months later his father died, and his mother, Fatina Hasham Corey, renamed her son Elias in memory of his father. By this time, the Great Depression (1929–39; a period of time in America when the economy suffered, banks and businesses closed, and many people lived in extreme poverty) had begun, and it was very difficult for a single mother to support a family. Naciby and John Saba, Corey's aunt and uncle, moved in and became like a second set of parents to Corey and his siblings.

Times were difficult, but Corey's family was strong. In his 1990 autobiography Corey wrote, "My grandparents on both sides, who emigrated from Lebanon to the United States, also knew how to cope with adversity, as Christians in a tragically torn country, under the grip of the [Muslim] Ottoman empire." The Corey children learned the value of hard work and the joy of close family ties. From his family, Corey explained, "I learned to be efficient and to take pleasure in a job well done, no matter how mundane [boring]."

Living up to his father's name

Knowing that he had been renamed for his father placed a sense of responsibility on Corey. He had no memory of his father, but he learned from family and friends that his father had been a successful businessman who was well liked in the community. Corey wanted to be worthy of his father's name and of the devotion his mother, aunt, and uncle had given him. At the same time, he was an active boy who would rather go hiking or play sports than work.

After attending a Catholic elementary school, Corey went to a public high school. He enjoyed all of his classes, so it was hard for him to decide what career he wanted to pursue. When he graduated in 1945, Corey chose to study electronic engineering because it was an exciting new technology and it used mathematics, which was the subject he enjoyed most.

College whiz

Corey was only sixteen years old when he entered the Massachusetts Institute of Technology (MIT), one of the best colleges in the country. Freshmen (first-year students) take a variety of introductory courses, and Corey liked chemistry the best. He saw chemistry as central to all the sciences. His teachers were enthusiastic and interesting, and he enjoyed working in the laboratory. He wrote in his autobiography that "Organic chemistry was especially fascinating with its intrinsic [natural] beauty and its great relevance to human health."

Although it normally takes four years for a full-time student to earn a college degree, Corey received his diploma in only three years. He stayed at MIT to do graduate work. During this time he helped one of the professors do research on synthesizing the important antibiotic penicillin. It usually takes a year or two to earn a master's degree and another two or more for a doctorate, but Corey received his Ph.D. (doctor's degree) in chemistry in only two years.

Builds a foundation

Corey completed his graduate studies in 1950 and began teaching at the University of Illinois in Urbana-Champaign. Rather than specializing in one area of chemistry, he decided to teach and do research in a wide range of topics. He was interested in so many areas of chemistry that he took an unusual view of the subject. He saw it as a broad field rather than a collection of individual but related topics.

After seven years of teaching, Corey won a Guggenheim fellowship that would pay his salary for a year while he took a sabbatical (a break from teaching in order to do research). During that time he would be able to visit other researchers and explore new ideas. He began this year by working on chemical synthesis with a professor at Harvard University in Boston, Massachusetts. At that time, figuring out how to make a certain organic chemical from other compounds was more of an art than a science; it amounted to guessing what chemicals might react with each other in a way that would produce the desired substance.

Shortly after Corey arrived at Harvard in the fall of 1957, his uncle John died. Because this uncle had been like a father, Corey felt a great sense of loss. To escape his grief, he immersed himself in his work. According to his autobiography, within a few weeks "several of the key ideas for a logical and general way of thinking about chemical synthesis came to me."

During the rest of his sabbatical, Corey spent time working with chemists in Switzerland, England, and Sweden. After returning to Illinois and teaching for another year, Corey was offered a teaching and research job at Harvard. He was delighted to accept the position for two reasons: he considered Harvard's chemistry department to be the best in the world, and the move would put him close to his family in Methuen (which is 30 miles from Boston). He took the job in 1959, and the following year his aunt Naciby died.

There were happy moments in Corey's personal life too. In 1961 he married Claire Higham, whom he had known at the University of Illinois. They raised three children, John, David, and Susan, all of whom eventually graduated from Harvard. David became an organic chemist. John was interested in the composition of classical music and earned a graduate degree from the Paris Conservatory of Music. Susan studied education after earning a degree in anthropology.

Breakthrough

The first decade of Corey's professional life was spent building a foundation for the breakthrough that would make him famous. The idea he began to develop in 1957 bore its first fruit in the mid-1960s. He published his first descriptions of the process in 1967, but it would take years to become widely accepted and decades to be formally honored. The breakthrough, a process he called "retrosynthetic analysis," turned the field of synthetic organic chemistry upside down.

Before Corey's breakthrough, there had been some important successes in synthesizing organic compounds. For example, Robert Woodward (1917–1979) earned a Nobel Prize in 1965 for his work in chemical synthesis. The difficulty for other chemists was that there were no general rules to follow. When a chemist decided to try to synthesize a certain organic compound, he or she looked for simpler or more readily available compounds that had part of the structure of the desired molecule. Then a chemist tried to figure out ways to manipulate the chosen substance to transform it into the target chemical. Unfortunately, there were hundreds or thousands of compounds to choose from when selecting the beginning substance, and countless ways of adding to it or subtracting from it to change it into the target. Often luck or intuition were the keys to success. Not only did this mean that the process was rarely successful, but it was also impossible for a successful scientist to teach someone else how to synthesize other compounds.

During the 1960s, Corey was working on trying to synthesize certain chemicals that didn't have recognizable parts that could be used as starting substances. Unable to find a starting point, he decided to look at the result he wanted to achieve, and then work backward from it to get to a starting point. He took the target molecule, looked at its structure, and started peeling parts of it away to find simpler compounds. When he identified a basic component that was easy to find or to make, he then reversed the steps of his analysis. This gave him a sequence of steps for building the target molecule.

Corey was not the first chemist to think of working backward from the target. However he was the first one to look for and find a logical process that would work for *any* organic substance. He told *Science* magazine, "What I've tried to do is find the deep logic behind it and put it in the most fundamental form." His technique accomplished three things: it greatly increased the success rate for synthesizing organic chemicals, it made it possible to teach students how to go about solving problems, and it enabled scientists to use computers to help them solve synthesis problems. In fact, Corey wrote a program called LHASA (Logic and Heuristics Applied to Synthetic Analysis) that would help a researcher break a target molecule down into its building blocks.

Why it's important

Corey proved how well his method works by synthesizing more than 100 important organic substances between 1967 and 1990. Many of them are used in medicines to control blood pressure, treat arthritis, regulate the body's immune system, manage asthma symptoms, and control blood clotting. As one example, in 1988 Corey found a way to synthesize ginkgolide B, which is used to treat several ailments including heart and lung problems; previously this substance could only be obtained in small amounts from the ginkgo tree. Medicines using the synthetic product sell for $500 million each year and improve the lives of thousands of people. Another group of substances he succeeded in synthesizing in the 1960s had only been available in milligram amounts at that time. They had to be extracted from sheep or humans. As soon as the synthesis was found, though, the substances became available in kilogram amounts (a million times the former amount). This amount is enough to meet the medical and research needs of the entire world.

Wins but keeps working

In 1990 one research chemist told *Nature* magazine, "No one embarks on a synthesis these days without applying the retrosynthetic method." Because the process changed the entire field of synthetic organic chemistry so completely, Corey was awarded the Nobel Prize for Chemistry that year. The prize brought him worldwide fame and a reward of $700,000.

Now that synthetic organic chemistry has been tamed, Corey has turned to new puzzles. For example, his research group at Harvard is developing what are called molecular robots. When added to other chemicals, these molecules (called "chemzymes") can actually pull together other molecules and attach them together in a very specific way.

A *Science News* article quoted Corey as saying that synthetic chemists are people who can get "something valuable from almost nothing" by turning cheap materials "into new materials or substances of relatively great, or even lifesaving, value." He considers his work to be very important for humanity, but he also truly enjoys doing it. One of his fellow professors even told a reporter that chemistry seemed like a hobby to Corey. However, the man who had preferred hiking and sports to work as a child still spends free time enjoying outdoor activities and music.

FOR FURTHER READING

"Autobiography of Elias James Corey." *The Nobel Foundation Web Site*. 1997. http://www.nobel.se/laureates/chemistry-1990-1-autobio.html (Mar. 28, 1998).

McGrail, Kimberly. "Elias James Corey." *Notable Twentieth Century Scientists*. Detroit, MI: Gale Research, 1994, pp. 399–400.

Pool, Robert. "Chemistry 'Grand Master' Garners a Nobel Prize." *Science* (October 26, 1990): 510–11.

Waldrop, M. Mitchell. "'Chemzymes' Mimic Biology in Miniature." *Science* (July 28, 1989): 354–55.

Dick Dale

Lebanese-American musician

Born May 4, 1937
Beirut, Lebanon

"I STAND ON STAGE FOR TWO HOURS UNTIL I'M READY TO DROP. I'M NOT GOING TO RETIRE TO A ROCKING CHAIR. WHEN I DO GO, IT'LL BE UP THERE ON STAGE—IN AN EXPLOSION OF BODY PARTS."

Before the musical groups The Beach Boys and Jan & Dean made surf music popular in the 1960s, there was Dick Dale, a teenager who created surf music in the late 1950s. Using thick guitar strings and heavily reverberating (echoing) amplifiers, Dale's music mimics the sounds of untamed nature: the roar of an approaching wave, the growl of a wild tiger, the rumble of a volcano. Dissatisfied with recordings that failed to capture his live sound and unwilling to go on tour, Dale was a Southern California legend bound for musical obscurity until 1993, when Dale resumed performing to sold-out crowds.

A new generation became acquainted with Dale's unique sound when his 1962 song "Misirlou" (based on a traditional Middle Eastern song) ran as the melodic roller coaster accompanying the opening credits of the movie *Pulp Fiction* (1994). With the resurgence of his fame in the 1990s, Dale finally received recognition from the music industry for his contributions as the father—some even say king—of surf guitar.

Cowboy with a cardboard ukulele

Born Richard Monsour in 1937 in Beirut, Lebanon, Dale immigrated with his parents to the United States as a young child. He grew up in Boston, Massachusetts, and at age eight he got his first musical instrument: a cardboard ukulele he earned by selling jars of Noxema skin cream. As a teenager, Dale hung out with local musicians and bought a used guitar for eight dollars, making weekly payments of twenty-five cents. Most guitars are strung for right-handed players and need to be strung differently for left-handed musicians. Not realizing this, left-handed Dale learned how to play his guitar (which was strung for a right-handed player) upside down, with the chords backwards. He has played the guitar that way ever since.

Growing up, Dale spent his free time listening to his father's collection of records by country crooner Hank Williams, Sr. (1923–1953) and jazz drummer Gene Krupa (1909–1973). In 1954, as a senior in high school, Dale moved to Southern California. Once he finished school, he began pursuing a music career, winning the "Rocket to Stardom" contest as a country music performer. At the suggestion of a local disc jockey, Dale changed his name from Richard Monsour to Dick Dale—a fitting name for a country singer—and went on to perform at Los Angeles clubs and on country TV shows like *Spade Cooley* and *Town Hall Party*.

The majesty of the waves

Dale changed his musical style after he learned how to surf. Although it would later become very popular, surfing in the late 1950s was still a Hawaiian sport practiced by only a few. Dale found himself drawn to the water, ready to ride the waves at dawn. "It's a wonderful, spiritual experience, to stand in the water at 5 A.M. and face the majesty of those waves," he told the *Washington Post* in 1993. "You paddle out to a 15-footer, stand up, and the wave comes over your head, going tiddle-tiddly-dee. Then you're sucked down in a roll in a big roar. When you witness the power of mother nature that way, it makes you humble."

Dale became so intrigued by the strength of the ocean that he used his guitar to duplicate the sounds and sensations of surfing. He developed a frantic, staccato (choppy, with a

Dale (third from the right, wearing a dark suit) in an early 1960s publicity shot with his first surf band, the Del-Tones. Reproduced by permission of AP/Wide World Photos.

distinct break between each note) method of picking at his guitar strings to recreate the rush of an oncoming wave. He used thick guitar strings and echoing amplifiers to evoke the rumbling of the undertow of a current. He employed spiraling melodies (tapping his Arabic musical heritage) to replicate the rising and falling of waves.

Dale used few lyrics in his music—relying instead on a throbbing drum beat to drive each song. Rhythm is arguably the most important element of Dale's music, as the surf guitarist cites jazz drummer Gene Krupa as his main influence. "He mesmerized me," Dale told an interviewer. "He learned his rhythms from indigenous [native] sources, not from other so-called schooled musicians, and that's an approach I've always appreciated, and have tried to incorporate in my own music."

ARABIC MUSIC

"Miserlou," a song popularized by Dick Dale and used during the opening credits of the 1994 movie *Pulp Fiction,* is actually a traditional Middle Eastern song (the movie version can be found on the *Pulp Fiction* soundtrack and the older version can be heard on Dale's *Tribal Thunder* album). From his use of melody to the unusual beats, Dale's music shows strong Arabic influences. Middle Eastern folk songs are typically monophonic (consisting of a single line of melody, as opposed to several melodies blended in harmony) and are played on an *'ud* (pronounced ood), a four- or five-stringed instrument similar to the Western lute. Notes are grouped in sets, called *maqamat* (pronounced mah-KAHM-at) which define scales, favored notes, and popular melodies and rhythms. Within the rules of each *maqam*, artists are encouraged to improvise, and the use of other music devices keep the songs from being too similar.

Dramatic variations in pitch (the highness or lowness of a note) and the use of minor keys gave a winding, longing sound to each tune. Staccato notes and vibrating membrane instruments (such as tambourines and drums) produce patterns of pauses and strong and weak beats that drive the melody. Sometimes horns or other wind instruments carry the melody from the *'ud*. Many of these classical Arab music elements found their way into Dale's songs. "That staccato sound," musician Jonathan Richman told *The Atlanta Journal and Constitution,* "that Middle Eastern minor-key sound and that raucous, trebly, wild rock 'n' roll sound that says America, that says youth—now isn't that Dick Dale?"

In 1957, Dale began playing for high school dances and for surfers who went to the Rinky-Dink Ice Cream Parlor. When the parlor owner refused to give Dale and his band, the Del-Tones, a $5 raise, the group started looking for a new place to play. Dale set his sights on the city-owned Rendezvous Ballroom in Balboa, California. In order to hold shows there, he had to obtain a city permit to play rock 'n' roll and promise to keep the crowd from going wild. "They thought anybody who played guitar was evil," Dale told interviewer Godfrey Daniels. "They said, 'They [audience members] gotta wear ties!'" So Dale bought a box of cheap ties and stood there at the door on opening night, handing out ties to the bare-footed surfers who came through the door. Seventeen surfers came to Dick Dale and the Del-Tones' first gig, but within a few weeks, the crowd grew to be more than 4,000 strong.

The real surf guitar sound

Financed by his father, Hughes Aircraft machinist Jim Monsour, Dale's 1958 debut album, *Surfer's Choice,* sold an impressive 88,000 copies and produced the hit "Let's Go Trip-ping." Capitol Records pounced on the promising young star, signing a record deal with Dale that gave him $50,000 in advance—more money than Radio Corporation of America (RCA) paid for rock 'n' roll singer Elvis Presley (1935–1977). Between 1961 and 1964, Dale and his Del-Tones produced five albums—none of which became major hits, although several of his songs (including "Surf Beat" and "Misirlou") enjoyed popularity in Southern California.

A staple of the surf scene, Dale costarred with Annette Funicello (1942–) and Frankie Avalon (1939–) in *Beach Party* and *Muscle Beach Party.* He told *Newsweek* magazine in 1963 that his music "seemed to bring out the primitiveness in the surfers" and said other surf musicians like The Beach Boys and Jan & Dean were only singing surfing lyrics to rock 'n' roll music. "I'm the only one with the real surf guitar sound."

Still, Dale failed to achieve the global commercial suc-cess that The Beach Boys and Jan & Dean did. The main rea-son for that, he told the *Washington Post,* was that his albums never really captured his stage sound. "I was always fighting with engineers who'd tell you how many years they'd been in school, how you couldn't do this and you couldn't do that," he said. "So I did what they said, and when I heard the records, I hated them and smashed them against the wall." If he couldn't be recorded right, Dale decided, he wouldn't be recorded at all. He also refused to go on national tour to promote his albums. "I was surfing every day, and I was only playing on the weekends," Dale told the *Chicago Tribune* in 1993. "So why would I want to go traveling all over the country?"

In 1964, at age twenty-seven, Dale's career came to a grinding halt when he was diagnosed with rectal cancer and given only three months to live. He took a break from every-thing and went to Hawaii to rest. He stopped eating red meat and quit smoking. And he surprised his doctors by making a full recovery. Disillusioned by the music industry, Dale immersed himself in other projects. He learned how to fly a twin-tailed Cessna airplane, dabbled in architecture (he designed his parents' single-story, 7,000-square foot dream home in the California high desert), and became a martial arts expert. Dale's love for nature extended to wild animals,

and he has collected a private zoo of panthers, lions, and ocelots (medium-sized American wildcats).

An explosion of body parts

In the late 1980s, Dale returned to the music scene to contribute to several projects. He performed a duet with singer and guitarist Stevie Ray Vaughan (1954–1990), for which the two picked up a Grammy nomination. He also worked with guitarist Joe Satriani (1956–) and The Beach Boys' Brian Wilson (1942–) on a cut of musician Paul Shaffer's (1949–) album. In 1993, several Californian writers persuaded Dale to make a couple of nightclub appearances, all of which sold out. Dale agreed to cut an album with High Tone records, and this time was paired with a cooperative sound engineer. "I finally found an engineer who didn't have an ego

Dale's 1993 album Tribal Thunder *was popular with both younger and older generations. Dale went on a U.S. tour for the first time in his career. Reproduced by permission of Hightone Records.*

problem," he told the *Post*. "He just said, 'Dick, it's going to be tough, but we won't leave here until we got it the way you want it.'"

With its robust melodies and manic percussion, Dale's album *Tribal Thunder* finally embodied what he meant by surf guitar. Although he never wanted to go on tour before, Dale found himself touring—and loving it. "Now I can't stop," he told an interviewer. "I stand on stage for two hours until I'm ready to drop. I'm not going to retire to a rocking chair. When I do go, it'll be up there on stage—in an explosion of body parts."

Dale's performances are as vigorous as ever. He still plays with such intensity that his fingers bleed, his guitar picks melt down (he often goes through at least twenty picks per show), and his thick guitar strings snap like brittle strands of spaghetti. The inspiration for his newer music is his wild animals, but the song that most young people know him for is "Miserlou." The success of "Miserlou" and Dale's comeback led to his belated recognition within the music community. In 1996, he was inducted in the Hollywood Rock Walk of Fame and the Surfing Hall of Fame. He also received the Lifetime Pop Music Culture Award from University of California at Berkeley.

On the road, members of Dale's family sometimes join him for a set on stage, with his wife, Jill, on bass and his son Jimmy (born in 1992) on drums. Dale is still an avid animal rights activist and is dedicated to environmental issues. In the 1980s, after surfing with some open wounds, Dale's hip became infected from pollutants in the water, and he almost lost his left leg. He said the water that inspired his surf sound is now too dangerous to even enter. "Being a pilot, when I fly over the water, I see what's in the water that the people don't see," he told the *Chicago Tribune*. "I don't really want to go in the water."

FURTHER READING

Bourgoin, Suzanne, ed. *Contemporary Musicians,* vol. 13. Detroit, MI: Gale Research, 1995, pp. 67-69.

Dahl, Bill. "Surf's Back Up." *Chicago Tribune* (August 6, 1993): sec. 5, p. 3.

Himes, Geoffrey. "Dick Dale's Second Wave." *Washington Post* (October 15, 1993): 13.

Martin, Annabel, and Lorna Damms, eds. *Encyclopedia of Rock Stars.* New York: DK Publishing Inc., 1996, pp. 239-40.

Newsweek (August 26, 1963): 71.

Pareles, Jon. "Surfin' Again." *New York Times* (May 1, 1994): 5.

Michael Ellis DeBakey

Lebanese-American surgeon and inventor

Born September 7, 1908
Lake Charles, Louisiana

"CERTAINLY, I AM PLEASED TO SEE MY WORK RECOGNIZED—EVERYONE IS—BUT I DON'T DWELL ON IT. YOU JUST GO ON WITH YOUR ACTIVITIES AND INTERESTS."

Dr. Michael Ellis DeBakey (de-BAY-kee) developed several new types of lifesaving surgery on the heart and blood vessels, including what is now commonly known as *bypass surgery* (in which a section of vein from a patient's leg is patched onto a clogged artery near the heart, forming a bridge that carries blood past the blockage). He also invented revolutionary medical devices such as artificial arteries and the blood pump used in heart-lung machines. His army service during World War II (1939–45; when the United States and certain European countries went to war against Nazi Germany and Japan to stop their aggressions) brought about major changes in military medicine. He built Texas's Baylor College of Medicine into one of this country's most respected medical research and teaching institutions, and he led the effort to establish the National Library of Medicine.

Begins adventurous life

DeBakey's parents, Shaker Morris and Raheega Zorba DeBakey, emigrated from Lebanon as children. Originally members of the Greek Orthodox Church, DeBakey's parents joined the Episcopal Church in America. His father became a successful businessman. Both parents were energetic, intelligent people who taught their five children to develop their talents and help others. DeBakey is the oldest of five siblings, with three sisters and one brother. All the DeBakeys loved to learn, and each of the children read the entire *Encyclopaedia Britannica* before finishing high school.

When he was twelve years old, DeBakey and his family spent a year abroad. They crossed the Atlantic Ocean by ship, drove across France, and took another ship to Cairo, Egypt, stopping briefly in Naples, Italy. Their destination was Jedeidet, Lebanon, the hometown of DeBakey's grandparents. While staying there, they explored the surrounding area, including the Holy Land (Palestine—a region on the eastern shore of the Mediterranean Sea that is a place of pilgrimage for several religions). During that time, DeBakey learned to read, write, and speak Arabic fluently.

Before embarking on their year-long adventure, DeBakey had visited the editor of a local newspaper. He asked if the editor would publish DeBakey's weekly letters so the boy wouldn't have to write to each of his friends individually about what he has doing and learning on his trip. The editor gladly agreed, allowing DeBakey's classmates and neighbors to share in his adventure.

Trains his hands

As a youngster, DeBakey learned to play the piano, then changed to the saxophone so that he would be able to play in a band. While he was a student at Tulane University in New Orleans, Louisiana, he taught himself to play the clarinet so he that he could join the symphony orchestra as well as the marching band. He also joined the handball team and played billiards while at Tulane.

"If you can use your hands, let's say, on a musical instrument, somehow I think that helps your ... coordination," DeBakey said in a 1996 interview with William Roberts, editor of the *American Journal of Cardiology*. "It is that kind of ... coordination with your hands that you either have genetically, like a good athlete, or you don't. I think a surgeon needs that same quality—athletic coordination."

Pumps up his career

After two years at Tulane, DeBakey had enough credits to be admitted to the medical school, but he still wanted to earn his bachelor's degree. He took his first two years of medical school and his last two years of college at the same time. During his third year of medical school, he worked as a laboratory technician. The professor in charge told him to find a pump that could change the pulse wave that pushes blood through the arteries (blood vessels carrying blood from the heart to other parts of the body). DeBakey could find little information on pumps in the medical library, so he mentioned the problem to a close friend who was studying engineering. The friend suggested that DeBakey look in the engineering library, where he found a lot of information about the history of pumps and how they work.

DeBakey read about an early nineteenth-century pump that worked by squeezing a rubber tube. He started thinking about different ways in which he could press hard enough on a rubber tube to force blood through it without damaging the cells in the blood. To DeBakey, it seemed that some type of roller might be the answer. After a year or two of experimenting with different types and combinations of rollers, he made a pump with which he was satisfied.

Several years later, DeBakey saw a demonstration of a heart-lung machine designed to pump and oxygenate (to supply with oxygen) a patient's blood during heart surgery. The only problem with the machine was that the pump didn't work well enough. DeBakey realized that the pump he had invented would be more effective, so he offered it to the heart-lung machine inventor, John H. Gibbon, Jr. The improved device made open-heart surgery possible: bypassing the heart and using the machine to perform its functions during surgery allows a doctor to open the heart and replace valves, repair damage, or clear clogged arteries.

Joins the army

After finishing medical school in 1932, DeBakey spent two years in surgical residency at a New Orleans hospital. He then traveled to France and Germany to study with two of the world's leading surgeons, learning two more languages in the process. Returning to Louisiana in 1936, he married a nurse named Diana Cooper and began teaching at Tulane. When the United States entered World War II in 1941, DeBakey volunteered for the army and was stationed in Washington, D.C., at the Office of the Surgeon General, as the head of the U.S. Army's medical service. His job was to write the surgical orders (describing how to perform an operation) for nearly every type of surgery performed by army doctors.

DeBakey's efforts to make the army medical service more effective led to the establishment of mobile army surgical hospitals (known as MASH units) that saved thousands of lives during the Korean War (1950–53; when the United States helped South Korea battle its communist neighbor North Korea for control of Korea as a whole) and Vietnam War (1965–73; when the United States sent troops into South Vietnam to help them fight off their aggressive communist neighbor, North Vietnam). Believing that learning more about specific medical problems would lead to better treatments, DeBakey proposed a long-term program to keep track of veterans with certain disorders; this program became the Veterans' Administration Medical Research Program. He helped organize a system of specialized medical and surgical centers for treating people after they came home from World War II; this system became what is now known as the Veterans' Administration Medical Center System.

Invents new surgical procedures

DeBakey left the army and returned to his job at Tulane in 1946. Two years later, he moved to Houston, Texas, to become chairman of the Department of Surgery at Baylor University College of Medicine. Within a few years, he became famous for doing things no other surgeon had ever done. For example, in 1952, he performed the first successful repair of an aortic (ay-OR-tic) aneurysm in the United States. The aorta is the largest artery (blood vessel) in the human body that starts at the heart and carries blood to every part of the body except the lungs. An aneurysm (AN-yur-ism) is a weak spot in the wall of a blood vessel; the blood pressure pushes on the weak spot, stretching it out into a bubble that can burst and result in dangerous bleeding. DeBakey fixed an aneurysm in a patient by taking a section of aorta from another person (who had died) and attaching it to the patient's aorta on both sides of the aneurysm, rerouting the blood flow around the weak section.

Unknown to DeBakey, a few months earlier, a French surgeon had successfully performed a similar repair to an aneurysm in the abdomen (the part of the body containing the stomach and intestines). In future operations, however, DeBakey was the first surgeon to apply the technique to sections of the aorta in other parts of the body. He also used a similar technique, now called bypass surgery, to reroute blood past a section of artery that was partly or completely blocked by a blood clot or fatty deposits. One of his inventions was an artificial artery made of Dacron (a synthetic polyester fiber) fabric; using skills he had learned as a child, he borrowed his wife's sewing machine to stitch together the first sample.

Builds Baylor

When DeBakey first began working at Baylor, he was not very impressed by the school (DeBakey described it to Roberts as being "third-rate" at that time), and the university was not involved in doing any government-funded research. In fact, the school was not affiliated with a teaching hospital, so it didn't even have a residency program (in-hospital training program for doctors after they have graduated from medical school). Before long, DeBakey formed partnerships on Baylor's behalf with several Houston hospitals. During this time, he also created the first intensive care unit, based on knowledge he had gained during his military service.

Thanks to news of his surgical breakthroughs, DeBakey became very popular, attracting patients from all over the world. Early in his career he had earned small salaries, and his parents helped support him even after he finished going to school. By 1950, he was earning enough money to support himself and contribute personal funds to help him run the Department of Surgery at Baylor. He continued to support the department with his own money for nearly twenty years. In fact, in the late 1960s, the Baylor University College of Medicine was in serious financial trouble, and nine college and department heads quit. DeBakey was asked to become dean of the college. Under his leadership, the college was removed from the Baylor University system and became a separate organization with DeBakey as president. The new Baylor College of Medicine raised $30 million to get itself out of debt and operate successfully. DeBakey recruited talented doctors from many specialties who would bring research contracts to the college, giving the institution more money and prestige. By the late 1990s, Baylor ranked sixteenth in the nation in research grants from the National Institutes of Health.

Wins many awards

For DeBakey's efforts to improve military medicine during World War II, the U.S. Army gave him its Legion of Merit Award in 1945. While in the army, DeBakey spent a lot of time in the Surgeon General's Library, which he described to Roberts as "a national treasure." He was upset that the library was in an old building that leaked when it rained, and he knew that military spending would continue to be more important than money for a new library building. He eventually helped reorganize the library as the National Library of Medicine under the control of the National Institutes of Health. It is now the largest and best-known medical library in the world.

> **WORDS OF PRAISE**
>
> "Dacron arteries, arterial bypass operations, artificial hearts, heart pumps and heart transplants are common procedures in today's medicine, thanks to Dr. DeBakey." (From his International Samaritan Living Legacy Award given by the Women's International Center)
>
> "He was among the earliest proponents of blood banks and transfusions and wrote about their importance.... DeBakey was among the first surgeons involved in open-heart surgery." (From his Presidential Medal of Freedom award)
>
> "The great contribution [DeBakey] made was to make the aorta a very treatable entity." (Dr. William C. Roberts, editor of *American Journal of Cardiology*)
>
> "As a child, he accompanied his parents each Sunday to a local orphanage, where they delivered clothes and food for the children.... 'I realized that giving to others was a characteristic of my parents, and I saw the pleasure it gave them to share God's blessings with those less fortunate,' he says. 'That impressed me, and influenced my own determination to help others in any way I could.'" (From DeBakey's Horatio Alger Award)

During a fifty-year period, DeBakey served as an advisor to nearly every U.S. President as well as leaders of other countries. President Lyndon B. Johnson (1908–1973) presented him with the nation's highest civilian honor, the Presidential Medal of Freedom with Distinction, in 1969. President Ronald Reagan (1911–) awarded him the country's highest scientific honor, the National Medal of Science, in 1987. He has received a great many other awards from public and private organizations around the world.

"Certainly, I am pleased to see my work recognized—everyone is—but I don't dwell on it," he told Roberts. "You just go on with your activities and interests. I don't mean in any way to diminish [my awards'] value, but you can't live in the past. You have another day, a new day."

Enjoys life

As a child, DeBakey and his brother and sisters had to get up early each morning to do their chores. Although the family was wealthy, DeBakey's parents wanted to teach their children responsibility and self-discipline. When he went to college, DeBakey found that his habit of early rising came in handy. The dormitory was too noisy in the evenings for him to study, but he was able to sleep. He would wake up at three or four in the morning and study while it was quiet.

Known as the "Texas Tornado," DeBakey still arises each morning at five o'clock and spends the first part of his day on paperwork—he has written more than 1,500 publications (articles, book chapters, and complete books). After this, he goes to work at Baylor, where he became chancellor of the medical school in 1978. He has performed more than 65,000 surgeries in his long career, averaging a dozen a day even when he had reached the age of seventy-five.

DeBakey credits his genetic makeup with allowing him to get by on only five or six hours of sleep a night. Having learned as a child to enjoy fruits and vegetables, he eats a healthy diet that includes a lot of fish. He does not use tobacco or alcohol. Although he doesn't deliberately exercise, he does choose to use stairs rather than an elevator when given the choice. He also tries to use his time as efficiently as possible so he can do all the things he wants to do.

Although he might be described as a workaholic, DeBakey values his family too. He and his first wife had four sons. They were very happy together until her sudden death from a heart attack in 1972. Two years later, DeBakey married Katrin Fehlhaber, a German artist and actress. Their daughter was just starting college when DeBakey, at eighty-eight, described her to Roberts as "the joy of my life right now."

FURTHER READING

Altman, Lawrence K. "Dr. DeBakey at 90: Stringent Standards and a Steady Hand." *New York Times* (August 31, 1998).

McMurray, Emily J, ed. *Notable Twentieth Century Scientists,* Detroit, MI: Gale Research, 1994, pp. 466–68.

Roberts, William C. "Michael Ellis DeBakey: A Conversation with the Editor." *American Journal of Cardiology* (April 1, 1977): 929–50.

Farouk El-Baz

Egyptian-American geologist

Born January 1, 1938
Zagazig, Egypt

How does a geologist get involved with space exploration, archaeology (the study of the remains of past human life), and oceanography (the study of the oceans)? Ask Farouk (far-OOK) El-Baz. His professional career has taken him from planning moon missions to exploring undersea coral reefs. He has found vast deposits of water under deserts and oil under the ocean. He developed tools for archaeologists to find and explore important artifacts (human-made objects from certain time periods) without damaging them or even removing them from their resting places. Not content to discover new knowledge, he also loves to share it with others through school visits, published and broadcast interviews, and museum exhibits.

Playing on the pyramids

For the first twelve years of his life, Farouk El-Baz lived in the ancient town of Zagazig in the Egyptian desert. He was in the seventh grade when his family moved to Cairo, Egypt, and he saw the pyramids for the first time. Comparing them

"IT WAS WONDERFUL TO TAKE THE THINGS I'D LEARNED FROM THE SPACE PROGRAM—THE MOST SOPHISTICATED TECHNOLOGY THAT CURRENTLY EXISTS—AND APPLY THEM TO STUDYING ONE OF THE WORLD'S OLDEST CIVILIZATIONS, WHICH IS ALSO MY CULTURAL HERITAGE."

117

to fifty-story buildings, almost as high as the Washington Monument, El-Baz told interviewer Thomas Bass in 1990, "It's not just their height that's impressive. It's their bulk. They are absolutely immense structures." He and his brothers and sisters visited the pyramids often; they would race each other to the top or crawl inside to explore. (Access is more restricted now that the Egyptian government is more aware of the need to preserve and protect the monuments.)

El-Baz's interest in geology (the study of the earth's history as recorded in rocks) began with the field trips he enjoyed taking with his Boy Scout troop. He also liked to take his two younger brothers to the mountains outside Cairo. "We didn't have any money for public transportation, so we'd spend most of the day walking there and back, with a couple of hours remaining to make tea and explore the caves and mountains," he told Bass.

Revolution

Since before El-Baz was born, King Farouk (1920–1965) had ruled Egypt. But in 1952, the Egyptian military took over the country and expelled the king. By 1956, a new government had been established with Gamal Abdel Nasser (1918–1970) as president. "After the revolution the government decided who was going to get an advanced degree and in what. This depended solely on the needs of the country," El-Baz explained to Bass. El-Baz had been a good student in high school. When he graduated, the government told him he could go to either dental school or the school of science at Ain Shams University in Cairo. Having no interest in being a dentist, he chose science.

El-Baz described to Bass what happened next: "I took my papers to the registrar's office at Ain Shams and said, 'What do you teach here?' That's when I heard the word 'geology' for the first time. 'What's geology?' I asked. 'It has to do with people who go to mountains and collect rocks,' said the registrar. 'I want that one!' I said."

In 1958, El-Baz graduated with a bachelor of science degree in chemistry and geology. The following year, he earned a master's degree in paleontology (the study of fossils to reveal the history of life on earth). Because he was one of the best students in the country, the Egyptian government decided to send him abroad to get a Ph.D. degree. On the advice of an older brother who had visited the Soviet Union several times, El-Baz declined an offer to go there. A few months later, he received a Ford Foundation scholarship to study in the United States.

Few choices

When El-Baz arrived in the United States, he found that once again he had little choice about where he would study. Under the terms of his scholarship, the U.S. Bureau of Mines was responsible for assigning him to a school. The man who interviewed him had graduated from the School of Mines and Metallurgy, a division of the University of Missouri-Rolla. Assuring El-Baz it was a very good school, he assigned El-Baz to attend the University of Missouri.

El-Baz's older brother was attending Harvard University in Boston, Massachusetts, so El-Baz had been hoping to go to the nearby Massachusetts Institute of Technology (MIT), one of the most famous science colleges in the United States. He was disappointed to be sent to a school he'd never heard of in Missouri. Eventually, he changed his mind, as he told Bass: "It really turned out to be one of the best things that ever happened to me, because the education I got there was first class."

In the early 1960s, while he was working on his Ph.D., El-Baz did spend a year studying at MIT. During that year, he frequently visited the Boston Museum of Fine Arts, which has the largest collection of mummies (bodies preserved for burial) outside Egypt. He was already developing a greater sensitivity for the past than he had felt as a boy scampering up the pyramids. He told Bass, "When you stand next to [a mummy] for a long time and think of it as a person, with a life of its own so many thousands of years ago, you develop tremendous fellow-feeling for this creature. You begin to think, 'Isn't it terrible to be exposed like this?'"

Going home

After earning his Ph.D. in geology from the University of Missouri in 1964, El-Baz taught for a year at the University of Heidelberg in Germany. He and his wife, Catherine O'Leary El-Baz, planned to experience Europe for a year or two and then settle in Egypt. In preparation for that move, El-Baz

started to teach his wife Arabic (she already spoke Spanish, Italian, and French in addition to her native English). He couldn't find a book to use, so he wrote *Say It in Arabic: Egyptian Dialect,* which was published by Dover Publications in 1968 and again in 1982.

Eager to use his education and experience to establish a school of economic geology (geology related to valuable minerals and petroleum) that would benefit his country, El-Baz returned to Egypt in 1966. Besides his family's personal items, El-Baz shipped four tons of rocks from Germany to Egypt— geological samples he had collected in North America and Europe. To his disappointment, the government assigned him to teach chemistry at a technical school that didn't even have a geology program. "This was during Nasser's regime, when Egypt was a police state," El-Baz explained to Bass. "No one spoke his mind, and you didn't say no to the government." The only way to refuse the government's decision was to leave the country. He took his family back to the United States.

Egyptian Apollo

El-Baz went to Washington, D.C., where he worked for a company that was interpreting photographs of the moon's surface for the National Aeronautics and Space Administration (NASA). During the next several years, he became increasingly involved with NASA's program of manned missions to the moon. The program was named "Apollo" after a god of ancient Greece and Rome. As supervisor of lunar science planning and exploration, he was in charge of several aspects of the program, including selecting the landing sites on the moon and training the astronauts in geology. Based on earlier lunar photographs, he figured out what type of surface, such as hard, sandy, or powdery, the astronauts should expect when they first stepped out of the spacecraft. He also decided what types of samples the astronauts should collect on the moon and designed procedures for collecting the samples without contaminating them with material from earth.

El-Baz told interviewer Kevin Carleton that the first lunar astronauts resisted his training efforts because they thought of themselves as test pilots rather than scientists. But he won them over with his attitude and expertise. One of the astronauts surprised the ground control team by speaking an Egyptian greeting from lunar orbit as a tribute to El-Baz, whom they had nicknamed "King Farouk."

"The Apollo days were very exciting to me," El-Baz told *Aramco World* magazine. "I don't know if it was more the scientific work, or the things I did on behalf of Arab culture, such as teaching the astronauts some Arabic, and naming features on the moon." He named at least three dozen lunar features after historically significant Arab scientists like tenth-century astronomer Ibn Yunus (who developed an important formula for doing astronomical calculations) and ninth-century mathematician Mohammed ibn-Musa al-Khwarizmi (who developed algebra).

Searching sands

After working with his adopted country's space program for six years (El-Baz became a U.S. citizen in 1970), he undertook a new challenge in 1973. He became the first research director for the new Center for Earth and Planetary Studies at the Smithsonian Institution's National Air and Space Museum in Washington, D.C. During the ten years he held that post, he did extensive research around the world in addition to preparing space science exhibits for the museum.

His primary interest during this period was to learn more about deserts, particularly through the use of remote sensing (gathering information or images from a distance), a technique he had used extensively in the Apollo program. He told *Science* magazine that although deserts occupy one-fifth of the earth's land surface, they are the least understood of the world's ecosystems (an ecological community that includes the plants, animals, microorganisms, and weather of an area)—probably because the science of geology developed in Europe, the only continent without a desert. Even when he studied geology in Egypt, he "studied everything but the desert." He explained that money for research on deserts only began to appear after NASA's Viking program produced photographs that showed the surface of Mars to be an enormous desert. "We came in through the back door," he said, referring to scientists seeking to understand earth's deserts.

Using not only remote sensing, but also the knowledge he has gained from exploring deserts in the Middle East, the United States, Australia, India, and China, El-Baz has made some important contributions to society. For example, in 1981, he asked friends at NASA to take radar images (which are formed by sending out radio waves and detecting the waves that are reflected back by various objects) of the Western Desert in Egypt. To his surprise, the radar passed through the sand and produced images of the solid surfaces buried under the sand. By identifying long-hidden ancient river

SHAPING THE MONUMENTS

His knowledge of geology has led Farouk El-Baz to interesting conclusions about ancient Egyptian structures. For example, he realized that the Sphinx began as a wind-sculptured rock, which the ancients fine-tuned into a decorative figure. Understanding why the rock originally whittled away would help preservationists figure out how to keep similar forces from continuing to wear it down.

Similarly, El-Baz thinks the idea for building pyramids came from natural desert forms. "I was flabbergasted when I began exploring places that humans may not have seen for five thousand years," he told Thomas Bass. "You find conical structures where nothing should be standing. The wind is so fierce that everything around them has been totally leveled. Did the ancients notice these forms and realize they were durable?"

El-Baz believes the building of the monumental stone pyramids was part-time work done during the months that normal flooding kept farmers from working in the fields. Signatures and slogans carved on the building blocks convinced him that the workers were proud of their accomplishment. "This Hollywood version of slaves laboring under the whip simply doesn't work," he told Bass. "There was singing and joy and pride in building these beautiful structures."

beds, El-Baz located large stores of underground water that can be used to grow crops and sustain people in deserts in Egypt, Somalia, and Sudan.

Remote chance

After leaving the Air and Space Museum in 1982, El-Baz worked until 1986 for a company that was responsible for photography on NASA's space shuttle program. Then he accepted the challenge to head a new Center of Remote Sensing at Boston University. The center would help develop remote sensing as a tool for many fields. For example, infrared images taken from equipment on a satellite (a human-made object that orbits Earth or another celestial body) can show temperature patterns in the ocean, which can help meteorologists (people who study the atmosphere and weather) forecast weather patterns. Satellite photographs can help environmental scientists track oil spills in the sea, and guide geologists to promising sites to search for underwater or underground deposits of water, oil, and other natural resources. Satellite images can also help scientists monitor the growth or deterioration of underwater coral reefs, which are endangered ecological systems that support the earth's atmosphere by transforming carbon dioxide into oxygen.

Breath of stale air

Although El-Baz has shared his skills with various types of scientists, he has particularly enjoyed his chance to help archaeologists apply remote sensing technology to explorations of Egypt's pyramids. "It was wonderful to take the things I'd learned from the space program—the most sophisticated technology that currently exists—and apply them to studying one of the world's oldest civilizations, which is also my cultural heritage," he told Bass.

An ancient cedar boat found at the Great Pyramid in 1954 began to deteriorate within decades after it was removed from the chamber in which it had lain for 5,000 years. Archaeologists asked El-Baz to help them figure out how to preserve the wood and also how to explore a second, unopened chamber that might contain a similar boat, without triggering its deterioration. El-Baz was excited at the possibility that the chambers might have remained airtight for thousands of years. Being able to examine a 5,000-year-old sample of air would give scientists a rare chance to compare the air pollution created by modern societies with natural pollution from events like volcano eruptions.

El-Baz and his team spent two and a half years planning and designing equipment for drilling into the chamber and collecting a sample of the air without letting it mix with air from outside the chamber. When they finally carried out their plans in 1987, they found that the chamber was not airtight after all. However, their carefully planned and executed excavation allowed them to explore the chamber through only a small opening, using a tiny television camera. After examining its contents, the chamber was closed again.

Look but don't touch

Despite the disappointment over not finding an ancient air sample, El-Baz is excited about his work in applying remote sensing technology to develop "nondestructive archaeology." He told Bass, "The era of archaeology as high-class grave robbing is over. It's time we realize that archaeological sites are often as important as the objects they hold." He believes that tombs and other archaeological sites should be explored without disturbing them. He explained, "I say this not out of religious feeling, but because the sites themselves—the way they were planned and executed—have archaeological significance."

Furthermore, he cautions that archaeologists shouldn't be impatient to explore ancient sites with more traditional techniques. "The technology is developing so fast that there's no need to rush into one of these discoveries," he told Bass. "We have to leave some things for the next generation."

FURTHER READING

Bass, Thomas A. "Exploring Time." *Reinventing the Future: Conversations with the World's Leading Scientists*. Reading, MA: Addison-Wesley, 1993, pp. 130–49.

Bass, Thomas A. "Interview: Farouk El-Baz." *OMNI* (December 1990): 74–80, 134.

Carleton, Kevin. "Farouk El-Baz: Michel T. Halbouty Human Needs Award." *AAPG (American Association of Petroleum Geologists) Bulletin* (June 1996): 934–35.

Holden, Constance. "Egyptian Geologist Champions Desert Research." *Science* (September 28, 1979): 1357–360.

Kesting, Piney. "Taking the Long View." *Aramco World* (March/April 1992): 12–13.

Fadwa El Guindi

Egyptian-American anthropologist

Born July 16, 1940
Cairo, Egypt

"FILM IS ONE OF THE MOST POWERFUL WAYS TO CONVEY CULTURE."

The first thing Fadwa El Guindi did as an anthropologist (a scientist who studies cultures) was watch a society say goodbye to its way of life. Actually, she was more deeply involved than that: by living with the Kenuz Nubians in southern Egypt for an entire year before their homeland was destroyed and they were moved to a different region, she shared the final annual cycle of their traditional way of life. A few years later, she immersed herself in a different culture half a world away—a culture not as immediately threatened as the Nubians.

The Zapotec culture in Mexico expanded El Guindi's horizons and gave her a comparative base for her anthropological studies. Her book on Zapotec rituals broke new ground in anthropological methods; it was the first in modern times to formally recognize that a member of the subject society could help the anthropologist study and describe his or her culture. Eventually, El Guindi began to study the Egyptian culture in which she grew up and the Arab American community in which she lives as an adult.

Surprise student

Fadwa El Guindi grew up in a suburb of Cairo, Egypt. Her father was a civil aviation engineer, and his job frequently took him on trips to other countries. Her mother was a homemaker. When El Guindi was two years old, her mother didn't realize that rather than playing outside with the neighbors each day, the little girl was following her three-year-old brother across the street to his school—not only playing in the school yard, but even attending classes. Finally, the school surprised her parents with a bill for her tuition. Her parents paid it, deciding that if she was that eager to go to school, they should enroll her.

For her elementary and high school education, El Guindi attended the American College for Girls, a school that prepared Egyptian women for social responsibilities but also produced many prominent leaders in Egypt. She graduated with honors and was the valedictorian (student with the best academic record) in her class. After graduating from high school, she attended The American University in Cairo (AUC), graduating in 1960 with a bachelor's degree in political science.

A new Nubian

El Guindi went to work at AUC in the Social Research Center, which sponsored sociological and anthropological studies in Egypt. At this time, the enormous Aswan High Dam was being built in southern Egypt; when completed, it would create a 300-mile-long lake. The Social Research Center assigned El Guindi to study the culture of the Kenuz Nubian people, whose homeland would be covered by the new lake. The Egyptian government planned to move the people to new homes, but first the researchers wanted to learn about the people's traditional way of life, which would be disrupted by the move.

For an entire year, El Guindi lived in the Nubian village, observing the people's daily lifestyle as well as special events like births, weddings, and funerals. "My outlook on humanity began to change," El Guindi recalled in a book she wrote in 1986. "This occurred in the process of my close contact with the Nubian people, sharing their experiences, participating in their day-to-day activities, and being part of their joy, their mourning, their conflicts, their accomplishments, and, particularly, the uncertainties in the lives of the women who waited months and years for their husbands, brothers, and sons to return from migrant labor in the cities of Cairo and Alexandria."

After her year of simple village life, El Guindi spent the next three years in Cairo analyzing what she had observed and writing about the Kenuz Nubian culture. The research project was sponsored by the Ford Foundation, an American organization, and El Guindi worked with both Americans and fellow Egyptians. As she completed her work on the project, she began to think about two things: becoming an anthropologist and studying in America. She had a chance to do both when she received a scholarship to earn her Ph.D. (doctor's degree) in anthropology in the United States. Her advisors suggested that she get involved with a different cultural area than what she had previously experienced. This is why she attended the University of Texas in Austin, a school that is well known for its strength in Latin American studies.

Joins Zapotec family

Part of El Guindi's graduate work at the University of Texas was to do original research. In 1967, she participated in Stanford University's Summer Field School with an assignment in San Francisco Lachigoló, a village in southern Mexico. Living with a local family, she began to familiarize herself with the Zapotec Indian culture.

In her 1986 book, El Guindi wrote about Zapotec life-crisis rituals. She described her first summer with the Indians as "a memorable experience combining moments of fear, uncertainty, warmth, support, challenge, conflict, and love.... I was enriched by expanding my family to include the Zapotec, transcending barriers of faith, culture, and continents."

El Guindi's work with the Zapotec continued even after she earned her Ph.D. in anthropology from the University of Texas and began teaching at the University of California at Los Angeles (UCLA) in 1972. Between 1967 and 1978, she spent a total of thirty-two months in Lachigoló, including an entire year that started in 1969. Her daughter, Magda, was only three months old when they began that year-long stay. Four years later, El Guindi took another three-month-old, her

When anthropologist Fadwa El Guindi studies a society, she doesn't just observe it, she actively participates in it. She becomes one of the people she is studying, learning to experience life in their way.

For example, in her book *The Myth of Ritual,* she described how the Zapotec villagers first came to accept her presence. They were used to having anthropology students live with them during the summers. But as an Egyptian, she was different from the other students they had met.

She wrote, "They searched for a way to accept me—an Egyptian anthropologist, from the United States, living with them in a Zapotec village. They then made the connection between being Egyptian, being Arab, being Andalusian [from a region in southern Spain], and the Andalusian mixing with Mexican Indians after conquest. I was then ritually welcomed as a 'relative.' Later, when people invited me to baptize children I reminded them that, not only was I not Catholic, I was not Christian at all. Their answer was 'We don't care, do you?'" When a Zapotec child she had baptized died while El Guindi was at home in California, the anthropologist returned to the village to fulfil her role as godmother by conducting the funeral ceremony and burial.

son Khalid, to the village while she directed a summer school program there for UCLA students.

"It is difficult to measure and evaluate the experience of having my children with me in the field," she wrote in her 1986 book. "These times were full of joy, but not without moments of intense fear, worry, and doubt as I faced their occasional health problems. When I was able to conquer those fears, I found the children's participation in my field experience most rewarding."

Makes movies

After she had taught at UCLA for ten years as a professor of anthropology, El Guindi received a Distinguished Fulbright Scholarship to spend a year as a visiting research professor at Ain Shams University in Cairo. Returning to the United States in 1982, she was invited to join the faculty at the University of Southern California (USC). She arrived at USC at a time when a new anthropology program was being developed in a relatively young field called visual anthropology—studying cultures using the visual medium. El Guindi was particularly interested in ethnic filmography, which captures and explains ethnic traditions by filming cultural events and adding interpretive voice-overs to a carefully edited film.

"It was an exciting, emerging field and I got the bug," El Guindi told *Aramco World* magazine. "Film is one of the most powerful ways to convey culture."

El Guindi was aware that few anthropological films about Arab life were available in the United States. Her first three films, which she recorded in Egypt, addressed this gap. *El Sebou'* (1986) is a half-hour presentation of the celebration held on the seventh day after the birth of a child in both the Muslim and Coptic Christian cultures. *El Moulid* (1990) is a forty-minute record of a religious festival honoring a thirteenth-century Muslim holy man. *Ghurbal* (1995) is a film that does two things. First, it shows the craft of sieve-making (a sieve is a hand-held sifter used to separate grain from other particles) and, second, it demonstrates the process of interviewing people to learn ethnographic information. All three of these films were sponsored by the Smithsonian Institution, and all have received international honors.

El Guindi has shifted her focus from Egyptian traditions to the more recent development of Arab American culture. Her next few film projects focus on aspects of Arab American life. The making of ethnographic films has become so important to El Guindi that since 1985 she has divided her time between teaching (at both USC and UCLA) and operating a research organization she founded, called El Nil ("The Nile"). Her teaching and her research focus on both cultural studies and ethnographic filmmaking.

Explains Islam

Considering that El Guindi studied political science in college and that her work in anthropology has focused on current cultural practices, it is not surprising that she has been interested in Middle Eastern public affairs. Since 1978, she has taught classes for U.S. State Department diplomats assigned to serve in Middle Eastern countries, explaining religious and cultural practices and attitudes. For example, she explains that westerners have misinterpreted the Islamic (Muslim) values, emphasizing political and militant dimensions while ignoring cultural and social aspects. "For ordinary Muslim Egyptian men and women, Islam has inspired not militancy but silent resistance," she told the National Press Club in 1997.

As another example, she explains that westerners generally interpret the veiling of Muslim women's faces as a form of male oppression. But El Guindi explained in a *Los Angeles Times* column that many modern, educated, "liberated" Muslim women prefer to wear veils and traditional clothing: "Their Islamic dress, so mystifying and misunderstood in the West, is in fact an anti-consumerist claim for their right to modesty, to control of their own bodies, to sexual space and moral privacy." El Guindi further examined that complex topic in her book *Veil: Modesty, Privacy and Resistance*.

El Guindi is frequently invited to speak to groups around the world on topics like "Islamic Feminism," "Values Shared by Islam and the West," and "Arab American Concerns in the Middle East: The Palestinian Situation." She is active in professional organizations; for example, she has been president

El Guindi interviewing Hoksha, master craftsman in the art of sieve-making in rural Egypt. Reproduced by permission of El Nil Research.

of the Middle East Section of the American Anthropological Association (AAA) and the Society for Visual Anthropology of the AAA. She was also an editor of the AAA journal. She is active as a private individual as well; for instance, she was president of the Los Angeles chapter of the American-Arab Anti-Discrimination Committee (ADC) and was a speaker at a 1994 walk-a-thon sponsored by the Greater Los Angeles chapter of the Palestine Aid Society. This event raised funds for needy Palestinians in Gaza, the West Bank, and Lebanon.

On stage, on screen

El Guindi has come up with a creative way of studying Arab American culture while enriching it and showing it to both outsiders and the Arab American community itself. In the early 1990s she founded an organization called Al-Funun Al-Arabiya (Arab Arts). "It is the nation's first contemporary forum devoted exclusively to presenting and promoting the visual, literary and performance arts, created by Arab Americans," according to its online brochure. Music concerts, poetry readings, and theater and film presentations are some of the events Al-Funun supports.

One of Al-Funun's productions was a two-act play called *Mahjar* (mah-ZHAR: immigrant). The bilingual drama is a story of the "lives and concerns, conflicts and doubts, fears and joys" of Arab Americans. El Guindi coauthored and codirected the production. When the lead actress quit a few days before the play's first performance, El Guindi was the only one who was willing and able to take her place. Not thinking of herself as an actress, she hadn't intended to appear on stage, but she agreed to do it to save the production.

To her surprise, a few months later El Guindi received a telephone call from a television casting agent who had seen the play. The agent invited her to audition for a part in an upcoming episode of *Star Trek: Deep Space Nine,* playing the mother of one of the show's regular characters, Dr. Bashir. "My first instinct was that when such an opportunity falls in the lap of the Arab American community, it should not be missed," El Guindi told the *ADC Times.*

At the audition, she competed with many experienced actresses, but within an hour she was offered the part. She had a great time filming the show and was happy with the program, which was first broadcast in February 1997. Although she didn't start looking for other acting opportunities, she told *ADC Times* that she might be willing to consider another part "if it makes Arabs look good and if it does not interfere with my principal career as an anthropologist."

FURTHER READING

"ADC Member Plays Dr. Bashir's Mom on Star Trek." *ADC Times* (February-March 1997).

Clark, Brian. "Celebrations of Life." *Aramco World* (September 1990): 40.

El Guindi, Fadwa. "Feminism Comes of Age in Islam." *Los Angeles Times* (February 17, 1992): B5.

El Guindi Website. http://www-bcf.usc.edu/~elguindi (June 1998).

Rosalind Elias

Lebanese-American opera singer

Born March 13, 1931
Lowell, Massachusetts

A talented singer and actress, Rosalind Elias entertains opera lovers in productions ranging from tragedy to comedy. In addition to performing in operas, she has appeared as a soloist with major symphony orchestras, acted in live stage productions, and directed operas. She has won Emmy and Grammy awards for her television performances and recordings. Whether she is starring or playing a supporting role, she continues to enjoy her career after more than forty years of professional performances.

Breaks the mold

Elias was the youngest of thirteen children born to Salem and Shelahuy Rose Namay Elias. Her parents had moved to the United States from Lebanon, and Elias spoke Arabic before she learned English. Elias had decided that she wanted to be an opera singer by the time she was in her early teens. Willing to work hard for her goal, she began taking singing lessons. She won starring roles in her high school's musical shows. After graduation, she continued her training at the

New England Conservatory of Music in Boston. She was the only member of her family to be interested in music. "My father felt that performing was not a respectable pursuit for a serious person," she later told the the *New York Times,* "until he saw me winning scholarships and actually performing with respectable contracts."

Hits the stage

At the age of seventeen, while studying at the conservatory, Elias made her debut with the New England Opera. She appeared as the character Maddalena in *Rigoletto,* a classic opera written by Italian composer Giuseppe Verdi (1813–1901). In 1951, the year she turned twenty, she appeared in three different operas, including Verdi's famous *Falstaff.*

The following year Elias went to Italy, where she took lessons from two prominent opera singers. She also found work on two productions. At La Scala Opera House in Milan, she was chosen to understudy the title role in *Danae,* by Austrian composer Johann Strauss (1825–1899). This meant she would fill in if the star was ever unable to perform. The lead performer didn't miss any performances, however, so Elias didn't get on stage. Shortly after that contract ended, Elias went to Naples where she got a part in *The Magic Flute,* which had been composed by Austrian composer Wolfgang Amadeus Mozart (1756–1791).

Although she had planned to stay in Europe for two years of instruction and practice, Elias came home a year early because her mother was ill. After a little more training with the American Theater Wing (the organization that presents the Tony Awards), the young singer decided she was ready to reach for her ultimate goal—a position with New York's Metropolitan Opera (the "Met").

A difficult choice

Elias entered a Met-sponsored competition called Auditions of the Air, knowing that if she won the competition she would be offered a fairly important role in an upcoming production. Her backup plan, in case she didn't win, was to return to Europe and build a reputation that would attract the Met's attention.

Elias (standing) on stage with Barbara Daniels and Deidre Palmour, during a performance of Falstaff. Reproduced by permission of the Baltimore Opera Company.

Before the second round of the auditions, however, she had to make a difficult decision. A cast member in that season's production of *Die Walküre,* by German composer Richard Wagner (1813–1883), had become ill. The Met needed someone to fill the minor role; they asked Elias to withdraw from the auditions and take the part. She was afraid that the part was so small no one would notice her. If she withdrew from the auditions, she would give up her chance of winning a much better part the following season. On the other hand, if she turned down the part and stayed in the auditions, she might not win. If that happened, she wouldn't have even a small role with the company of her dreams.

She accepted the small part. A week later, on February 23, 1954, she made her debut with the Metropolitan Opera. The minor role of Grimgerde the Valkyrie turned out to be one of seven small parts Elias would play in Met productions during her first season. One of her parts was even sung from off-stage. Although her parts were relatively minor, she continued to perform with the Met the following two years. By her third season, some theater critics were mentioning her in their reviews.

Takes another chance

The Met was preparing for a 1958 premiere of *Vanessa*, a new opera composed by Samuel Barber (1910–1981). Barber and Gian-Carlo Menotti (1911–), who wrote the libretto (text) of the opera, held auditions for Vanessa and Erika, the two main female roles, both of which were written for sopranos (the highest female vocal range). One of Elias's friends arranged for her to sing in the audition.

Because she was a mezzo soprano, with a lower natural voice, "the whole idea seemed pretty pointless to me," Elias later told Marjorie Samuel, a reporter for the *Christian Science Monitor*. "With the Met contract, it had looked like risk. Here it looked like futility. However, they were both important composers and I thought once they had heard me they might think of me for future works. So I sang for them."

Barber and Menotti thought Elias's personality and appearance were just right for the part of Erika. They also decided that Elias would be able to handle the soprano part. After offering her the role, Barber wrote an aria (an elaborate solo) for Erika in the mezzo soprano range.

A star!

Vanessa was a smash hit. Theater critics praised Elias, saying that she had achieved stardom with this role. Barber, who told Elias after the first performance, "You're my lucky charm!," won the 1958 Pulitzer Prize for Music for *Vanessa*.

The role of Erika has turned out to be a great opportunity for other singers too. Major parts in operas are usually written for sopranos. Erika's part gives mezzo sopranos a rare opportunity to be in the spotlight.

Although her performance in *Vanessa* made her a star, Elias hesitates to call it the turning point of her career. "I don't think there's such a thing as one turning point," she told Samuel. "Every opportunity that comes along seems to me to have a turning-point potential." She thinks it is important to explore every chance that comes along. As she told Samuel, "You can't always judge the significance of an opportunity in advance. You can waste a lot of time if you insist on waiting for the 'right' opportunity."

A friendly and fun-loving person, Elias enjoyed the chance to be a celebrity as a young adult. She dressed with style and designed many of her own clothes—including some of her opera costumes. Once, wearing a diamond ring on her toe, she joked that it was "an old Lebanese custom."

Speaks out

By 1961, Elias was a true celebrity, and she decided to use her status in a powerful way. It was the first year of John F. Kennedy's presidency, and there was great tension (called the Cold War) between the world's super-power governments— the United States and the communist Soviet Union. The fear of a nuclear war was so widespread that basements of public buildings around America were stocked with food, water, and medical supplies so survivors of a nuclear war could take refuge in these "fallout shelters." School children rehearsed what to do in case of a missile attack.

Elias announced her reaction to this national mood in a half-page advertisement in the *New York Times* that October. It said, in part, "I shall, as an American, continue to walk upright in the open sunlight of my home.... My faith in God and in my country is far too great for me to ever feel anything but strong and secure. I am not afraid!" People all over the country praised her statement, and the Freedom Foundation at Valley Forge gave her an award. When asked to explain why she had placed the ad, Elias said, "I am so proud to be an American that I wanted everyone to know it. My father came here from Lebanon many years ago a penniless emigrant. He raised and educated thirteen children and became prosperous. Where else in the world could that have happened?"

Roles change

During a career of more than forty years, Elias has played many different kinds of roles. She is as good at comedy as she is at tragedy. Sometimes she appears as the lead character, and other times she performs a small part. As time has passed, she has expanded her experiences to take on other kinds of roles as well. For example, in 1967, she sang the role of Gretel in the Met's production of German composer Engelbert Humperdinck's (1854–1921) *Hansel and Gretel,* and in 1982, she appeared in the same opera as the witch, giving a performance one critic called "a real treat." Two years later she directed *Hansel and Gretel* for the Memphis (Tennessee) Opera. In 1997, Elias appeared in a new production of *Vanessa* at the Opera Festival of New Jersey; this time, she sang the part of the Old Baroness rather than the youthful Erika. "My crossovers [into smaller character parts] have just begun," Elias told Lesley Valdes, a *Philadelphia Inquirer* music critic, as she rehearsed the baroness part. "I don't mind cameo roles. It doesn't matter to me if a role is five pages, as long as there's substance to it. I like the acting part of it all."

Elias clearly does love her career. To her, it is more important to make a show successful than it is to attract personal attention. "What's wonderful about Rosalind [is] she continually shows us just what a pro she is," Albert Takazauckas, the director of the 1997 production of *Vanessa,* told Valdes. "She's always so thoroughly prepared and ready to work … and she never, ever tells us how things were done for the Met premiere."

FURTHER READING

"Elias, Rosalind." *Current Biography Yearbook 1967.* New York: H. W. Wilson Company, 1965, pp. 105–07.

Samuel, Marjorie. "It's Hard to Judge an Opportunity." *Christian Science Monitor* (December 30, 1964): p. 11.

Shepard, Richard F. "Rosalind Elias Is Singing New Kind of Repertory." *New York Times* (August 9, 1985).

Valdez, Lesley. "Elias Returns to a Barber Favorite." *The Philadelphia Inquirer* (July 11, 1997).

Mansour Farah

Lebanese-American manufacturer

Born 1885
Beskinta, Lebanon

Died May 11, 1937
El Paso, Texas

Born in a small Lebanese village, Mansour Farah became a successful businessman in America. His success resulted from his willingness to work hard at even the least glamorous of tasks and his flexibility in changing the company's direction when necessary. The menswear manufacturing company he founded became a multimillion-dollar national company under the leadership of his sons, who managed the business after Farah's death.

> "THE ROLE OF A RETAILER ... WAS NOT ONE WHICH SATISFIED THE RESTLESS, CREATIVE URGE WITHIN THE MAN.... MANSOUR FARAH WANTED TO CREATE HIS OWN PRODUCTS FOR THE MARKET."

Searching for "farah"

Mansour Farah was born in the small village of Beskinta near Beirut, Lebanon, in 1885. In Arabic, the word *farah* means *joy* or *happiness;* perhaps it was to seek that happiness that Farah's parents decided to move their family to Canada in 1905. From there, they moved again to New Mexico, a U.S. territory that was not yet a state. At the age of twenty, Farah settled in Las Cruces, after having lived in several other New Mexico towns.

Farah and his brother Andrew opened a hay and dry-goods store in Las Cruces, a city in south-central New Mexico. Although the business succeeded, "the role of a retailer ... was not one which satisfied the restless, creative urge within the man. Even then, Mansour Farah wanted to create his own products for the market," family biographer Antone Haywood wrote.

In 1915, Farah married Hana Abihider from Lawrence, Massachusetts, the second of sixteen children of a Greek Orthodox priest (unlike the Roman Catholic church, the Greek Orthodox church allows its priests to marry). Also a native of Lebanon, Farah's wife had come to America at the age of fourteen. The couple returned to Farah's home in Las Cruces, where they settled and had two sons.

Creativity wins

In 1920, Farah's restlessness with the retail business stirred him to action, and he took his family on a trip to the east coast. Leaving his wife and children in Massachusetts to visit their relatives, Farah went to New York City to learn about garment manufacturing. At that time, the garment manufacturing industry was undergoing drastic change by adapting the meet their demands) and national boycott (when people band together as a group and make a conscious effort not to buy or use services or products from a certain source in order to express disapproval), then the second largest in the nation's history, lasted nearly two years and heavily damaged both the company's reputation and its financial health. In another miscalculation, William misjudged fashion trends in the mid-1970s, and the company again suffered substantial losses.

Forbes magazine wrote in 1981, "It is not that Willie Farah ... is inept. On the contrary, even his most vehement critics tout his genius in production, his intuitive grasp of the most efficient way to make a garment.... The production engineer's mind, though, is antithetical [directly opposite] to that of the marketer." From the production engineer's perspective it is often more cost-effective to manufacture large quantities of something at one time as opposed to making smaller quantities on an as-needed basis, while from a marketing perspective it is better to be able to offer new products quickly, and to offer new products often. William was removed from company leadership in 1976 but regained control two years later. In the mid-1980s, he aggressively expanded the company, building new plants; however, this growth happened too quickly. The company developed problems such as poor-quality products and late shipment of orders. William lost his position in the company in 1990 at the age of seventy-one. He died March 10, 1998, in El Paso.

assembly line concept recently developed for the automobile industry by Henry Ford (1863–1947), who developed the first popular low-priced automobile and founded the Ford Motor Company. Farah was able to see the most modern techniques for designing, cutting, and assembling shirts.

Farah and his family then moved to El Paso, Texas, a larger city forty-five miles southeast of Las Cruces. Farah rented a building and opened a garment factory. At first, he produced only one style of work shirt under the label name Apache. The shirts sold in stores for about thirty-five cents each.

Sons pitch in

In 1930, Farah's sons, James (age 14) and William (age 11), started spending more time working at the factory after school. The boys had different interests and talents, both of which helped their father's business. James learned to handle paperwork in the office, while William worked on the machinery in the factory. Although he employed twelve to fifteen seamstresses at this time, Farah still did much of the work himself—designing and cutting the garments, selling them to stores, and even serving as the company janitor.

Shirts out, pants in

The early 1930s were hard years for all American businesses because of the Great Depression (1929–39; a period of time in America when the economy suffered, banks and businesses closed, and many people lived in extreme poverty). There was little money to finance business operation or expansion, and with as many as one-fourth of the country's workers unable to find jobs, customers couldn't afford to buy much. In the midst of this difficult climate, Farah's shirt factory was suddenly faced with tough competition from an unexpected source. Inmates at a U.S. prison were put to work manufacturing shirts. Because inmates could be paid less than Farah's employees, the prison-made shirts sold in stores for only twenty-five cents apiece.

Farah responded quickly to this threat to his business. Realizing he couldn't compete in the shirt market, he began manufacturing blue denim pants and, later, bib overalls. Further broadening its product line in 1935, Farah's company began producing matched sets of khaki shirts and pants that were popular as work clothes.

Strong legacy

In the midst of this period of company growth, Farah died on May 11, 1937, after a short illness. He was fifty-two years old. James Farah, then twenty-one years old, took over the company. William Farah, who had graduated from high school four months before his father's death, attended the Texas College of Mines and then served as a bomber pilot and instructor in the U.S. Air Force during World War II (1939–45; when the United States and certain European countries went to war against Nazi Germany and Japan to stop their aggressions) before returning to work for the family business in 1945.

During the war, Hana Farah helped her elder son operate the factory as it produced various types of uniforms and combat clothing for the U.S. Army. Continuing Mansour Farah's dedication to quality clothing produced economically, the company was presented an award by the government. Brigadier General J. A. Porter, who presented the award in 1944, called the Farah factory "the perfect war plant."

FURTHER READING

Antone, Evan Haywood. *William Farah: Industrialist.* El Paso, TX: Carl Hertzog, 1969.

Mack, Tony. "A Painful Lesson." *Forbes* (January, 19, 1981): pp. 51–52.

Poole, Claire. "'We did what we had to do.'" *Forbes* (December, 9, 1991): pp. 148–50.

Jamie Farr

Lebanese-American actor

Born July 1, 1936
Toledo, Ohio

> "AS A KID I *HAD* TO BE FUNNY. THAT WAS THE WAY TO KEEP MY NOSE FROM BEING BROKEN."

Jamie Farr is one of the few male celebrities who is most recognizable in women's clothing. Corporal Maxwell Q. Klinger, the character Farr played on the TV show *M*A*S*H*, frequently donned feminine apparel in attempts to convince his army superiors that he was crazy and should be sent home. Farr's zany Klinger helped make *M*A*S*H*, a show about U.S. Army doctors serving in the Korean War (1950–53; when the United States sent troops into Korea to help South Korea fight off its communist neighbor North Korea), one of the most popular TV series of the 1970s and 1980s. Farr has continued acting, appearing in numerous movies and Broadway productions.

A small boy with a large nose

Farr was born Jameel Joseph Farah in 1936 to Lebanese immigrants Samuel, a butcher and grocer, and Jamelia, a seamstress. Joking that his birth name is "the only name you can say and clear your throat at the same time," Farr eventually changed his name to sound more English because "people couldn't pronounce my name."

Raised in a Jewish-Polish-Arab neighborhood in industrial Toledo, Ohio, Farr was an altar boy at the Antiochian Orthodox Church and the runt of the neighborhood gang. As a small boy with a large nose, Farr told *People* magazine, his sense of humor prevented him from being picked on. "As a kid I *had* to be funny. That was the way to keep my nose from being broken."

Farr became interested in acting at an early age. He practiced singing and dancing for his family, and he went to the movies as often as three times a day with his friends. In the 1940s, movie tickets cost only twelve cents, and Farr and his friends would scrounge up the money by reselling parts they stole from the local junkyard. After graduating in 1952 from Toledo's Calvin M. Woodward High School—where he was a three-time class president, feature editor of the school newspaper, a writer and performer for the school's annual variety show, and an honor student—he decided to become an actor.

Heads to Hollywood

Based on an ad he saw in *Theater Arts* magazine, Farr went to the Pasadena Playhouse, a theater company in Pasadena, California. A year later, a talent scout for Metro-Goldwyn-Mayer (MGM) spotted Farr and brought him in for a screen test. Farr landed the key role of Santini in the hit movie *The Blackboard Jungle* (1955). "I thought I was on my way to stardom," he told *People*. "[But] I didn't get work for a year after that."

He made one more movie appearance—*No Time for Sergeants* (1958) with actor Andy Griffith (1926–)—before enlisting in the army for a two-year stint in South Korea (making him the only member of *M*A*S*H*'s cast to have actually served in South Korea). When he returned from duty in 1959, Farr found he had been forgotten by Hollywood. He worked a variety of odd jobs—including delivery boy, post office clerk, and "pooper scooper" at a ranch for chinchillas (rabbit-like rodents)—while looking for acting roles. His movies *Santa Claus Conquers the Martians* (1964), *The Greatest Story Ever Told* (1965), *With Six You Get Eggroll* (1968), and *Heavy Traffic* (1973) were all box office busts, but he began gaining recognition from his frequent appearances on the comedy/variety programs *The Red Skelton Show* (1951–71) and *The Danny Kaye Show* (1963–67).

THE KOREAN WAR

The Korean War (1950–53) was a conflict in which the United Nations—with the United States as chief participant—defended South Korea from an invasion by North Korea. The United States was on friendly terms with South Korea and did not want to see it become part of North Korea, a communist state that was backed by the Soviet Union and China (the United States' main enemies at the time). When North Korea invaded South Korea on June 25, 1950, the United Nations voted to send in forces to halt the invasion.

At first, troops sent by the United States and other United Nations countries successfully drove the North Koreans out of South Korea. In December 1950, however, thousands of Chinese soldiers came to the aid of the North Koreans, who were then able to launch a second major offensive. Fighting continued with no apparent victor until July 27, 1953, when the United Nations and North Korea agreed to a treaty that reaffirmed the border between North and South Korea. There was no "winner" in the short war, but with a total of 3 million casualties in only three years, all sides were eager to bring the conflict to a close. Approximately 54,000 Americans died in the Korean War.

Playing it straight

In 1972, a seemingly insignificant part was offered to Farr: a one-time appearance as Corporal Klinger on the TV show *M*A*S*H*. It was early in the first season of the Korean War sitcom about army doctors stationed at the 4077th Mobile Army Surgical Hospital (M*A*S*H), where wounded soldiers from the front lines were sent for medical attention. One episode of the show called for a male GI (a person in the armed forces) dressed as a woman to jump out from behind a bush, surprising a general who is walking by. The general reacts to the cross-dressed GI, saying: "Ah, Corporal Klinger, still trying to get out of the Army, I see." Because Klinger's role was so small and the show's producer, Gene Reynolds (1925–), knew exactly who he wanted, no auditions were held. "Gene said there is only one person in the world who can play this part," Farr told an interviewer in 1995. "That's when he called on me."

Farr suited up in a woman's army outfit—blouse, skirt, and high heels—and gave the "limp-wristed and rather effeminate" performance the producers requested. When the producers saw the takes, however, they realized that wasn't how they wanted the character played. Klinger was supposed to be a heterosexual *pretending* to be a gay cross-dresser—all so he

Farr in costume as Corporal Klinger from the television series M*A*S*H. *Reproduced by permission of the Corbis Corporation (Bellevue).*

could get himself discharged from the army. When the producers asked for Farr's take on the character, he told them, "I think I should just play it straight. Use my regular voice and I don't pay attention to the clothes I'm wearing but everybody else does. Let's see how that works."

Farr's performance was an instant hit, and the producers brought Klinger back for later episodes, making him a regular the following season. Klinger's role helped bring humor to what was otherwise a dark premise for a sitcom—the Korean War. "That's what made it very special," Farr told an interviewer, "because you had these people trapped in situations ... they couldn't get out of. And of course they had to provide entertainment for themselves so they wouldn't go crazy."

During the eleven seasons he played Klinger, Farr's outlandish costumes included Statue of Liberty garb, a Scarlett O'Hara (a Southern belle from the book and movie *Gone with the Wind*) chiffon dress, and a golden Ginger Rogers (actress; 1911–1995) evening gown. Exquisitely color-coordinated and accessorized, the outfits were comically set off by Farr's hairy chest, bowlegs, and masculine strut. "The ruse is so transparent, it's funny," *M*A*S*H* producer Larry Gelbart (1928–) told *TV Guide*. "He is merely a well-meaning little guy—trapped, wanting out and willing to do almost anything to achieve it. People identify with that."

Farr's fame

Farr—who was thirty-eight by the time he was offered the role of Klinger—savored his belated celebrity status. He was a frequent guest on *The Gong Show, The $100,000 Pyramid,* and *The Love Boat,* among other shows, to expand his audience base. His distinctive look (particularly his large nose) made him an easily recognizable actor. This recognition factor helped him command top dollar. At some times, however, Farr felt like his fame was a dream that could end at any moment. "I still remember the days when I was hoping to make enough money to buy a can of tuna for dinner," Farr told *People* in 1979. "I think what has happened to me is not real, but fake. I'm frightened it will end."

When *M*A*S*H* finished its final season in September 1983, Farr's career didn't end, but it did slow down. The end of the series was both sad and exhausting, Farr told an interviewer, because "when you're doing that kind of a show ... you're part of everybody's household." Farr appeared as Klinger in the *M*A*S*H* spinoff, *After M*A*S*H,* which lasted for one season. His later movies include *For Love or Money* (1984), *Combat Academy* (1986), *Happy Hour* (1987), and *Curse 2: The Bite* (1988). He has also established himself on Broadway, appearing as Nathan Detroit in *Guys and Dolls* and as Ali

Hakim in *Lend Me a Tenor*. In 1997, he starred opposite William Christopher (1932–) in a Canadian production of *The Odd Couple*. More than anything else, Farr said he would like to be the first actor to create a certain character on Broadway, "as opposed to replacing somebody on Broadway or doing a revival of something on Broadway."

Personal notes

Farr married former model Joy Ann Richards in 1963, and the couple have a son, Jonas Samuel, and a daughter, Yvonne Elizabeth-Rose. Besides being an avid gardener, Farr collects old movie books. He also remains a proud native son of his hometown, Toledo, Ohio, where he returns frequently to visit old friends and hold his 4th of July golf tournament. "They treat me the same way they did when I was growing up and I love it," Farr told an interviewer, "because they don't have any airs about them and I certainly don't have any airs about myself."

FURTHER READING

Farr, Jamie. *Just Farr Fun.* Clearwater, FL: Eubanks Donizetti Enterprises, Inc., 1994.

Jackovich, Karen G. "Angling for a Discharge Has Made Jamie (Klinger) Farr of 'M*A*S*H' a Big Fish in the Hollywood Pond." *People* (July 23, 1979): 57–58.

Oulahan, Richard and Cable Neuhaus. "When Corporal Klinger Finally Gets There, It's Jamie Farr Who is the Toast of Toledo." *People* (May 16, 1983): 127–29.

Whitney, Dwight. "It's—Uh, a Real Drag." *TV Guide* (September 27, 1975): 26–28.

Doug Flutie

Lebanese-American football quarterback

Born October 23, 1962
Manchester, Maryland

"Fame is fleeting, especially for college athletes. But that play has given me a mystique or an aura. Everybody believes now that there is no situation that is out of the question for me."

Doug Flutie's success and popularity as a football player have been compared to those of Wayne Gretzky in hockey and Michael Jordan in basketball. As the quarterback for Boston College, he won the Heisman Trophy as the United States' outstanding college football player in 1984. His greatest success in professional football came in the Canadian Football League, where he was named the league's Most Valuable Player (MVP) for six of the eight years he played there in the 1990s. During those eight years, he led his teams to the national championship finals four times, winning the title three times. He is also dedicated to public service, particularly through the Doug Flutie, Jr. Foundation he founded to help families with children, like his son, who suffer from autism (a development disability that appears during the first three years of life and affects the normal functioning of the brain).

Sporty kid

Douglas Flutie was born in Manchester, Maryland, a town near Baltimore. When he was six, his family moved to Melbourne, Florida. Flutie, along with his older sister and brother (Denise and Bill) and his younger brother (Darren), played all sorts of sports. Besides learning traditional games like football, baseball, and basketball, he loved to improvise. For example, on a rainy afternoon, he might start a family game of indoor baseball in his basement, using a crumpled paper cup as a ball and an open hand as a bat.

Flutie was eight when he started playing Little League baseball. "Doug was usually the best player," his mother told writer John Devaney. "But more than that, he was always doing the unexpected." She described a time when Flutie was playing shortstop: with a runner on second base, Flutie fielded a ground ball; he faked a throw to first base and then tagged the runner who thought it was safe to try to reach third base.

When Flutie started playing tackle football at the age of nine, he returned kicks and played the free safety position. The next year, he made the all-star team as a running back. He played quarterback the year after that, but he recalled in his autobiography that "I was bored because all I did was hand off, so the following year I asked to play running back. I enjoyed that a lot more and my running skills really came through."

Loves strategy

When Flutie was thirteen, his family moved to Natick, Massachusetts, about fifteen miles west of Boston. He was already a good strategist when he played quarterback on his junior high-school football team. He wrote that his coach "was probably one of the first people to realize I was thinking ahead of the other guys. He made me memorize all the plays and the formations that go with them so I could call my own plays." When he watched professional football on television, Flutie concentrated on points of strategy, such as whether the team should pass the ball or run with it or when it would be wise to call a time-out.

In high school, Flutie played three varsity sports, lettering eight times. His favorite sport was actually basketball, in which he played point guard. His baseball career ended during his sophomore year when he quit the sport to work at an ice cream stand; his family often had financial problems, and he wanted to earn money to reconnect their telephone service so he could call his girlfriend. Football was his most successful sport. He was named to the all-state team, whereas in basketball and baseball the highest he achieved was all-league status.

Flutie's brother Bill played quarterback in high school, so Flutie joined the senior-high team as a sophomore free safety and wide receiver. In the fifth game of his first season, after four agonizing losses, the coach moved Flutie to quarterback and his older brother to wide receiver. After that point, neither player ever left the field. They returned kicks and punts, and Flutie kicked field goals and kickoffs, while his brother punted and held the ball on field goal attempts.

Colleges uncertain

During his senior year, major colleges recruited Flutie as a football player, but only Division 1-AA schools offered him scholarships. The problem was his size; unfortunately he was just under 5 feet 10 inches tall and weighed 175 pounds, and Division 1-A coaches were afraid he wasn't big enough to play at that level. Finally, he was offered a scholarship at Boston College, a Division 1-A school, when the quarterbacks it had been recruiting decided to go elsewhere.

Soaring Eagle

During his four years, from 1981 to 1984, as a Boston College (BC) Eagle, Flutie proved that he could play with the big guys. He began as the fourth-string quarterback, but he got a chance to play in the fourth quarter of the fourth game of the season. The first-string quarterback was injured and the next two candidates had not been able to produce a score; the team was trailing Penn State 38–0. Coach Jack Bicknell decided he would take this chance to see what Flutie could do. "It was just like somebody turned a switch and all of a sudden, everything was going at a faster pace," Bicknell recalled in the 1998 autobiography *Flutie*. Flutie completed eight of eighteen passes including BC's only touchdown of the game. For the rest of his college career, Flutie started every game.

By the end of his freshman year, Flutie was ranked as the ninth best passer in college football. It wasn't because of weak opponents, either; BC's 1982 schedule was ranked the fifth toughest in the country. That year, as a sophomore, Flutie broke the school record for yards passed in a season. The team was invited to its first post-season bowl game in more than forty years; even though the Eagles lost in the Tangerine Bowl, Flutie was named the game's MVP.

When Flutie started playing for BC, his team wasn't even ranked in the top fifty; by his junior year, the team was in the top ten. Season ticket sales doubled. *Sports Illustrated* profiled Flutie as "A Little Man On Campus"; the cover photo showed him standing on a chair to throw the ball over the heads of the offensive line. The team finished the year with a one-point loss to Notre Dame in the Liberty Bowl and Flutie was again chosen as the game's MVP.

The pass

Flutie's younger brother, Darren, joined the BC team as a freshman in 1984. It was a great year for Flutie—he broke the National Collegiate Athletic Association (NCAA) Division 1-A records for both yards passing in a career (10,579) and total offense (11,317). The year ended with a play so spectacular that a 1997 Columbia Broadcasting System (CBS) SportsLine poll ranked it as the second-greatest single play in college football history, with 30.6 percent of the votes.

The famous play came at the end of BC's game against the University of Miami, the defending national champion. With six seconds left in the game and Miami leading 45–41, Flutie called a "flood tip" pass. That meant that the three best receivers would head for the end zone and Flutie would throw a high pass; if the closest receiver couldn't catch the ball, he would tip it as high as he could to give one of his teammates a chance to catch it. The play started at the Miami 48-yard line. Trying to scramble long enough to give his receivers time to get to the end zone, Flutie back-pedaled to the BC 40-yard line before throwing the ball. Teammate Gerard Phelan caught the pass in the end zone, giving the Eagles a 47–45 win.

"Fame is fleeting, especially for college athletes," Flutie told *USA Today.* "But that play has given me a mystique or an aura. Everybody believes now that there is no situation that is out of the question for me. If anybody's gonna do it, I'm gonna do it."

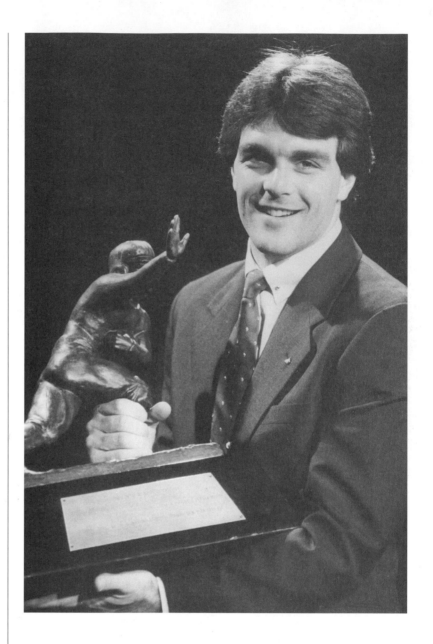

He's number one

A few days later, Flutie won the Heisman Trophy as college football's most outstanding football player of the year. It had been thirteen years since the trophy had gone to a quarterback. "The Heisman was something I never dreamed of winning," Flutie wrote in his autobiography. "I was always concentrating on the football seasons and [winning the trophy] just kind of happened.... It didn't matter what they would say about my height or whether I played in the NFL [National Football League] or played professionally or even if I didn't play another down of football. I had won the Heisman Trophy and that was something I was going to be proud of for the rest of my life."

Flutie's college career ended with a 45–28 victory over Houston in the Cotton Bowl. He broke the Cotton Bowl record by throwing three touchdown passes in the first half; by the end of the game his team had broken another record by gaining 541 yards of total offense. Boston College finished the year ranked fifth in the country.

Straggling into the pros

Despite his spectacular college record, NFL teams were still concerned that Flutie wasn't big enough to succeed at their level of play. Unsure of his chances to be drafted by the NFL, he accepted an offer from the United States Football League (USFL), an alternative league that played its games in the spring. He played his first professional game with the New Jersey Generals on February 6, 1985. He broke his collarbone on June 1 and missed the rest of the season.

During the summer of 1985, Flutie married Laurie Fortier, a legal secretary he had been dating since getting his telephone reconnected when they were high school sophomores. Their daughter, Alexa, was born three years later, and their son, Doug Jr., was born in 1991.

The USFL struggled through the summer trying to prove in court that the NFL was preventing it from competing fairly. With the USFL on the verge of collapse, and the Generals merging with another team, Flutie was released from his contract, allowing him to look at other offers. Hoping to hear from an NFL team, he went home to Boston, where he finished his college degrees in communications and computer science. He kept in shape by running, lifting weights, and working out with the Boston College football team.

A year and a half after Flutie's last USFL game, he signed with the Chicago Bears. After one season he was traded to the New England Patriots, where he played backup quarterback. In NFL games he started, Flutie's record was nine wins and five losses, but he still faced criticism that he was too short. He told

Esquire about watching a televised NFL game in which a tall quarterback got *"three passes in a row* batted down. When it happens with a taller quarterback, it's great defense. When it happens with me, I'm too short."

Canadian Football League (CFL)

In June 1990, Flutie signed with the British Columbia Lions of the CFL. He played his first preseason game in Winnipeg. "When I went into the stadium, I kind of shook my head. I thought, I guess it's okay, it's kind of adequate," he wrote. "To me it looked like a small college stadium, but I just kind of accepted it." Fans were excited about seeing him, and a stadium-record crowd of 34,000 showed up. CFL rules are somewhat different from those of the NFL, so the style of play is also different. "It just felt like it was fun. There was a lot of room out there [on the larger field] to do things and guys would get open," Flutie wrote.

The stadium in the team's hometown of Vancouver, Canada, was great, but overall, Flutie didn't enjoy his first season. His second season was a different story. He set a league record for passing yards, including thirty-eight touchdowns, with a personal best 64 percent completion rate. At the end of the season, he was named the league's MVP—an honor he repeated in five of the following six seasons (he didn't win the honor in 1995 because he missed part of the season for surgery to repair a torn tendon in his passing arm).

After his second CFL season, he was traded to the Calgary Stampeders. The team had made it to the Grey Cup game (the CFL championship) the year before, and Flutie led them to the title in his first season. The 1995 season was a bad one; not only did Flutie have arm surgery, but the Stampeders' owner went bankrupt (didn't have enough money to pay his debts) and couldn't pay Flutie's salary. In 1996, Flutie signed

with the Toronto Argonauts and led them to Grey Cup victories that year and the next.

Backup Bill?

"To me football is about having fun," Flutie wrote in his autobiography. "If I go to the NFL at some point, it's because it's the right situation and it's the right thing for me; it's not just to prove a point." He didn't have to wait much longer for the right situation to arise. In January 1998, he signed a two-year contract with the NFL's Buffalo (New York) Bills. At the age of thirty-five but still in great shape, Flutie felt confident in his ability to compete for the starting quarterback slot. However, three weeks after Flutie signed with the Bills, the team announced hiring Rob Johnson as its "number one" quarterback.

Flutie led the Toronto Argonauts to two consecutive championships. Reproduced by permission of Archive Photos, Inc.

"Flutie didn't sound off in public. But, privately, he seethed," the New York *Rochester Democrat and Chronicle* newspaper reported. However, calling him "The Little Quarterback That Could," the paper also reported that Flutie was working hard on competing for the best position he could win. "If Rob Johnson becomes the starter and I'm the backup, that's the role I'll play," Flutie said. "But I'm going to prepare as if I'm taking every snap. This isn't going to change the way I compete."

During the season's first three games, Flutie saw limited playing time, with Johnson starting each game. But Johnson was injured in the first quarter of the fourth game, and Flutie was sent in. Completing twenty-three of twenty-eight passes, he led the Bills to a 31-24 victory. After winning another three games in a row, Flutie was named the team's starting quarterback for the rest of the season, regardless of Johnson's health. The Bills won ten of their sixteen regular-season games before losing in the playoffs. In January 1999 the Associated Press named Flutie the NFL's Comeback Player of the Year.

Off the field

When Flutie's son, Doug Jr., was about three years old, his development started going in reverse. Although he had been speaking normally for his age, within six months he no longer spoke, and he became totally withdrawn. He didn't react to the presence of anyone, even his parents. He had developed autism, a developmental disorder in which people live "in a world of their own," as described on the Doug Flutie, Jr. Foundation Web site. "I wouldn't trade him for anyone in the world. He's the happiest kid I've ever seen," Flutie wrote in his autobiography. "Yeah, he struggles and doesn't speak and we're working with him on his education. But if anything it makes you stop taking things for granted." In 1998, Flutie established The Doug Flutie, Jr. Foundation for Autism with three goals: "to provide funding for services for financially disadvantaged families who need assistance in caring for their autistic children, to fund research and education into the causes and consequences of childhood autism, and to serve as a clearinghouse and communications center for new and innovative programs and services developed for autistic children."

For recreation, Flutie and his brother Darren (also a CFL star) play in a rock band called The Flutie Brothers; he plays drums and Darren plays a guitar. Their first album, *Catch This,* was released by Danger Records in 1996. Flutie wrote in his autobiography that "probably the biggest rush I've ever had" was when rock star Jon Bon Jovi (1962–) called him on stage during a show and invited him to play drums.

FURTHER READING

Devaney, John. "Doug Flutie: 'The Little Rascal.'" *Winners of the Heisman Trophy.* New York: Walker, 1990, pp. 7–16.

Flutie, Doug, and Perry Lefko. *Flutie.* Los Angeles: Warwick Publishing, 1998.

"Flutie, Doug." *Current Biography Yearbook 1985.* New York: H. W. Wilson Company, 1985, pp. 118–21.

Lupica, Mike. "Remembrance of Flings Past." *Esquire* (September 1989): 97–98

Pitoniak, Scott. "Flutie's Plans: Prepare as If He Could Still Start." *Rochester Democrat and Chronicle* (April 26, 1998).

Kahlil Gibran

Lebanese-American poet, writer, and artist

Born 1883
Besharri, Lebanon

Died April 10, 1931
New York, New York

"ONE *LARGE THOUGHT* IS FILLING MY MIND AND MY HEART; AND I WANT SO MUCH TO GIVE IT FORM."

Kahlil Gibran's most famous book, *The Prophet,* is the second-best selling book in twentieth-century America, behind only the Bible. A deeply spiritual person, Gibran rejected organized religion because of the conflict it caused among different factions and because it was "destructive to man's freedom and growth." He wrote poetry, novels, plays, essays, and short stories in both Arabic and English. As an artist, he is best known for the illustrations he created for his own books. His basic message of kindness, unity, and hope continues to appeal to readers around the world. As evidence of his popularity, *The Prophet* has been translated into at least twenty languages.

A sad childhood

Kahlil Gibran, who was originally named Gibran Khalil Gibran, was born in a village near the famous cedar groves of northern Lebanon. His birth date was not recorded; it was either December 6 or January 6, 1883. His mother, Kamila Rahme Gibran, was married twice, first to a man who abandoned his family, moved to Brazil, and died there. Her second husband was a violent man who gambled and drank too much. She had a son (Peter) by her first husband, and a son (Kahlil) and two daughters (Marianna and Sultana) by her second husband.

"As a child I did not know I was sad," Gibran later told his dear friend Mary Haskell. "I just knew I was longing to be alone, making things. And they could never get me to play." He enjoyed the peacefulness of the forest and the quietness of his room, where he drew pictures and wrote stories. When he was about eight, he became very interested in casting figures out of lead; he used sand and sardine cans as molds to make figures of gods and goddesses. "The pleasure was while I was doing the thing. The result was never what I wanted," he told Haskell. "I was always unhappy because my vision was so far beyond anything I could do."

As Maronite Catholics, Gibran's family experienced severe discrimination in their Muslim-ruled society. For example, the Maronites had been required to wear black and were not allowed to own horses. If accused of a crime, they could not ask a Muslim to testify in their defense. And they remembered suffering various episodes of violence, even massacres. The fact that groups of people would treat each other so harshly in the name of religion turned Gibran away from ever wanting to belong to an organized church.

When Gibran was eight, his father was arrested for theft and spent three years in prison awaiting trial. He was finally convicted, and his family's home and all their belongings were taken. To escape the shame of this episode, Gibran's mother took her children to America in 1894. They settled in Boston, Massachusetts, where some relatives lived. After a year of peddling laces and linens, Gibran's mother saved enough money to open a dry goods store; her older son managed the store, and her daughters worked there.

He's not here

In Lebanon, an older friend had informally taught Gibran to read and write Arabic. When his family arrived in Boston, he attended school for the first time. His English teacher suggested that the boy drop the first "Gibran" from his name and change the spelling of his middle (now first) name from

"Khalil" to "Kahlil" so it would be easier for Americans to spell and pronounce.

Gibran was still a sad child. He later told Haskell that his first two years in Boston were the most difficult time of his life: "[My teachers] really loved me. And I felt it. But we had nothing in common." He still liked to be alone, and his mother was very understanding of his quiet nature. "When I was a boy, say from nine to thirteen, sometimes [my mother] would smile at someone who came in and look at me and lay her finger on her lip and say, 'Hush. He's not here.'"

A new world opens

The Gibran family lived in the Chinatown area of Boston, which was actually a slum of sorts where poor people of many nationalities lived. Concerned people from Boston's wealthier areas opened "settlement houses" in Chinatown to help improve the lives of the immigrants. These houses offered play areas and enrichment activities for children and social events for adults and families. Gibran enjoyed attending plays, poetry readings, and music concerts. He was able to take art classes and begin developing his natural talent for drawing.

In 1897, when Gibran was fourteen, his art teacher introduced him to Fred Holland Day, a book publisher who would teach Gibran about English and American poetry. Day was also interested in the arts, especially new, experimental forms; his personal hobby was portrait photography, and his favorite models were immigrant children with exotic features. Gibran's friendship with Day lasted many years, and it opened the door to a new world of elegance and culture. Gibran became part of an arts-centered society.

At the age of fifteen, Gibran returned to Lebanon for two reasons—he was homesick, and he wanted to get an advanced education. He attended college in Beirut, concentrating on Arabic and French language and literature. He became an accomplished poet, winning a contest that established him as the school's official poet for his final year. He spent the summers in Besharri with his father. He later wrote Haskell about a certain dinner party his father gave. A famous poet was among the guests, and he asked Gibran to read some of his poems after dinner. "They all listened—and I shall never forget it—They liked it—it touched them—they all looked kindly at me.... And my father said—'I hope we shall never have any more of this stuff—this sick-mindedness.' That hurt deep into my innermost being."

A year of death

Gibran was on his way back to America in 1902 when he read in a Paris newspaper that his younger sister had just died of tuberculosis (a disease of the lungs). He was deeply touched not only by her death, but by the extent of her suffering. Gibran's brother was also suffering from tuberculosis by this time, and seven months later he too died from the deadly disease. Gibran's mother was becoming increasingly ill from cancer; three months after her elder son's death, she passed away. By this time, Gibran was selling some of his poetry, but while his family members were ill he set his writing aside to run the family store. A friend wrote, "Pegasus [the mythical winged horse] harnessed to an ash-wagon would suffer less." After his mother's death, he sold the store and turned his attention back to writing and drawing.

In 1903, some of Gibran's drawings were included in an art exhibit at Wellesley College in Boston. English-speaking audiences knew only of his visual art at this time; he was writing solely in Arabic because he was not yet fluent enough in English to express his thoughts in the language. His poetry first appeared in Arabic-language periodicals published for immigrants in America. In a 1991 biography of Gibran, his cousin and namesake wrote, "Four years of college in Beirut had not fully equipped him to perfect his writing in Arabic.... He was forced to resort to his essentially peasant's ear when putting down his thoughts. Ignoring much of the traditional vocabulary and form of classical Arabic, he began to develop a style which reflected the ordinary language he had heard as a child in Besharri and to which he was still exposed in [Boston]. This use of the colloquial [common language] ... appealed to the thousands of Arab immigrants who responded to this unique and simplified treatment."

Meets Mary

In 1904, Gibran met Mary Haskell, the headmistress of a school for girls. Although she was not wealthy, by living a frugal life, Haskell was able to give money to several artists and writers who were not yet able to support themselves by selling their work. Not only did she give Gibran money, but they developed a deep friendship that would last the rest of their lives. For a while, they considered getting married, but she was not comfortable with the fact that she was ten years older than he was. They understood each other so well that she began helping him find the right words to translate some of his writings into English. Later, she helped him with his language when he composed works in English.

By the time Gibran was twenty-two, he was a respected member of the Syrian-American community. About this time, old tensions between members of the Maronite and Orthodox Christian churches flared up. Biographer Kahlil Gibran (the poet's cousin) wrote that the feud was a "bitter urban war" that "affected the social and business lives of both Syrians and Lebanese.... In a conciliatory effort, the [Arabic language *al-Mohajer*] newspaper ran a front-page drawing by Gibran, which showed an angel extending both hands to the conflicting factions." About a year later, another controversy arose among the "people to whom religious dissension was a way of life, but [Gibran was] determined to preach the doctrine of brotherhood.... He sincerely believed that the readers of *al-Mohajer* needed a spokesman who could say with conviction, 'For the earth in its all is my land.... And all mankind my countrymen.' He firmly believed he was destined to be that spokesman."

Although he was frustrated by the conflicts between different religions, Gibran was a deeply spiritual person who often had mystical dreams. In 1908, he wrote to Haskell, "My soul is intoxicated today. For last night I dreamt of Him who gave the Kingdom of heaven to man.... I do not remember His words—and yet I feel them now as one feels in the morning the impression of the music he heard the night before.... I cannot write nor draw nor read. I can only sit alone in silence and contemplate the Unseen."

Artistic growth

Gibran was trying to develop himself as both a visual artist and a writer. With Haskell's support he spent nearly two and a half years in Paris, studying drawing and painting. In Paris, he met Ameen Rihani (1876–1940; see entry), another Lebanese philosopher and writer. After returning to the United States, Gibran prepared the illustrations and cover picture for Rihani's *The Book of Khalid,* the first novel written in English by an Arabic writer. Partly because it was where his friend Rihani lived, Gibran moved to New York City. As Gibran's career progressed, he began writing more in English and less in Arabic, and eventually he drew and painted only to illustrate his books.

Masks

The first book Gibran wrote in English, *The Madman,* was published in 1918. Like many of his books, it is a collection of parables and poems. The title character becomes a madman when someone steals the masks he has worn in his seven lives (Gibran believed in reincarnation). He says, "I am not what I seem. Seeming is but a garment I wear—a care-woven garment that protects me from thy questionings and thee from my negligence."

In his own life, Gibran wore masks also. He made up details about his early life to make himself sound more exotic or impressive. The biographer Gibran wrote, "In 1912, he had first tried to define his concept of 'creative truth versus dead truth.' 'The Arabs distinguish between the two kinds,' he told [Haskell]. 'They dislike impertinent questions and the trivial. Ask one what he had at a supper, and he may tell you nectar and birds of heaven—and you may find it was really potatoes, mushrooms, and beans. But he's not lying; he's refusing to answer—what he doesn't like is your asking.'" Gibran also told Haskell, "I meet curiosity a great deal—and I hate it. There isn't anything about me that can't be seen—in my work—in my face, in me. But people don't want to find it out—they want me to tell them in words. They don't want to work for it."

Prophet

"One *large thought* is filling my mind and my heart; and I want so much to give it form," Gibran wrote to Haskell in 1918. He wrote three-fourths of *The Prophet* in less than a month, but it would take several years to finish writing and revising it until he considered it complete. One reason was that there were other demands on his time; he was writing new pieces for the Arab immigrant press, encouraging young people to be proud of their Syrian origins but to also devote themselves to becoming good citizens of America. He was also writing articles for the Middle Eastern press, urging independence for Lebanon, and he was heavily involved in an Arab American literary society. Answering fan mail was also taking increasing amounts of his time. And although *The Prophet* is a small book, it is a profound work that took a great deal of thought and effort to write.

Gibran considered *The Prophet* to be a culmination of his life's work. "All these thirty-seven years have been making it," he told Haskell. "Everything that I have done is already over for me. And they have all been just my schooling. But in *The*

Prophet I have imprisoned certain ideals—and it is my desire to live these ideals." The book tells the story of a man about to leave a country of exile and return to the land of his birth; as he prepares to leave, people ask his thoughts on important subjects like love, marriage, work, joy, sorrow, and death. The prophet's poetic, profound answers are the heart of the book.

"I'm not trying to write poetry in these," he told Haskell about the prophet's words. "I'm trying to express thoughts—but I want the rhythm and the words right so that they shan't be noticed, but shall just sink in, like water into cloth—and the thought be the thing that registers."

Finally published in 1923, *The Prophet* became one of the most popular books in the world. Suheil Bushrui, director of the Kahlil Gibran Research and Studies Project at the Center for International Development and Conflict Management, wrote, "Inspired by his experiences in a country far from the land of his origins, [Gibran] strove to resolve cultural and human conflict, in the process developing a unique genre [type] of writing, and transcending the barriers of East and West as few have done before or since."

Jesus

Three years after *The Prophet* was published, Gibran began an even more ambitious project. He wrote to Haskell, "My greatest hope now is to be able to paint the life of Jesus as no one did before." Stories about the experiences of Jesus have been retold in Lebanon for nearly 2,000 years. Drawing on these stories that he heard as a child, Gibran wrote *Jesus, The Son of Man.* Some of the seventy episodes are told from the point of view of Biblical persons like Mary Magdalen or John the Baptist, while others are unknown people who saw or spoke to Jesus.

Death and beyond

Gibran was in poor health by the time he was writing his book about Jesus. To control the pain he felt, he drank too

---

THOUGHTS OF THE PROPHET

When someone asked Almustafa, the prophet in Kahlil Gibran's most famous book, to speak about talking, he says, "You talk when you cease to be at peace with your thoughts; And when you can no longer dwell in the solitude of your heart you live in your lips, and sound is a diversion and a pastime. And in much of your talking, thinking is half murdered. For thought is a bird of space, that in a cage of words may indeed unfold its wings but cannot fly."

Asked to speak of joy and sorrow, Almustafa replied, "The deeper that sorrow carves into your being, the more joy you can contain.... Is not the lute that soothes your spirit the very wood that was hollowed with knives?"

Asked to speak of work, he answers, "Work is love made visible."

much alcohol, which in turn contributed to his poor health. He died of tuberculosis and a diseased liver in 1931 at the age of forty-seven. Hundreds of people filed past his casket during a two-day wake in New York. His body was then taken to Boston, where several memorial services were held. Finally, his body was sent to Lebanon for burial.

Gibran's biographer told how the poet had once described the room in which he envisioned being buried: "a square room of gray stone, 'simple, with one narrow door like the Egyptians', and light from above only.' Opposite the door would be an old Buddha from India, with a crucifix hanging above.... A Muslim prayer rug would cover the floor and on the rug would stand a silver incense bowl. He concluded, 'When I die, of course my friends will bury me under the stones of the floor.'" In fact, Gibran's sister bought Mar Sarkis, an old monastery carved in a rock near Besharri, and buried him there.

Biographies of Gibran were published in 1934 and 1945, but they contained either deliberate or accidental mistakes. Gibran's cousin biographer, also named Kahlil Gibran, spent fifteen years researching a true account, which he and his wife published in 1991. In it they wrote, "Constantly the theme of divided loyalties to two languages, two careers, two often conflicting sets of associates, dominated [Gibran's] development, with the result that biographers and historians have been biased, aware of one perspective and neglectful of the other.... We have attempted in our work to show Gibran's several worlds, and the way he lived in them all." They concluded, "It seems that Gibran's reputation, whether challenged by biased reporters, enhanced by an expanding world audience, or analyzed by a widening number of Arabic scholars, remains intact. His words continue to comfort and illuminate, and that, he would agree, was his intent."

FURTHER READING

Bushrui, Suheil. "Kahlil Gibran of America." http://www.alhewar.com/Gibran.html, July 17, 1998.

Gibran, Jean, and Kahlil Gibran. *Kahlil Gibran: His Life and World.* New York: Interlink Books, 1991.

Gibran, Kahlil. http://leb.net/gibran, July 17, 1998.

Twentieth Century Literary Criticism, vol. 9. Detroit: Gale Research, 1983, pp. 81–94.

Philip Habib

Lebanese-American diplomat

Born February 25, 1920
New York, New York

Died May 25, 1992
Puligny-Montrachet, France

P hilip Habib is responsible for some of the United States' major acts of foreign diplomacy from the 1960s to the 1980s. His achievements as a diplomat include attempts to negotiate peace in the Middle East and to stop the fighting in Vietnam (1965–73; when the United States sent troops to help the South Vietnamese fight off their aggressive communist neighbor, North Vietnam). Habib worked mostly behind the scenes to bring together opposing sides in order to negotiate compromises that each could support. One of the foremost experts on Asian political affairs, Habib crossed over in the late 1970s to Middle Eastern diplomacy, an area where he arguably made his greatest contribution. Habib is widely credited for arranging the negotiations between Egyptian President Anwar al-Sadat (1918–1981) and Israeli Prime Minister Menachem Begin (1913–1992). These negotiations resulted in the historic 1978 Camp David Accords, which put an end to Egyptian-Israeli conflicts. Habib was called out of retirement several times during the 1980s to serve as a special representa-

> "DIPLOMACY, AS AN ALTERNATIVE USE OF FORCE, NEEDS A BASE OF NATIONAL STRENGTH, CLEARLY DEFINED OBJECTIVES, AND PUBLIC SUPPORT."

tive to Lebanon and Central America before his death in 1992 from a heart attack.

Ranger Habib?

Philip Charles Habib was born in 1920 to Lebanese immigrants Alexander Habib, a grocer, and Mary Spiridon. He grew up in the Bensonhurst neighborhood of Brooklyn, New York, a predominantly Jewish community. While learning Arabic from his parents, Habib picked up Brooklyn slang and a Yiddish vocabulary from his Jewish neighbors. He helped his neighbors by turning on the lights and running errands for them on the Sabbath (according to Jewish law, every Saturday is a day of worship and rest, and most forms of work are banned). But he still felt a strong tie to the Arab American community. "It took a long time for the Lebanese to come up the ladder of success in America," he told author Gregory Orfalea (1949–; see entry). "We lived in ghettos, were very clannish, and used to think of ourselves as second-class citizens. We're not." Habib's multicultural awareness as a youth would later help him work with both the Arab and Jewish factions in attempts to restore peace to the Middle East.

Habib helped out at his father's store, stocking shelves and writing prices on canned goods with a black crayon. Later he got an after school job making metal boxes at a sheet metal factory in Brooklyn. After graduating from high school in 1938, Habib planned on becoming a forest ranger. He enrolled at the University of Idaho's College of Forestry and Wildlife and Range Sciences, graduating with a bachelor of science degree in 1942. He served in the army during World War II (1939–45; when the United States and certain European countries went to war against Nazi Germany and Japan to stop their aggressions), reaching the rank of captain before receiving his discharge in 1946.

Still intent on being a forest ranger, he enrolled at the University of California at Berkeley, where he earned his Ph.D. (doctor's degree) in agricultural economics in 1952. While at the university, he saw a sign publicizing a test that students could take to enter the State Department. On a whim, Habib decided to take the test. When he passed, he started taking diplomacy assignments—all while continuing to work on his thesis on the economics of the lumber industry.

Behind-the-scenes diplomacy

Habib's early assignments took him to the United States' embassies (the official residence for ambassadors) in Canada (1949–51), New Zealand (1952–54), and Trinidad and Tobago (1958–60). During this time he worked his way up from third secretary to United States consul general. After a brief stint as a foreign affairs officer at the State Department in Washington, D.C., Habib was sent in 1962 to the embassy in Seoul, South Korea. There he served as the counselor for political affairs. As American involvement in Vietnam began heating up in the mid-1960s, Habib was reassigned to Saigon, South Vietnam. There he served as the chief political advisor to U.S. Ambassador Henry Cabot Lodge (1902–1985). Described by the *New York Times* in 1968 as "the State Department's most knowledgeable expert on Vietnam," Habib was chosen to head the department's Vietnam task force. The task force issued a report recommending that the United States ease up its bombings of North Vietnam and pursue peace talks—a strategy President Lyndon Johnson (1908–1973) decided to follow after America's devastating loss from the 1968 Tet Offensive. The Tet Offensive was a surprise North Vietnamese attack that started on the first day of the Vietnamese Lunar New Year. The month-long attack produced heavy casualties all around and brought both sides to the negotiating table in 1969. When Johnson's ambassadors were replaced by newly elected President Richard M. Nixon's (1913–1994) appointees in 1969, Habib stayed on to preserve the continuity of U.S.-Vietnamese talks.

Habib was not a high-profile diplomat—in fact, he shunned publicity for himself. He did, however, play a crucial role in "unofficial talks" with opposing parties. He worked behind-the-scenes to bring diplomats together and prepare them for the necessary compromises. He was known for being a "straight-shooter" who spoke frankly with all sides. "He's able to use rough language without giving offense," one State Department official told the *Christian Science Monitor*. "You always know where you stand with Habib." He also was known for being direct and getting right to the point of a discussion. "He has a simple, earthy way of going to the heart of an issue," said former Assistant Secretary of State Harold Saunders. Former State Department counselor Helmut Sonnenfeldt added that Habib was "not stuffy at all," but had "a good sense of humor, which he sometimes turn[ed] on himself."

Because he was not one of the high-profile negotiators, Habib was not accepted by the North Vietnamese as the head of the American delegation. Even though Nixon had promoted Habib to the post after Henry Cabot Lodge and Lawrence E. Walsh resigned, the North Vietnamese saw Habib as a lower-ranking U.S. representative. They felt his promotion indicated a decreasing U.S. interest in resolving the conflict or signaled an attempt to sabotage the peace talks. Although he laid much of the crucial groundwork that led to the 1973 withdrawal of American troops, Habib was unable to end the conflict. He was replaced by David K. E. Bruce in 1970.

Helps broker peace at Camp David

The following year, Habib was appointed U.S. ambassador to the Republic of Korea, where he served until 1974. When he was promoted to assistant secretary of state for East Asian and Pacific Affairs, he returned to the State Department headquarters in Washington, D.C. Habib's focus changed from Asian to Middle Eastern affairs in May 1976, when President Gerald Ford (1913–) appointed him undersecretary of state for political affairs (a position he kept when President Jimmy Carter [1924–] took office in 1977). Although he held that post for only two years, he helped negotiate one of the most important treaties of the century—the 1978 Camp David Accords between Egypt and Israel. The Accords ended nearly thirty years of hostility between the two countries. It was an important first step in resolving the tensions between Arabs and Israelis who held competing claims to lands in the Middle East.

Shortly after the Camp David Accords, heart problems began taking their toll on Habib's health. He suffered a severe heart attack in 1978 and resigned from the State Department. After his recovery, Habib served as the diplomat-in-residence at Stanford University and worked as a senior research fellow at the Hoover Institute. In 1981, President Ronald Reagan (1911–) called Habib out of retirement to serve as a special ambassador to the Middle East. He tried to prevent violent attacks in Lebanon from escalating into a full-fledged war between several countries. Habib worked long hours to set up

CAMP DAVID ACCORDS

Signed on September 17, 1978, the Camp David Accords were two agreements that provided the outline for the Egyptian-Israeli peace treaty signed the following year. The first agreement ended the war between Egypt and Israel, which had started with the creation of Israel in 1948. Under this agreement, Israel would withdraw its troops from the Sinai Peninsula, a portion of Egyptian territory that the Israelis had seized during the Six-Day War of 1967. In return, Israeli ships would be allowed passage through Egypt's Suez Canal. Egypt and Israel would establish normal diplomatic relations, with embassies in each other's countries.

The second agreement of the Camp David Accords was a more general outline toward reaching peace in the Middle East. It called for Israeli troops to eventually grant self-government to Palestinians living in the West Bank and the Gaza Strip—contested areas that the Israelis occupied by force but neighboring Arabs believed rightly belonged to them.

The Accords between Egyptian President Anwar Sadat and Israeli Prime Minister Menachem Begin signaled the first negotiated peace between Israel and any of its Arab neighbors. Relations between the two countries began thawing in November 1977, when Sadat visited Jerusalem to address the Israeli government—the first Arab leader to do so. When subsequent peace negotiations stalled, U.S. President Jimmy Carter invited the two leaders to the presidential retreat at Camp David, Maryland, for another round of talks. Although Sadat and Begin had taken the initial steps toward peace, Carter's middleman role in the accords is the foreign policy highlight of his administration.

an agreement that would decrease Syrian and Israeli presence in Lebanon. But continued fighting and a deeply-rooted distrust in the region prevented any constructive resolution. When Israel invaded Lebanon in 1982, Habib's intense efforts were still not enough to restore peace to the region.

Habib came out of retirement again in 1987 to serve as Reagan's special ambassador to Central America. At this time, Central America was experiencing rampant revolutionary activity. The United States was supporting the El Salvadorian government against left-wing rebel forces that wanted to establish a communist regime. It was also giving aid to revolutionaries trying to overturn the communist Sandinista government in Nicaragua. The Central American peace accords Habib helped draft in 1987 would put have an end to all foreign involvement in Central American politics. Some members of the Reagan administration, however, resisted a treaty because they wanted to continue actively opposing foreign left-wing groups. Frustrated by American opposition to the accords, Habib resigned for good from diplomacy.

From left: Secretary of State George Schultz, Special Mideast Envoy Philip Habib, Habib's assistant Morris Draper, and President Ronald Reagan, in 1982. President Reagan asked Habib to come out of retirement to help with the Middle East situation. Reproduced by permission of AP/Wide World Photos.

The Diplomatic Equation

Although he recognized the complex fears and varied goals that diplomats brought to the negotiating table, Habib believed that the art of diplomacy boiled down to a simple equation. "Diplomacy, as an alternative use of force, needs a base of national strength, clearly defined objectives, and public support," he said in his 1985 Sandy D. Berger Memorial lecture for the Institute for the Study of Diplomacy at Georgetown University. "Without economic and military strength, diplomacy will falter in a world of confrontation and competing ideologies. Without public support, diplomacy cannot be sustained any more than the use of force." With these elements backing their policy, diplomats should come to the table with realistic and fair aims. "Every move in the diplomatic chess game need not be spelled out in advance," he said. "But the objectives must be clear, and their relevance to national purposes understood."

Even after he declared his final retirement, Habib remained active as a member of the board of directors of the American University in Beirut, Lebanon, and of the Audi Bank of California. He helped set up the Philip Habib Endowment for the Study of Environmental Issues and World Peace at his alma mater, the University of Idaho. The honors he received during his accomplished career include the Rockefeller Public Service Award (1969), the National Civil Service League award (1970), the President's Award for distinguished federal service (1979), and decoration as commander of France's Legion of Honor (1988). In his leisure time, he was an avid gourmet cook and a skilled poker player. Habib died in 1992 of a heart attack while vacationing in France. He left behind his wife of fifty years, Marjorie Slightam, and their daughters Phyllis and Susan.

FURTHER READING

"Habib, Philip C(harles)." *Current Biography Yearbook 1981* New York: H.W. Wilson, pp. 185–88.

Hofmann, Paul. "U.S. Delegation's Vietnam Expert." *New York Times* (December 26, 1968): A2.

Manegold, Catherine S. "Philip C. Habib, a Leading U.S. Diplomat, Dies at 72." *New York Times* (May 27, 1992): D21.

Orfalea, Gregory. *Before the Flames: A Quest for the History of Arab Americans.* Austin: University of Texas Press, 1988, pp. 227–28.

Southerland, Daniel. "Habib—a 'Diamond in the Rough' Who Sparkles." *Christian Science Monitor* (June 9, 1981): 5.

Joseph Marion Haggar

Lebanese-American manufacturer

Born December 20, 1892
Jazzin, Lebanon

Died December 15, 1987
Dallas, Texas

"YOU CAN MAKE AN
HONEST MISTAKE ... AND
COST ME A THOUSAND
DOLLARS, AND I WILL
NEVER EVEN CALL YOU
INTO THE OFFICE. BUT IF
YOU MAKE A DISHONEST
MISTAKE AND COST ME A
NICKEL, I'LL FIRE YOU IN
FIVE MINUTES."

When J. M. Haggar came to the United States at the age of sixteen, he had no money and spoke no English. At the time of his death, the company he had founded was one of the country's leading manufacturers of men's clothing. Under his leadership, the Haggar Corporation added several major innovations to the men's apparel industry (he even invented the word *slacks* for casual pants). During his lifetime, he gave more than $200 million to charity.

First Spanish, then English

Joseph Marion Haggar was born in the small, mountain village of Jazzin, Lebanon, in 1892. His family lived in a one-room house in the farm country outside the village. His father, Kalil Hajjar (pronounced Hah-ZHAR, the name means "stone-mason" in Arabic), made leather by tanning animal hides. Young Haggar was only two years old when his father was thrown from a horse and killed, leaving his mother, Manney (Saba) Hajjar to raise him, his brother, and his sisters. When

Haggar was thirteen, he decided to leave because "we were starving to death," he later told Joy Spiegel, his biographer.

An older sister had already left Lebanon. In 1905, Haggar went to join her and her husband in Torreón, Mexico. After enduring a stormy, forty-day ocean voyage on a cattle ship, Haggar literally kissed the ground when he walked onto dry land. Three years later, he struck out on his own again, this time walking across the border into Laredo, Texas. All it took to enter the United States was payment of a two dollar "head tax."

Some of this, some of that

Haggar promptly got his first job in America. Just after crossing the border, he noticed a crew of Mexican laborers working on a railroad, and he asked if they could use another worker. His railroad work took him gradually northward, and he stopped in a town near Austin to work on a cotton farm. After harvest, he hit the road again and went to New Orleans, where he washed dishes in a large hotel. His knowledge of Spanish and some French he had learned as a child helped him get by as he learned English. A couple of months later, he moved on again, this time to St. Louis, Missouri. His aimless wandering ended when he met Rose Mary Wasaff, a fellow member of the Maronite Catholic church in the city's Lebanese community. He was so intrigued with her that he rented a room in the large Wasaff home so he could spend his evenings with her (under the watchful eye of her mother).

Around 1914, the Wasaffs moved to Bristow, Oklahoma, and, approximately one month later, Haggar moved there too. He got a job at a cotton processing plant owned by a man he had met in the St. Louis Lebanese community. Haggar was now in his early twenties, and he began to settle down. (Around this time he changed the spelling of his name from the original Hajjar to a more American form.) He rented a house, applied for U.S. citizenship, and practiced his English. He learned all he could from his new job—everything from how to grade cotton to how to run a business. He even moonlighted as a grocery store clerk to build up a "nest egg." When he felt his savings were large enough, he proposed to Wasaff; they were married on August 22, 1915.

No foolin'

Since childhood, Haggar had been taught the importance of honesty. He not only practiced it himself, but he required it from those around him. Even as a young cotton buyer, he was up-front about how strongly he felt about honesty. When farmers brought cotton seeds in to sell to the company where he worked, it was his job to reach deep into the wagon load to see whether the seeds had been soaked with water to increase their weight (they were sold by the pound). His boss told him that if the load was wet, he should guess how much weight the water added to the load and, without saying anything about it, discount the farmer's pay by an appropriate amount. Haggar, though, preferred to be more open. "You put water on that seed, and I'm gonna deduct you," he told the farmers. "If that's not satisfactory, you don't have to sell it to me. Just take it back. But if you're gonna sell me cotton, you're not gonna put any water in it!" Having warned them, he applied heavy penalties for water-logged seeds, deducting 150 pounds of weight from the load for every 100 pounds of water that had been added. It wasn't long before the problem disappeared; the farmers stopped adding water to their cotton.

In 1916, Haggar moved his wife and his son, Ed, back to St. Louis. The city was a major trading center for the dry-goods industry, and Haggar went to work for a large wholesale company that supplied cotton fabric to stores in the United States, Mexico, and Central America. Haggar's knowledge of Spanish helped him sell to companies south of the border. After five very successful years with the company, Haggar quit in protest after being insulted by a company officer. "I gave 'em the thirty days [notice] before I quit," he later told Spiegel, "and during that thirty days I never worked harder in all my life. I wanted 'em to know they lost a good man."

Simple and fair

One of the reasons Haggar became a successful businessman was that he didn't think something had to be done a certain way just because it was usually done that way. For example, while he was working as a traveling salesman for a Dallas, Texas, manufacturer of overalls in the early 1920s, Haggar saw the weakness in the clothing industry's customary pricing strategy. He was supposed to offer his customers different prices on each item, and his commission was different for each price. That is, if a customer bought pants for $11 per dozen, Haggar was paid a 6 percent commission, or sixty-seven cents a dozen; but if the customer paid only $10 per dozen, Haggar's commission dropped to 3 percent, or thirty cents. Haggar realized that he could sell more pants at a lower price, so his total income might be larger, even though the percent of commission was smaller. For example, selling two-and-a-half dozen pairs at $10 per dozen earned him seventy-cents, which was more than the sixty-seven cents he would earn by selling one dozen pairs at $11 a dozen. While the company's other salesmen were working to sell pants at the higher price to get the highest percent of commission, Haggar found customers who happily bought more pants at a lower cost, making him the most successful.

The mid-1920s brought many changes to Haggar's life. His second son, Joe, and his daughter, Rose Marie, were born. His mother came from Lebanon to live with his family for two years (she died in 1929). In 1926, the company Haggar had been working for decided to get out of the retail business. Seeing this not as the loss of his job as a salesman, but as a chance to pursue his dream of owning his own business, Haggar started manufacturing and selling clothing.

As he traveled around the region selling his products, he saw another example of how impractical current pricing practices were. He was in a general store in a small Texas town, talking to the owner about ordering some merchandise. A local cowhand came into the store, looked at a shirt, and asked its price. The owner said it was eight-five cents. The customer put the shirt back on the display table and walked toward the door. The owner called after him, "You can have it for seventy-five cents." The cowboy kept walking. The owner called out, "It's yours for sixty-five cents." The customer had reached the door by this time, and he leaned out the door to spit some tobacco juice. It turned out this (not the shirt's price) was the reason he had headed for the door in the first place. After the man bought the shirt and left, Haggar told the store owner, "Good thing the door wasn't ten feet further. You'd have *given* him the shirt!"

It was this incident that sparked Haggar to pioneer the concept of pricing products with a single, fair price. He realized that this would be best for both the customer and the seller. Other companies followed his lead, and this new pricing policy became common.

Fair but not cheap

Haggar worked eighteen hours a day—traveling around the region to sell his products, going to New York a couple of times a year to buy fabrics, and supervising the factory. By 1929, his "Dallas Pant Manufacturing Company" employed 250 workers and occupied a 6,000-square-foot factory. That's when the Great Depression (1929–39; a period of time in America when the economy suffered, banks and businesses closed, and many people lived in extreme poverty) began. During the next few years, companies all over the country went out of business; many banks closed and their customers lost the money they had deposited; the number of people who couldn't find jobs climbed to fifteen million. Haggar's business, though, remained strong.

Many factors contributed to that success. Haggar himself worked hard, and he expected his employees to do the same. He made sure there was as little waste as possible in the company's operations. His goal was not to make the least expensive product but a good one with a fair price. He insisted that employees, customers, and suppliers be treated fairly. During the sixty years he ran his company, he repeatedly told his salesmen, "You can make an honest mistake on the road and cost me a thousand dollars, and I will never even call you into the office. But if you make a dishonest mistake and cost me a nickel, I'll fire you in five minutes." When he had to, he proved he meant what he said.

Rewards

Except for the time they spent in the armed service during World War II (1939–45; when the United States and certain European countries went to war against Nazi Germany and Japan to stop their aggressions) in the early 1940s, Haggar's two sons helped run the family business. Their talents complemented their father's, and each took on a different role in the company. Ed concentrated on merchandising and marketing, while Joe supervised factory operations and the building of new plants.

In the mid-1950s, Haggar decreased his involvement in the company, leaving more of the responsibility to his sons and other employees. After his wife died in 1965, however, he renewed his involvement in the business to ease his loneliness. By the time he died at the age of ninety-four, the company he founded employed more than 7,000 people and had sixteen factories.

Haggar believed wholeheartedly in the "American dream"—that anyone is capable of success if he or she is willing to work for it. A 1980 story about him in *Forbes* magazine said, "Having come up the hard way, he doesn't weep for people who have to do the same." Although he expected others to work for their dream as he had for his, he was willing to help. During his lifetime, he gave more than $200 million to various charitable organizations such as St. Jude Children's Research Hospital and Notre Dame University (from which his son Ed had graduated). When Gregory Orfalea (1949–; see entry) was gathering information for his book *Before the Flames: A Quest for the History of Arab Americans,* he asked Haggar about his donations. "Easy come, easy go," replied Haggar, adding, "That 'easy come' is hard work."

FURTHER READING

Berman, Phyllis, with Toni Mack. "Renaissance on the Rio Grande: Building on a Rock" *Forbes* (September 1, 1980): 40.

Orfalea, Gregory. *Before the Flames: A Quest for the History of Arab Americans.* Austin: University of Texas Press, 1988, pp. 277-80.

Spiegel, Joy G. *That Haggar Man: A Biographical Portrait.* New York: Random House, 1978.

Khrystyne Haje

Arab American actress

Born December 21, 1968
Los Angeles, California

> "EVERY TIME I DID A COMMERCIAL, I WOULD GET THIS LITTLE SPURT OF HAPPINESS. SO I FIGURED IF I WERE AN ACTRESS, THERE WOULD BE EVEN MORE OF THAT."

Khrystyne Haje (pronounced Haj) is best known for her role as Simone Foster, the quiet intellectual on the American Broadcasting Company (ABC) television series *Head of the Class* (1986–91). Haje turned success as a model into an acting career. By age seventeen, her role on *Head of the Class* earned her national recognition. During the 1990s she also appeared in several movies and plays.

Sounds like "Christine"

Khrystyne Haje was born in California in 1968. Her father, who was from the Middle East, met her American mother, who was traveling around the world, in an airport in Beirut, Lebanon. Haje's first name is a variant spelling of "Christine," the name chosen by nuns who had prayed for Haje's mother while she was sick during her pregnancy. "'Christine' was picked, but there was no stopping my mother. She wanted to spice it up," Haje told *TV Guide*. "She gathered my four older brothers and a group of friends in the liv-

MODELING

Modeling is a highly competitive profession that requires not just looks but training and persistence. For some world-famous models, getting "discovered" was the easy part—Kate Moss (1974–) was picked out of a crowd at New York's Kennedy Airport, while Naomi Campbell (1970–) caught a recruiter's eye as she walked through London's Covent Garden wearing her school uniform. Recruiters for modeling agencies hang out in heavily traveled public areas and look for a pretty face who might be the next Cindy Crawford (1966–). Major agencies require that female models have good skin and teeth, hips no wider than thirty-six inches, and that they stand between five feet nine inches and six feet tall. Beyond that, it's a matter of opinion as to who has the looks to make it as a model.

Runway modeling may not appear to be that complicated, but it takes time to learn how to do it well. Models have to be taught how to carry themselves with grace and confidence on the runway without being startled by the barrage of camera flashes.

Unfortunately, stories of aspiring models making it big are more of the exception than the rule. "The odds are against [young women who want to be models] if they're not a particular size and don't have a fashion look from head to toe," said one agency owner.

ing room. They all came up with different spellings and then they voted. This spelling was the winner."

Growing up in front of the camera

Influenced by her oldest brother who was working in Los Angeles as an actor, writer, and director, Haje decided to try acting herself when she was nine years old. She got her first taste of acting in a short Walt Disney educational film that shot for seventy-five days in Disneyland. Although the experience was thrilling for Haje, it was upsetting to her mother, who felt that wearing make-up and acting for a camera would force her daughter to grow up too fast. Her mother pleaded with Haje to postpone a career in acting, and Haje agreed.

In the meantime, Haje busied herself with schoolwork, Girl Scouts, the speech and debate team, and Little League. Her dedication paid off: she was an honors student and was voted most valuable player on her baseball team. Then at age fourteen, a discussion about whether Haje should take Spanish or French in school developed into a conversation about careers. Haje's mother thought Spanish would be more helpful in California, where the Hispanic population was growing, but Haje was thinking about a career in modeling—a profession that could take her to European countries where French would be a more helpful language to know.

Haje persuaded her mother to let her take French and allow a family friend to shoot some pictures of her to show modeling scouts. A modeling agent from France saw the pictures and tried to recruit Haje to model on the runways in Paris. Although this was what she wanted, Haje turned down the invitation. Her school work was important to her and she did not want to fall behind. She changed her mind, however, when she realized the invitation could be a once-in-a-lifetime offer.

Modeling and Michelangelo

Before Haje took off for Europe, she worked out an arrangement with her teachers to continue her homework assignments abroad. She even took advantage of her six weeks in Milan, Italy, to write a paper on Italian Renaissance painter and sculptor Michelangelo (1475-1564). She had a unique opportunity to actually see Michelangelo's work in Florence and Rome and hunted down every piece of art by him that she could find.

Haje fell in love with modeling after working in Milan and Paris, but once her eight weeks were up, she returned to California to finish the school year. That summer, she returned to Europe for another four months of modeling. The long hours and sometimes tough times finding work braced Haje for the trials that would later come with acting.

"There's a lot of self-discipline and a lot of rejection [in modeling], which prepared me for acting auditions later on," Haje told *Seventeen*. "I'd go on eight modeling interviews and get two jobs or no jobs—it was no big deal, nothing personal. I was doing the best I could, and if I didn't have the right look or the right build, it wasn't something I could do anything about."

When Haje came back from Europe, she found work doing TV commercials and magazine ads. "Every time I did a commercial, I would get this little spurt of happiness," Haje told *'TEEN* magazine. "So I figured if I were an actress, there would be even more of that." Haje hired an agent and starting going to auditions on a regular basis. She landed a few small roles, including appearances on *Murder, She Wrote* and

Growing Pains. She also picked up a bit part as a runaway in the Eddie Murphy (1961–) movie *The Golden Child* (1986). She only had two lines in the movie, but she got to work opposite Murphy, who is one of her favorite actors and someone she respects because "he always makes me laugh."

Rises to *Head of the Class*

In March 1986, Haje landed the part of poetic beauty Simone Foster in the series *Head of the Class,* a show about a class of gifted students at Manhattan's Fillmore High School. Haje described her character as a shy wallflower who had a lot of complicated feelings going on inside. The show's appeal, Haje told *Seventeen,* was its honesty. "*Head of the Class* doesn't make a joke out of being a teenager, but deals with problems every teen can relate to and have fun doing it."

After *Head of the Class* ended its successful five-year run in 1991, Haje had guest appearances in several television shows, such as *Parker Lewis Can't Lose* (1993). She parodied victimized ice skater Nancy Kerrigan (1969–) in the television movie *Attack of the Five-Foot-Two Women* (1994), and she appeared in a 1995 Perry Mason television movie, *The Case of the Jealous Jokester.* Her big screen movies include *Scanners: The Showdown* (1994) *Scanner Cop II* (1995) and *Cyborg 3: The Recycler* (1995), none of which enjoyed much success. Haje's latest projects have been in theater, where she has appeared in such productions as *Moon Over Buffalo* at the Pasadena Playhouse in California and *Featuring Loretta* (1998).

Personal notes

An ardent animal lover, Haje has four ducks ("child stars," she calls them, as they were born on an episode of *Head of the Class*), two dogs, and more than twenty rabbits. She used her time away from the *Head of the Class* set to lend a hand to her favorite causes. In 1989, she baked more than 1,500 chocolate-chip cookies for a world tour by a humanitarian group. She bought land in Northern California to help preserve "the redwoods and the environment that goes with them." Haje enjoys horseback riding, skiing, traveling, and whitewater rafting.

FURTHER READING

"Class Lass." *'TEEN* (August 1988): 112–13.

"Khrystyne Haje: Head of the Class." *TV Guide* (September 23–29, 1989): 14.

Miller, Edwin. "Two Young Actresses Are Going to the Head of the Class." *Seventeen* (November 1986): 105–06+.

Najeeb Halaby

Syrian-Scotch-English-American government
official and businessman

Born November 19, 1915
Dallas, Texas

Often thought of as one of the most prominent Arab Americans of his generation, Najeeb Halaby has been in the public eye for most of his life. A lawyer and businessman who liked to fly planes in his spare time, Halaby found a post that utilized all of his skills when President John F. Kennedy (1917–1963) nominated him to head the Federal Aviation Administration (FAA). Halaby went on to lead Pan American World Airways (Pan Am) and start up several of his own business projects. He also speaks his mind about the plight of Arabs, and he uses his influence on Capitol Hill and in the private sector to propose solutions to the economic and political problems of the Middle East.

The old man's tongue

Najeeb Elias Halaby was born in 1915 to Najeeb Halaby, a Syrian immigrant, and Laura Wilkins, an American of Scotch-English background. Halaby's father and uncle Habeeb came to the United States around 1900, bringing the family's gold, jewelry, copperware, rugs, and damask material (reversible fabric

"FLIGHT *CAN* BE A POETICAL, MYSTICAL, ALMOST RELIGIOUS EXPERIENCE; FOR ME, FLIGHT HAS ALWAYS EVOKED THE BIBLICAL GENESIS, IN WHICH 'GOD GAVE MAN DOMINION OVER THE EARTH AND OVER EVERY CREEPING THING UPON THE FACE OF THE EARTH.'"

Reproduced by permission of Archive Photos, Inc.

189

used for table cloths) to sell on the American market. The money from selling those goods was sent back to Syria so the rest of the Halaby clan could come to America. Halaby's father continued peddling goods to make money, and one summer he met former First Lady Frances Cleveland (1864–1947) while hawking his rugs and jewelry in Bar Harbor, Maine—a summer get-away for the rich. A letter of introduction from Cleveland opened other business doors for the elder Halaby, who expanded his import business. In the early 1910s he moved to Dallas, Texas, home to cotton and oil millionaires who would buy the fine Arab fabrics and artwork Halaby was importing.

Halaby's parents met and married in Dallas, where they ran a lucrative import and interior design company, Halaby Galleries. Although his parents divorced when he was twelve and his father died a year later, Halaby, an only child, picked up a love of golf and his Arab identity from his father. "Unlike many Syrians, Lebanese, and others from the Middle East, he refused to change his name or pretend to be something he wasn't," Halaby wrote in his autobiography, *Crosswinds: An Airman's Memoir.* But, Halaby continued: "To my later regret, we never spoke Arabic at mealtime, as did many Arab Americans, but I did pick up a few epithets in the old man's native tongue."

Halaby studied at a series of rigorous private schools where he learned to be independent and self-reliant. His greatest growth came during his high school years at the Leelanau school in Glen Arbor, Michigan, under his instructor William "Skipper" Beals. "He supplied me with my first real sense of ethical values and the capability to recognize in myself some capacity to persuade and lead others; to assume responsibility for someone other than Najeeb Halaby," he wrote.

Dreams take flight

Halaby's fascination with flight began as a boy, during the 1920s, when books, model airplanes, and air shows capitalized on the popularity of ace pilots from World War I (1914–18; when the United States and certain European countries fought the aggressions of imperial Germany and Austria-Hungary). His interest really took off at age seventeen, when he saw German World War I pilot Ernst Udet perform what he called "blood-chilling stunts" like flying close to the ground and tilting the airplane to pick up a handkerchief close to the ground with the plane's wing tip.

Halaby pleaded with his mother for permission and money to take flying lessons, and she agreed. After several lessons with a crop-duster who owned a biplane, Halaby took his first solo flight. He was far too nervous to experience "the mystical love of the sky" at first, but as he became a more able aviator, Halaby came to see the beauty of flight. "Flight *can* be a poetical, mystical, almost religious experience; for me, flight has always evoked the biblical Genesis, in which 'God gave man dominion over the earth and over every creeping thing upon the face of the earth,'" Halaby wrote.

While studying political science at Stanford University, Halaby had little money for flying. He graduated in 1937 and continued on to law school—first at the University of Michigan, then at Yale University. When he began working for the Los Angeles, California law firm of O'Melveny and Myers in 1940, Halaby put aside his interest in flying.

That changed in 1941 when the United States entered World War II (1939–45; when the United States and certain European countries went to war against Germany and Japan to stop their aggressions). Horrified by what was happening abroad, Halaby lent his aviation expertise to the U.S. forces, testing America's first jets and training United States airmen. Flying the Lockheed Shooting Star jet fighter from California to Maryland in five hours and forty minutes, Halaby logged the first U.S. transcontinental jet flight. The success of that flight was kept a secret for several years because the jet was part of the military's classified equipment. As a Navy pilot trainer, Halaby even taught his boyhood hero, aviator Charles Lindbergh (1902–1974), how to handle the military's high-tech jets.

The troubleshooter

After the war, Halaby got a job at the State Department's Office of Research and Intelligence—the precursor to the Central Intelligence Agency (CIA). His aviation expertise was put to use analyzing the flight and other technological capabilities of other countries. That expertise, along with his Arab roots, made him the perfect man to send to Saudi Arabia in 1947 to help the country reform its airline practices. On some SAUDIA (the major airline in Saudi Arabia) flights, livestock roamed the cabin while passengers barbecued food. Pilots needed better technology and techniques to fly through the fierce sandstorms and over the treacherous mountains.

Halaby returned to Washington, D.C. in 1948 and joined the newly-formed Department of Defense. One of his major undertakings there was to help draft the North Atlantic Treaty, which created an alliance of Western countries committed to resisting communist expansion in Europe. After World War II the communist Soviet Union competed with other western countries, especially the United States, for power and influence among the governments of world. The North Atlantic treaty was meant to stop the Soviet Union from expanding its influence in the world.

The low pay and constant infighting among government officials took its toll on Halaby, who left the Department of Defense in 1953 to work for Laurance Rockefeller. Halaby was a "personal troubleshooter" for the millionaire, watching Rockefeller's investments in McDonnell Aircraft and Eastern Air Lines. Halaby also compiled studies for Rockefeller on solar energy and evacuation plans in case New York City ever came under nuclear attack from the Soviet Union.

Presidential appointment

As the vice-chairman of the White House aviation facilities study group, Halaby was instrumental in drafting the 1957 Curtis Report, which proposed the renovation of the nation's airline facilities. The report recommended creating the Federal Aviation Administration (FAA) to regulate air business, control air space for use by both civil and military flights, and establish safety standards. Congress created the FAA in 1958, and President Dwight Eisenhower (1890–1969) appointed E. R. Quesada to head the agency. When President John F. Kennedy took office in 1961, he appointed Halaby to head the FAA. "That was a thrill in the sense that it was the first time anyone of Arab American background had ever had a presidential appointment," Halaby told Gregory Orfalea (see entry). "I don't think [Kennedy] was even trying to find a [token] Arab or anything like that. It was that I had achieved a certain technical expertise and capability which was sought by some of my friends in the administration."

Halaby was a hands-on administrator, making a point to discuss aviation issues with pilots during "hangar flying ses-

AVIATION SAFETY

As the number of planes in flight increased and the technology became more sophisticated, the government had to address new safety issues. The government has created agencies and passed laws to regulate the airline industry, but many safety lessons were only learned after devastating crashes. For the first twenty years of their existence, planes were not regulated by the U.S. government. As airplane accident rates increased, however, the government decided in the mid-1920s that it needed to create requirements for pilots to meet before receiving a license to fly.

Airline regulation did not really take off until after World War II (1939–45; when the United States and certain European countries went to war against Nazi Germany and Japan to stop their aggressions), when several domestic collisions occurred. Some planes did not have the right equipment (such as radios or radar) to detect where other planes were; at most airfields, there were no take-off or landing schedules to ensure that planes would not compete for the same space on the runway. In 1958, the Beacon Report proposed solutions to these problems. They required planes to have the necessary communications and plane detection equipment in order to use certain airports. Such equipment is needed because visual illusions (caused by sloping cloud tops and other natural elements) can distort pilots' views of how far they are from other planes.

The Federal Aviation Administration (FAA) was also created in 1958 to provide the government with an agency to specialize in regulating private, commercial, and military flights. Ten years later, the original Terminal Control Area proposal was drafted. This proposal provided for the building of control towers to supervise heavy plane traffic, telling planes when and where to land. Most of these policies came into place because of specific accidents that claimed the lives of hundreds of passengers and flight crew members. According to aviator Richard L. Collins, "From studying the relationship between accidents and rules, one can gather that the FAA is reactive and that we make regulations by smoke and flame."

sions" and test-flying planes to ensure their safety. He even inspected all plane crash sites in person. Halaby revised most of the agency's aviation guidelines but relied heavily on his regional FAA administrators to implement and enforce those measures. He set the standards for improved radar use to keep track of planes, using computers for air-traffic control, and requiring jets and low-speed planes to use different runways. While he headed the FAA, airline fatalities dropped by more than 60 percent.

All those innovations, Halaby said, were part of his greatest contribution to the FAA. "My most creative and lasting work was to change the culture and the attitude of the FAA," he told *Business and Commercial Aviation*. "In four and half years, we really converted an old basement operation of the

As head of the FAA, Halaby would personally test-fly new planes like this Boeing 747 jet to ensure their safety. Reproduced by permission of Archive Photos, Inc.

Commerce Department into a lively and able outfit. And I think it gained the respect of the public and the aviation community during the early 1960s."

Showdown with Arab terrorists

Halaby left the FAA in 1965 to become senior vice president of Pan Am airlines, and in 1969 he was promoted to chief executive. His seven-year tenure at Pan Am was, by all accounts, a turbulent one. He took the reins of leadership when the airline was drowning in debt, losing customers because of an economic recession (a declining economy), and facing additional competition due to government deregulation of the airline industry. As if those problems were not enough, Halaby also had the unfortunate distinction of being in charge of one of the first airlines faced with a terrorist situation.

On September 6, 1970, two hijackers from the Popular Front for the Liberation of Palestine (PFLP) took control of a Pan Am flight with revolvers and hand grenades they brought on board. Departing from Amsterdam, the Netherlands, the flight was scheduled to fly to New York, New York. Instead, terrorists demanded that the plane go to Beirut, Lebanon to refuel, and then continue on to Cairo, Egypt. Minutes after the 152 passengers and eighteen crew members deboarded in Cairo, the plane exploded. "It was ironical," Halaby told Orfalea. "The loss of the first jumbo jet in flames set by the craziest of the homeless, frustrated Palestinians, who missed their Israeli target and hit an airline headed by an Arab American aviator who had labored long to help get recognition of the rights of the Palestinian people—and in my father's homeland, too!"

For the twenty-seven months Halaby headed Pan Am, the company suffered a loss of more than $100 million. Halaby attributed the company's woes to a combination of difficult circumstances—some of which were already in place before he came to the company. The Pan Am board of directors blamed Halaby for the airline's problems, however, and in March 1972, the board demanded (and received) his resignation.

Speaks out on Arab issues

Freed from association with the government or any major corporation, Halaby felt he was finally able to speak publicly on the Arab-Israeli tensions. These tensions date back to the controversial 1948 creation of Israel that uprooted many Arabs who were living in the area. Halaby started personally lobbying congressmen and policy officials, pleading with them to stop aiding the Israelis and to start helping the warring sides arrive at peace. He worked with the group that wrote the groundbreaking Brookings Report, which served as the outline for agreements reached at the historic 1978 Camp David Accords. The Accords helped to end hostilities between Israel and Egypt. His suggestions to Secretary of State George Shultz (1920–) became part of President Ronald Reagan's (1911–) plan to deal with the 1982 Israeli invasion of Lebanon. To help the war-ruined areas of the Middle East rebuild economically, Halaby joined the Builders for Peace organization in 1993. The group brought together Jewish American and Arab American businessmen to invest in companies and properties in the West Bank and the Gaza Strip.

Halaby has continued to serve on aviation advisory boards, such as the Flight Safety Foundation, the Air Safety Foundation, and other FAA panels. He has also continued flying recreationally, now with his personal Piper Malibu plane. Over his lifetime, Halaby has logged more than 10,000 hours of flight in more than 125 different kinds of aircraft, including some foreign planes with no pilot's manual and a command panel printed in a foreign language.

Personal notes

On February 9, 1946, Halaby married Doris Carlquist, and the couple had three children: Lisa, Christian, and Alexa. In 1973 Halaby started Halaby International, a global venture capital group that brings together investors to provide financial backing for new businesses. He also teamed up with the national airline of Jordan, to form Arab Air Services. Halaby hired his oldest daughter, Lisa, to work for the airline. While she was in the Middle East designing an air university where pilots could be trained, she met King Hussein of Jordan. The two fell in love and married in 1978, adding "father-in-law of King Hussein" to Halaby's long list of titles.

Halaby and his first wife went through a difficult divorce in the mid-1970s, and in 1980, he married Allison Coates, a volunteer and trustee for several youth organizations. Halaby's second wife died in 1996, and two years later, Halaby married Libby Carter, a longtime family friend. The couple lives in McLean, Virginia.

FURTHER READING

"The Friendly Aviation Administrator." *Business & Commercial Aviation* (March 1994): 78–79.

Halaby, Najeeb. *Crosswinds: An Airman's Memoir.* New York: Doubleday, 1978.

"Halaby, Najeeb." *Current Biography Yearbook 1961.* New York: H.W. Wilson Company, 1961, pp. 189–91.

Orfalea, Gregory. *Before the Flames: A Quest for the History of Arab Americans.* Austin: University of Texas Press, 1988, pp. 103–04, 124–31.

"The Pilot President." *Time* (January 19, 1970): 55.

George A. Hamid, Jr.

*Syrian-American businessman
and circus owner*

*Born 1918
Jersey City, New Jersey*

Saying George Hamid (HAM-id) is a businessman is like saying the Grand Canyon is a big hole in the ground. Hamid's accomplishments are much more colorful than that. Besides owning and managing circuses and state fairs, Hamid operated the Steel Pier, a large amusement park that featured live entertainers; in addition, he regularly worked with the biggest stars in music—people like Frank Sinatra (1916–1998), Paul Anka (see entry), and The Beatles. He dabbled in other branches of the amusement industry, managing a world-champion boxer and running a motor speedway. However, the only operation that he kept going through a career that lasted more than fifty years was the circus business. He called the circus "a gem of a business" in a 1993 *Amusement Business* magazine interview. He explained, "I was dealing with stars on Steel Pier. It's easier to deal with elephants. They don't have too many problems and don't demand $40,000 a day."

Son of a tumbler

In 1906, a nine-year-old boy left his home of Broumana

in Syria (now in Lebanon) to join his uncle as a tumbler performing in the Buffalo Bill Circus that was touring Europe. The circus brought the boy to the United States the following year. Wild West sharpshooter Annie Oakley (1860–1926) taught him to read and write, and former U.S. scout William "Buffalo Bill" Cody (1846–1917) taught him the ins and outs of show business. A dozen years later, after his son was born, the young Syrian began a new career as a booking agent, signing performers for appearances at circuses and fairs.

The tumbler's son is George A. Hamid, Jr. During Hamid's childhood in Long Island, New York, he spent his summers traveling with his father as he booked grandstand shows for fairs throughout the northeastern United States. Meeting the different kinds of performers was exciting. In the *Amusement Business* magazine interview, Hamid remembered the childhood thrill of circling a dirt track with race-car driver Bob Robinson: "In those days, race cars had two seats—one for the mechanic."

Again recalling his early years, Hamid told interviewer Bill Kent in 1996 that his father "worked his way up to the point that he booked the Ringling Brothers circus. Through him, I got to know every cat act in the country. I know every high-wire act, every acrobatic team."

Circus family

Hamid was thirteen when his father went into partnership with Robert Morton to start the Hamid-Morton Circus. Using the resources of Hamid's father's talent agency, the Hamid-Morton Circus began its tradition of being freshly formed each season rather than keeping the same acts every year. It was one of the first circuses to produce shows for community fund-raising groups like the Shriners.

Tumble Bug to tiger

When Hamid was a teenager, he earned money not by working as a grocery bagger or a paperboy, but by operating an amusement park ride called the Tumble Bug. His father had given him the Tumble Bug, which he operated at White City Park in Worcester, Massachusetts. Operating the ride not only gave him spending money, it financed his college education. Hamid attended prestigious Princeton University in New Jer-

The circus owned by George Hamid's family was one of the first in the United States to team up with community groups that wanted to raise money for worthy causes. The group that is best known for using circuses as fund-raisers is the Shriners. The Moslem Shrine Temple in Detroit, Michigan, presented the first Shrine Circus in 1906. By the 1920s, cities all across the country were hosting Shrine Circuses. Even today, Shrine Circuses often enter a town with a festive parade. Local Shriners, each wearing the traditional red fez, march in the parade, sell advance tickets, and welcome customers.

The Shrine of North America was founded in New York City in 1872 by thirteen members of the Masonic Order. They used a Middle Eastern theme for the new organization, calling each chapter a "temple" and naming the original chapter Mecca Temple. Although the Shrine started out as a social organization, members decided to shift to a focus of service. They decided their mission would be helping children who suffer from orthopedic disabilities (deformities or injuries to the skeletal system); later they broadened the focus to include children with burn injuries. Proceeds from the Shrine Circuses (along with other fund-raisers and donations) are used to build and operate hospitals and conduct medical research. There are now twenty-two Shrine hospitals. Since the first one opened in 1922, more than 575,000 children have been treated, all free of charge.

sey. Through his father's circus bookings, Hamid probably knew more about tigers (the Princeton mascot) than most students! He majored in English, intending to become a writer.

When Hamid graduated from Princeton in 1940, his father was ready for his help with the family business; in fact, he even changed the name of his booking agency from "George A. Hamid Inc." to "George A. Hamid & Son." World tensions prompted Hamid to enlist in the U.S. Navy. Eight months later, on December 7, 1941, the Japanese attacked the American naval base at Pearl Harbor, Hawaii, drawing the United States into World War II (1939–45; when the United States and certain European countries fought to stop Nazi Germany and Japan from conquering the world). Hamid fought for his country in the South Pacific until the war ended. His father served as general chairman of outdoor amusements for the Navy Relief Society, and as chairman of the Army-Navy Emergency Relief Society, he raised $300,000 from the theater industry.

Fair deal

When Hamid returned home after the war in 1946, his father handed him a little black book and said, "Go book concerts at fairs." For the next fifty years, booking fairs would be part of Hamid's job. Each year the family booking agency put together three complete sets of acts and scheduled them on different fair circuits from Ottawa, Canada, to South Carolina. The process changed in 1960 when the family realized that "name talent" (nationally recognized entertainers) were becoming more popular at fairs and would draw bigger crowds than the entertainers they had been booking.

The Hamid family company continued to produce the New Jersey State Fair, however. Hamid's father had bought the rights to the fair's name in 1931 when the Great Depression (1929–39) nearly put the fair out of business. The Great Depression was a period of time when the American economy collapsed and many people lost their jobs. People struggled in poverty and were unable to buy groceries, much less tickets to the circus. Eventually, two of Hamid's sons joined the family's entertainment business. Tim Hamid managed the New Jersey State Fair until the company sold it in 1996, while James Hamid took charge of the family's circus, which was renamed the Hamid Circus Royale.

Star-studded pier

In 1945, Hamid's father bought another failing business that he turned into a big success. It was an amusement park located on the Steel Pier in the harbor of Atlantic City, New Jersey. The pier was almost half a mile long and as wide as a football field. At one end was a ballroom, at the other end was a circus, and in between there were theaters for live entertainment. For the previous twenty years, the elder Hamid had been booking the acts for the pier circus. World War II nearly destroyed the pier's business; especially because of its ocean-front location, it was required to stay dark at night to prevent enemy ships from using it as a landmark for navigation or as a target. This "black-out" requirement kept the park closed in the evenings, severely cutting its profits.

When wartime restrictions ended, the Steel Pier became profitable again. The elder Hamid continued to book the kinds of spectacular circus acts he had become famous for, like the Human Cannonball, the High-Diving Hawaiians, and Alvin "Shipwreck" Kelly (who sat atop a pole for a world-record seven weeks, setting off a fad as challengers around the country tried to break the record). Another circus act that

Steel Pier in Atlantic City, New Jersey, offered exciting attractions such as diving horses and a human cannon ball. Reproduced by permission of The Press of Atlantic City.

became a tradition at the Steel Pier was the Diving Horses. Responding to charges of animal cruelty, Hamid wrote to the Princeton University alumni newsletter in 1998, "From 1947 to 1975 our horses worked for three months each year. Their 'work' consisted of diving into a clean, warm pool and climbing out for their reward of apples and molasses.... As Phyllis McGuire [of the popular McGuire Sisters singing group] once told me, 'George, you are cruel. You care more for your diving horses than you do for your singers.' I gave her a brotherly hug and replied, 'But, my dear, you don't work for molasses and apples.'"

By 1960, Hamid had taken over the act-booking duties from his father, and he continued to bring the country's most famous entertainers to the pier's theaters and ballroom. At that time Steel Pier and the showrooms of Las Vegas, Nevada, were the best places in the country for seeing top performers like Frank Sinatra, Tony Bennett (1926–), and Wayne Newton (1942–). When rock singing sensation Rick Nelson (1940–1985) appeared at the Steel Pier in 1958, the enormous crowds prompted Hamid to invent "festival seating." In one day, the box office sold 44,211 tickets for a planned five performances. It was obvious after the first show that the 3,000-seat theater wasn't going to handle the crowds. In a spur-of-the-moment decision, Hamid moved Nelson into the ballroom, which could hold 10,000 people.

Hamid sold the Steel Pier in 1975; it closed a few years later but reopened in 1993. It was rebuilt by businessman Donald Trump (1946–) as part of his Taj Mahal casino operation.

What a sport

The circus, the New Jersey State Fair, and the Steel Pier were the most constant parts of Hamid's business, but other activities were added to the company roster from time to time. Several were sports-related. For example, the family operated the Trenton (New Jersey) International Speedway for twenty years. Originally a mile-long oval, the race-car track was redesigned into a mile-and-a-half irregular oval in 1969. Between 1958 and 1972, the track hosted eight National Association for Stock Car Auto Racing (NASCAR) Winston Cup Series stock car races.

Along with entertainer Danny Thomas (1914–1991) and clothing manufacturers Ed Haggar and Joseph Haggar (1892–1987), the Hamid family helped Joe Robbie (1916–1990; see entries) start the Miami Dolphins professional football team. The Hamids owned 10 percent of the team for several years until Robbie bought their share.

Hamid even managed heavyweight boxer Ernie Terrell for a while in the mid-1960s. Terrell was part of a singing group that performed at Hamid's Steel Pier entertainment center. When his scheduled fight with boxing legend Muhammad Ali (1942–) was canceled, Terrell ran out of money. He asked Hamid to become his manager. Hamid accepted, knowing he wouldn't have to figure out how to build Terrell's boxing reputation—the fighter already held the World Boxing Association (WBA) championship.

Guess wrong, guess right

In 1997 the *New York Times* profiled Hamid, who was nearing the age of eighty. He told the reporter about "the biggest mistake of [his] life," though he said it didn't seem like it at the time. In 1957, a major talent agency suggested that Hamid hire one of their clients for a performance—a young country singer named Elvis Presley (1935–1977). "[The agency] wanted the same money for Presley that I was paying Rick Nelson, and Rick Nelson was a name that made girls line up from Steel Pier to Hackney's restaurant at six o'clock in the morning," Hamid recalled. "Who was this Presley kid?" It wasn't long before Presley became the undisputed king of rock-and-roll music.

Hamid avoided a similar mistake in 1964, booking a new music group on its first U.S. tour. He brought The Beatles to Atlantic City for a concert at the city's convention center. After performing at Shea Stadium in New York, the group flew to New Jersey by helicopter. Between the flight and the concert, Hamid recalled, "I hid them away in a hotel." He told *Amusement Business* it was the highlight of his career. When he met them, the four-member singing group was beginning a period of dominance in popular music that would last long after they broke up in 1970. When the *Amusement Business* reporter asked Hamid for the secret of his success, he replied, "Keep your eye on the ball and do your homework."

FURTHER READING

Deckard, Linda. "Hamid Checks List of Things to Do; But What Hasn't He Done?" *Amusement Business* (April 5, 1993): 3+.

Kent, Bill. "King Emeritus." *New York Times* (August 8, 1997): section 13NJ, p. 16.

Raymond G. Hanania

Palestinian-American journalist and author

Born April 17, 1953
Chicago, Illinois

"MY MOM WANTED ME TO BE A DOCTOR OR A GROCER, BUT I NEVER REALIZED THAT I WOULD SOMEDAY GROW UP TO BE AN ARAB."

Ray Hanania (Han-na-NEE-ya) reported on city politics for local Chicago newspapers for fourteen years and hosted a radio talk show for nearly as long. In 1991 he was nominated for a Pulitzer Prize, the most prestigious award in journalism, for his series of newspaper articles about the treatment of Palestinians under Israeli occupation. In response to his personal experiences, he has become active in organizations that promote a positive image of Arabs in the United States. He also works, individually and in organizations, to help find a peaceful solution to the conflict between Israelis and Palestinians in the Middle East. His 1996 autobiography, *I'm Glad I Look Like a Terrorist: Growing Up Arab in America,* takes an often-humorous look at important issues of identity and prejudice.

Jerusalem, Bethlehem, Chicago

Ray Hanania considers himself both a Palestinian Arab and an American. His father, George Hanna Hanania, the son of a Palestinian peddler (a person who sells things door-to-door or on the street), was born in Jerusalem but came to America in 1923. "He didn't forget his Arab heritage, but he didn't wear it like a chip on his shoulder, either. Dad believed that 'blending in' was the key to a successful life here," Hanania wrote in his autobiography. His father, who served in the U.S. Army during World War II (1939–45; when the United States and certain European countries went to war against Nazi Germany and Japan to stop their aggressions), returned to Palestine in search of a bride after his first wife died. He married Georgette Dabdoub Kronfil, the daughter of a Bethlehem tailor, and brought her to Chicago to help him raise his first son Johnnie. George and Georgette eventually added two children of their own to the family: Ray and Linda.

Herman the Arab

Growing up in a Jewish neighborhood on Chicago's South Side was not a problem for the young Palestinian. Hanania believes that Arabs and Jews really have many things in common; in his autobiography he wrote, "Were it not for the Arab-Israeli wars, we would have had a fine existence together, eating the same foods, sharing the same ties to biblical history (my last name is a Hebrew word that means *God has been Gracious*)."

In fact, Hanania and his Jewish friends got along well together during childhood, even during the Six Day War in 1967 (a war that lasted six days when Israel defeated Egypt, Syria, and Jordan and reunited Jerusalem), which erupted when he was fourteen years old. "While they knew I was 'Arab' they also had embraced me as a friend and had nicknamed me 'Herman,'" he wrote. "Maybe they called me Herman because in Hebrew school and at the JCC [Jewish Community Center], they were taught that the Arabs were their enemies, just as in my community, I was taught that the 'Jews' were my enemy. I couldn't be an Arab to them, if I was a 'Herman.'"

Turn around

School was not one of Hanania's favorite activities. He had failed his high school writing classes several times before one of his teachers recognized his hidden talents. She asked him what his favorite hobby was; when he answered that it was playing the guitar in a band, she asked him to write a rock music column for the school paper. The column was so successful that he was chosen to serve as editor-in-chief of the newspaper the following year.

Reality check

When Hanania enrolled at Northern Illinois University in DeKalb, he became the first Arab student ever to be accepted into a fraternity on that campus. During his first two years of college, he was the social chairman for his fraternity. Paying more attention to that job than he did to his studies resulted in low grades; he dropped out of school in 1973 and enlisted in the U.S. Air Force.

Five months later, Hanania became the target of bitter anti-Arab attitudes from fellow servicemen and officers when Egypt and Syria attacked Israel in an attempt to regain land they had lost during the 1967 Six Day War. "I quickly recognized more than many others in my own [Arab American] community, that the real war was the war that we were losing in the American media," he wrote in *I'm Glad I Look Like A Terrorist.* "Americans want simple answers. The American media gave them simple explanations.... I needed to become involved in journalism. I took it for granted in high school, ignored it in college, recognized how important it was during my service in the military and during the 1973 Arab-Israeli War [also known as the Yom Kippur War to mark the day that Arab states attacked Israel; a cease-fire agreement was eventually signed with the help of the United States and the United Nations], and made a decision to master it."

FBI target

Hanania decided to begin writing a book on the history of the Palestinian struggle for independence. He spent his off-duty time in the air force base library reading every book he could find about the Middle East. He requested information from organizations representing all sides of the question, in this country and overseas. He received answers from, among others, the International Red Cross headquarters in Switzerland, former Israeli Prime Minister Menachem Begin (men-AH-hem BAYG-en; 1913–1992), and Palestine Liberation Organization (PLO) headquarters in both New York and Beirut, Lebanon. The PLO and several other groups he heard from were officially considered terrorist organizations by the U.S. government.

He wrote in his autobiography that air force officials noticed he was getting "letters with strange postmarks, and sent by organizations blamed for some of the worst terrorist bombings and airplane hijackings in world history." They considered him a troublemaker and reported him to the Federal Bureau of Investigation (FBI).

Hanania was discharged from the air force in 1975 when the United States downsized its military forces a few years after the end of the Vietnam War (1965–73; when the United States sent troops into South Vietnam to help them fight off their aggressive communist neighbor, North Vietnam). He then enlisted and served nine years in the Illinois Air National Guard.

Student activist

Now that his interests in journalism and Middle Eastern affairs gave him a real purpose for his education, Hanania enrolled at the University of Illinois in Chicago. He was elected president of the Organization of Arab Students on campus but was soon removed from office after being accused of "communicating with the Zionists" (that is talking with supporters of Israel).

Hanania began attending meetings of various Palestinian groups in the Chicago area. One of the people he met at these meetings was Ibrahim Abu-Lughod, a Northwestern University professor whom Hanania later described as "one of two chief motivators to push PLO Chief Yasir Arafat [1929–] to pursue peaceful negotiations with Israel in the late 1980s." Abu-Lughod invited Hanania to a meeting of the Arab American Congress for Palestine (AACP). Although the AACP was not considered a terrorist organization, it was under surveillance (careful watch) by the FBI for "criticizing the policies of a foreign country, Israel" (according to Hanania's autobiography).

Hanania was soon elected the spokesman for the Arab American Congress for Palestine. In that role, the twenty-four-year-old college student was invited to present the Palestinian point of view in a 1997 National Public Television debate with Abba Eban (1915–), a skilled public speaker who had held numerous positions in Israel's government. Hanania also presented his views on the pursuit for peace in the Middle East by writing letters to the editor that were published in major newspapers and national magazines like *Time* and *Newsweek*.

Fighting the FBI

Hanania still wanted to be a journalist. "I figured that as a reporter, I could influence the public, indirectly, and educate them on the real nature of the Arab community," he wrote in his autobiography. He worked on the school newspaper at the University of Illinois. He even published his own monthly newspaper, *The Middle Eastern Voice,* from 1975 until 1977.

In 1975 Hanania began to suspect that he was under investigation by the FBI. "Most of my friends and some business acquaintances reported they had been contacted by the FBI concerning my 'activities,'" he wrote in his autobiography. "As polite as they were, these FBI contacts regarding issues involving international terrorism caused great harm to how people looked at me and at other Arab Americans." Hanania requested information from the U.S. Justice Department. Finally, in 1977, he received a copy of a twenty-five-page report the FBI had prepared about him. He was outraged that the report unjustly made him appear to be sympathetic to terrorists. The report "began with the insidious [false] caution that they believed I was 'involved' in the activities of 'several organizations' supportive of Middle East terrorist organizations... but ended with the buried disclaimer that I was, in reality, 'concerned with bettering the Arab American community in Chicago.'"

Gets a beat

Hanania protested not only to the FBI, but also to his U.S. Representative, his two U.S. Senators, and his commander in the Illinois Air National Guard. Afraid that the investigation might keep him from finding a job, he asked that the report be destroyed. His request was denied. Nevertheless, he did get a job as a political reporter for the *Southtown Economist,* a Chicago neighborhood newspaper, in 1977. Assigned to the political beat, his job was to cover local government issues and events.

Hanania wanted to move up to the *Chicago Sun-Times,* the city's major daily newspaper. "I wanted the *Sun-Times* job because I believed that Arab Americans could never influence the news media from the outside as successfully as others were doing it from the inside," he recalled in his autobiography. By 1985, when he was finally hired by the *Sun-Times,* his reporting experience had changed his attitude. "My original motivation to become a reporter had changed from one of politics to one of profession. I loved being a journalist and I believed strongly in being objective," he wrote.

Different point of view

During his six years with the *Sun-Times,* Hanania covered city politics and rarely wrote about anything relating to the Middle East. There was one major exception, however. In 1990 he received a letter from an aunt who lived in Israel. Based on the letter, he proposed that his editors send him to the Middle East to write about the Palestinian experience. Although he argued that the paper had sponsored similar trips for Jewish reporters and had run articles presenting the Israeli viewpoint, his request was denied. He was given a leave of absence, however, so he took the trip at his own expense.

The *Sun-Times* published four articles Hanania wrote based what he saw in the Israeli-occupied West Bank. The articles, which are reprinted in his autobiography, drew complaints from some readers, but Hanania later wrote that "the editors agreed the stories were balanced and offered a compelling and insightful narrative of life under Israeli occupation, a perspective that was certainly unique." The following year, the newspaper nominated the series of articles for a Pulitzer Prize. Although Hanania did not win the prize, it was a significant honor to be nominated.

Hanania left the *Sun-Times* in 1991. He was accused of using his position at the newspaper to improperly influence a local political battle. He denied the charges and sued the newspaper for wrongful dismissal from his job and for damage to his professional reputation. He lost the lawsuit.

Adult activist

In his autobiography, Hanania wrote, "My mom wanted me to be a doctor or a grocer, but I never realized that I would someday grow up to be an Arab." Throughout his adult life, he has sought ways to understand what it means to be an Arab American and to try to share that understanding with both Arabs and Americans. In 1996 he began writing a weekly column on Middle East affairs for publication in several newspapers in the United States, England, the Middle East, and for distribution on the Internet.

He has served on the executive board of the Arab American Institute, whose objective is "to promote full citizenship participation among Arab Americans, by means of educational, research, and organizational projects for the advancement of Arab American leadership on all levels of U.S. society, [and] to impact domestic and foreign policy issues that affect Arab Americans." He has also served as national president of the Palestinian American Congress, whose goal is "to organize Palestinian Americans and empower them in the American political and social system."

Funny, serious man

Hanania's autobiographical book, *I'm Glad I Look Like a Terrorist,* is actually a collection of short articles and speeches Hanania wrote over a period of years. In the article that provided the book's title, he explained, "I am glad I look like a terrorist because it gives me a special sword to help destroy the stereotype that continues to injure my people, distort our image and to cause otherwise compassionate Americans to engage in hateful acts of bias." The book is subtitled "Humor and reality in the ethnic American experience." Hanania told *The News Circle* magazine that he feels "Humor can provide an excellent medium to break down the barriers that prevent people from understanding each other. That's what I hope this book achieves."

Hanania's second book, *Deir Yassin: Arab & Jewish Tragedy in Palestine,* first appeared on the World Wide Web in 1998, with a planned paperback edition to follow. A fact-based novel, it contains four stories about a Palestinian village that played a major role in the 1948 Arab-Israeli War (the first full-scale war between Arab states and Israel triggered by the formation of the Jewish state of Israel in what was Palestine). In the book's introduction, Hanania wrote, "I hope this novel will not only help people better understand Deir Yassin and the significant place it marks in the history of the Palestinian People. I hope it also helps objective people evaluate an event that had an impact on both Arabs and Jews, and allow Arabs and Jews, together, to consider each other's pain."

FURTHER READING

Hanania, Ray. *I'm Glad I Look Like a Terrorist: Growing Up Arab in America.* Tinley Park, IL: Urban Strategies Group Publishing, 1996.

"New Book Details Arab/Ethnic American Experience." *The News Circle* (April/May 1997): 76.

"Ray Hanania." *The Media Oasis.* http://www.hanania.com (June 3, 1998).

Samuel John Hazo

Lebanese-Assyrian-American poet

Born July 19, 1928
Pittsburgh, Pennsylvania

> "POETRY ... IS THE SOLE MEANS WE HAVE TO LEARNING THE ANSWER TO THE ESSENTIAL QUESTION, THE QUESTION OF WHO WE ARE."

Samuel (Sam) John Hazo, an athlete and former three-sport coach, contradicts the stereotype of a poet. His home office is furnished with a desk, a harp, and a weight-lifting bench. A former Marine, he writes powerful poems that capture the reality and inhumanity of war and says, "I find writing the most exhausting form of work." Hazo's poetry is an extension of his identity. A husband and father, he writes about the importance of love and family. A Christian, he records his search for the essence of human existence. A writer, he contends that the ultimate form of expression is silence—the absence of words.

Getting started

Sam Hazo was only six years old when his mother died. She came to the United States from the village of Atanit, near the biblical city of Sidon (now called Saida), in Lebanon. She was a nurse, but Hazo remembers her more for her musical abilities; she entertained at parties, singing and playing the oud (OOD: a mandolin-like instrument). Hazo's father, an

Assyrian immigrant from Iraq, was a peddler (a traveling door-to-door salesman) of linens and rugs. He traveled constantly, covering the east coast from Florida to New York. After their mother's death, Hazo and his brother, Robert, were raised by their mother's aunt, Katherine Abdou, who never married. It was not a typical childhood, but Hazo always felt loved.

Hazo grew up in Pittsburgh, Pennsylvania, and graduated in 1945 as valedictorian (highest-ranked student) of his high school class. Although his family couldn't afford to pay for college, Hazo was able to attend Notre Dame University in South Bend, Indiana, on a scholarship. After his sophomore (second) year, Hazo applied for a special program at Notre Dame that would combine the last two years of college with law school, which would allow him to become a lawyer faster than the traditional program. The dean rejected his application, thinking Hazo was too young for the program; World War II (1939–45; when the United States and other European countries went to war against Nazi Germany and Japan to stop their aggressions) had just ended, and many older, more mature veterans were attending college at that time.

Change of course

Disappointed about the law program rejection, Hazo changed his major to English. Looking back, Hazo is grateful for the rejection, as painful as it was at the time, because it redirected him to a career where he has found a deep sense of fulfillment. He attended a poetry reading for the first time while he was at Notre Dame. "It convinced me once and for all that the old saying about poetry was true: 'Poetry is to be said, prose read,'" he told *Notre Dame* magazine.

In addition to introducing him to poetry, Notre Dame also taught Hazo a philosophy he considers important. He learned, he told the university magazine, "what I have continued to believe ever since, namely that the final questions in literature are ethical, or, if you will, theological.... Literary creations confront us with man's nature as perceived by writers, and those perceptions are as complete or as limited as the author's view of man is."

College laid the foundation for Hazo's life work, but when he graduated in 1948 he still wasn't sure what he wanted from life. He worked first as a newspaper reporter, then joined the U.S. Marines in 1950. During his military service, Hazo started to get serious about writing poetry. "I had a lot of time on my hands, and I began rereading poems I'd read first in college," he told the *Renascence* literary journal. "I realized that it wasn't just a hobby anymore. It was a way of getting me through certain days, certain times, certain problems I was just working out in the writing."

For two years after leaving the U.S. Marines, Hazo taught high school; he also coached football, basketball, and baseball (he had played varsity softball in college). He married Mary Anne Sarkis in 1955. Their son, Samuel Robert, would eventually carry on the Hazo musical tradition by playing in a rock band as a teenager and later by directing the Duquesne (doo-KANE) University (a Catholic university in Pittsburgh), marching band.

By 1958 Hazo was developing a clearer sense of his career goals, and he began teaching at Duquesne University while he was working on a master's degree in English. He continued to teach at Duquesne while he earned his Ph.D. ("doctor of philosophy" degree is the highest academic degree in most fields of science, social science, and humanities) in 1957 from the University of Pittsburgh. In fact, he has stayed on the Duquesne faculty throughout his career. He told *Renascence* that even if he were offered a job at a larger or more famous university, he wouldn't be interested. "Things that would have tempted me ten or twenty years ago would now just be an annoyance to me." The things that matter to him are writing his poetry, being with his family and friends, and teaching at a school where graduates go on to become community leaders.

Filling the pages

Hazo's first book, *Discovery and Other Poems,* was published in 1959. During the next forty years, he composed thirteen additional volumes of poetry, wrote four novels, translated four volumes of essays and poetry, wrote a book of literary criticism, edited a collection of religious poetry and a set of essays, and wrote three volumes of his own essays. He even wrote a play that was recorded and marketed on videotape by Comstock Video (1994)—the production's musical score was composed by Hazo's son. Hazo's work has ranged from scholarly topics like *The Christian Intellectual: Studies in the Relation of Catholicism to the Human Sciences* to light-hearted poems like "Rhyme for the Very Pickled," which he wrote for the one-hundredth anniversary of the H. J. Heinz Company and read on a sound recording accompanied by the American Wind Symphony Orchestra.

However, most of Hazo's work has involved trying to examine and understand the most profound of human emotions and experiences. His play, *Until I'm Not Here Anymore!*, explores the struggle of a laborer in an industry that is barely staying in business. His novel *Stills* concerns news photographers covering Lebanon's civil war in 1975. Some of his poems, such as "Maps for a Son Are Drawn as You Go," look at the responsibilities of parenthood; others, such as "The Drenching," explore the nature of life and death; and still others, such as "Between You and Me," focus on love and human relationships. In his poetry, Hazo tries to follow an emotion so deeply into the human soul, peeling everything else away, that the "nothing that is left is everything."

Universal voice

Hazo is conscious of his Arab background, and he closely follows events in the Middle East. However, he told *Renascence* that he avoids writing about Arab topics because "you can write out of ethnic or national feeling and mistake it for inspiration. It has the same intensity. Some other people may be able to do it well. I can't." He told *Aramco World* that poems should speak "to everybody at all times," without being limited by the poet's individual frame of reference. "Being an American of Arab origin has nothing to do with it and shouldn't and can't have."

Hazo applied this concept to his novel *The Very Fall of the Sun*, the story of a guerilla (an independent soldier who uses violence and intimidation to further a cause) who kidnaps an American professor. Their experience is not limited to a particular country or political movement because Hazo kept the soldier's nationality vague. His reason, he told historian Gre-

> ## POETRY WITHOUT WORDS
>
> "Poetry by definition is an act of saying what can't be said. You hint at it.... With poetry, where the principle is basically less is more ... you try to reach a point in poetry where the language is so transparent that to the reader it's hardly there. The ultimate poetry, if you are the perfect poet, is silence.... Silence is ultimately the only universal language.... If you are incapable of that perfection without the poem, then the poem helps you create that silence. After you read a poem, after you see a particular play, or after you hear a particular piece of music, you don't want to talk for a minute or two. You want to just enjoy the silence that the poem has created."
>
> —*Samuel Hazo, as quoted in* Renascence.

gory Orfalea (see entry) in *Before the Flames,* was that "Violence has never been part and parcel of any one people and the question of fighting something within the limits of the law and finding out you can't is a universal struggle."

Power of poetry

Despite the fact that his writing encompasses many types of prose and verse, Hazo sees himself as a poet. "Poetry ... is the sole means we have to learning the answer to the essential question, the question of who we are," Hazo told the Pittsburgh *Standard-Times* newspaper. In fact, he believes that the dreariness and violence of modern American society is related to the fact that poetry is not widely read. "Poetry brings us face to face with our real natures, where feelings are as important as thoughts," he told *Notre Dame.* "If we lose contact with our real natures, we lose contact with ourselves, and that is tantamount [the same] to losing our souls. It can happen to anyone who is deprived of poetry. It can happen to a nation. That is why we cannot live fully without the insights and pleasure that poetry can give to us."

According to the publisher of Hazo's book *The Past Won't Stay Behind You: Poems,* "Samuel Hazo likes to think of poetry as art in the present perfect—that tense in English from which events in the past continue into the present." The publisher continues, describing the contents of the book: "Sometimes a poem ends with a kind of answer, sometimes in anger, sometimes in dismay or amazement, but every poem is a duel with reality."

"[Poetry] is a time when suddenly things come into focus, and you work under the imperative [power] of some impulse, something you did not will into being, that came to you, and you must work it out in words that are just now coming to you, that are making you put everything that you have at that moment right on the line," Hazo told *Renascence.* "I find writing the most exhausting form of work.... When you're finished, it's as if somebody has taken a sponge and squeezed it dry."

Technique versus content

Hazo told *Renascence,* "It is not just a matter of words and punctuation marks and ink and paper. It is your life that is being passed on. That is why those who think that writing is merely a craft are so far from the mark. It is as fundamental and mysterious a force as blood." Hazo sees the essence of poetry as a form of expression that is deeper than language or technique.

Hazo told *Notre Dame* that "Poetry is not technique. It is a visionary way of looking at life." Nevertheless, he is also aware that technique is important since poetry needs language for its vehicle. He told *Renascence,* "In some cases the best lines in a poem are the ones that you hear between the actual printed lines. It's what's evoked by what is there, the space between words or the pause between words or the space between sentences.... One aspect of language is a way of coming to terms with what we almost know."

Acts on conviction

Putting into action his conviction that people need poetry, as individuals and as a society, Hazo founded the International Poetry Forum in 1966. The forum's mission is to sponsor public performances of poetry, both by the poets themselves and by actors, musicians, and singers. During its first thirty years, the forum averaged twenty-five presentations a year, at sites ranging from school auditoriums to Pittsburgh's famous Carnegie Hall theater and the Smithsonian Institution in Washington, D.C. Poets from thirty-six countries in addition to the United States have participated, as have Academy Award-winning film stars.

In its fourth decade, the forum sponsors workshops that bring poets into schools to work with teenagers. The public poetry readings continue to be popular with a broad audience ranging from accountants to janitors. Adults who were once dragged to the readings as children keep coming back.

Official poet

In 1993, Pennsylvania named Hazo its first poet laureate, or official state poet. He was surprised at the honor, and he accepted it thoughtfully. For example, he asked that his term be limited to three years and that he not be paid for his services. He explained to *Notre Dame,* "A writer should not be an employee of the state. I did not want to be caught up in possibly being asked to write poems to celebrate political victories or other sideshows that I would have to refuse."

At his installation ceremony, he said that he did not intend to simply "cough up poems" for various official occasions. Rather, he promised, "I will try to enhance the presence of poetry in our public life."

FURTHER READING

Apone, Carl Anthony. "Art of the State." *Notre Dame* (Spring 1995): 28–31.

Hazo, Samuel John. *Once for the Last Bandit: New and Previous Poems.* Pittsburgh: University of Pittsburgh Press, 1972.

Kapsambelis, Niki. "Pittsburgh: Famous for Hoagies, Football, Steel and … Verse?" *Pittsburgh Standard Times* (March 8, 1998).

Orfalea, Gregory. *Before the Flames: A Quest for the History of Arab Americans.* Austin: University of Texas Press, 1988, pp. 242–44.

Simarski, L. T. "Poetry in the Blood." *Aramco World* (July–August 1990): 53.

Sokolowski, David. "An Interview with Samuel Hazo." *Renascence: Essays on Values in Literature* (Spring 1991): 163–93.

A. Joseph Howar

Palestinian-American builder

Born c. 1879
Tur, Palestine

Died February 27, 1982
Washington, D.C.

Joseph Howar made himself into a millionaire—two separate times. After arriving in America as a young man with only $65, he earned a fortune. After losing it to a trusted friend who cheated him, he started over and earned another fortune. A generous and compassionate man, he built a school and a mosque (a building where Muslims worship) for his home village near Jerusalem and shared his wealth with family and friends. He was involved in various businesses, but primarily he was a builder who constructed apartments in the Washington, D.C., area. His crowning achievement was building the Islamic Center, an elaborate mosque and Muslim studies center in Washington, D.C.

Runs away from home

Howar was born Mohammed Issa Abu Al-Hawa in about 1879 in the village of Tur on the Mount of Olives outside Jerusalem. The village was then in Palestine, but it would later become part of Israel. He was spoiled by his mother, Eva, because he was the firstborn of her two sons and five daugh-

> "I DECIDED TO RUN AWAY AND TAKE MY CHANCES FAR FROM HOME. IF I MADE GOOD, FINE; IF I FAILED, NOBODY WOULD KNOW ABOUT IT BUT ME."

WHAT IS A MOSQUE?

Christians conduct religious services in churches, Jews worship in synagogues, and Muslims meet for prayer in mosques. The word "mosque" (MOSSK) comes from the Arabic word "masjid," which means "place for prostration" (Muslims pray in a prostrate position, touching their foreheads to the floor). The first Muslim house of prayer was the home of Muhammad, the religion's founder. Other mosques are based on Muhammad's house and courtyard.

Worshipers remove their shoes as they enter a mosque, stepping into the room with the right foot first. The prayer hall contains no chairs or pews. Worshipers sit on the carpeted floor, and they also stand and bow in unison during the prayer service. The most important feature in a mosque is the *qibla,* a marker that indicates the direction toward the holy city of Mecca (which is in modern Saudi Arabia). Muslims face this direction for various purposes including prayer and burial. In a mosque the *qibla* is usually a *mihrab,* a chamber occupied by the prayer leader. Besides the prayer room, a mosque includes a courtyard that contains a fountain or well that provides water for ritual washing.

Both men and women may enter most mosques for prayer; however, they are separated by either space or time to minimize distractions.

For more information about mosques and Muslim prayer services, visit the CIAS Web site at http://i-cias.com/e.o/mosque.html.

---

ters and had suffered a nearly fatal childhood case of scarlet fever that left him frail. His father, Issa Abu Al Hawa, was harsh, demanding, and critical. When the boy was sixteen, the age at which young men normally became full-time farmers and got married, his father unleashed his frustration forcefully one day. He shouted to his wife, "This boy is worthless, and he will remain worthless if you continue to spoil him and fill his head with wild ideas. He won't be worth the peel of an onion."

"I was deeply hurt that day, and I made up my mind that if I stayed with my parents I never would amount to anything," Howar said in his biography. "I would turn out to be as worthless as my father already thought I was. I decided to run away and take my chances far from home. If I made good, fine; if I failed, nobody would know about it but me." During the night, he said a silent good-bye to his sleeping mother and left.

Having overheard people in Jerusalem talking about America, the boy decided to stow away on a ship and go to that land of opportunity. He went to the port of Jaffa and hid himself aboard the largest ship in the harbor, thinking it would be the one most likely to be taking such a long voyage.

False starts

The German crew discovered the boy the following morning and took him to their captain. Despite the language barrier, the boy explained he wanted to go to America. The crew laughed and said they were headed for Egypt. Rather than turning back, the captain told the boy he could stay on the ship but would have to work for his passage. He was assigned to assist the cook. In Egypt, he found work in a restaurant, which provided him with food and shelter while he prepared to try the voyage to America another time.

Returning to the docks, he again sneaked aboard the largest ship he could find. The next morning, he came out of hiding to throw himself at the mercy of the captain. Surprisingly, he found himself in front of the same German captain, who told him the ship was now headed for India. He went back to work in the galley. In India, he worked as a servant for a man he met at a mosque. After working for two years in India, he used his savings to buy a ticket on a ship, still intent on reaching America. He went as far as his ticket would take him, then he got a job and saved for another ticket. Eventually, he made his way back to Egypt, where he worked in a hotel. Three years after he had left Tur, he finally bought a ticket for England, knowing that from there he would be able to sail for America.

Incredibly, the England-bound ship turned out to be manned by the same German crew he had encountered twice before. On board, he met a Christian missionary who hired him to work as his servant in England. During the years he was saving for his next ticket, he enjoyed a pleasant life and began corresponding with his mother. In 1904, eight years after leaving home, the boy bought passage on a ship bound for New York.

Reaches America

Hearing a rumor that Muslims were not allowed to enter America, the boy began calling himself Ibrahim Yussef Hawa. When he landed at New York's Ellis Island, he gave his new name to the immigration officer. The official made the name sound more American and misspelled the last name; the boy became Abraham Joseph Howar.

When the immigration officer asked to what city Howar was going, Howar asked where the king lived. Hearing that America had a president instead of a king and that he lived in Washington, D.C., Howar replied, "Then, that is where I will live too. If it is good enough for the President, it will be good enough for me."

Up the job ladder

Howar's first job in Washington, D.C., was cleaning silver in a hotel restaurant. Soon, he met some Arab peddlers who convinced him that he could make more money selling merchandise door-to-door. "Peddling not only gave me more money, it gave me my independence," he said later. He sold needles and thread at first but then decided it would be more profitable to sell something more special. He began peddling fine laces and silk robes. The success of his new venture encouraged him to try other creative approaches to peddling. He bought a bicycle with a storage compartment on the back. With the bicycle he didn't have to depend on public transportation to reach market neighborhoods, and it enabled him to reach wealthier communities. One of his customers started making appointments for him to come at a certain time and then began inviting her friends to see his merchandise. This led to a trend of having "dress parties" at the homes of other regular customers.

In 1907, Howar applied for U.S. citizenship. His birth had not been recorded, so he nearly panicked when the judge told him he couldn't become a citizen without proof of where and when he was born. He asked an Arabic friend to come and swear that he was from the same village and knew when Howar was born. The friend agreed, the judge accepted the application, and Howar became an American citizen.

World War I (1914–18; a war that started as a conflict between Austria-Hungary and Serbia and escalated into a global war involving thirty-two nations) brought a wave of new people to the nation's capital, and many of them were reluctant to buy from peddlers. Howar convinced a friend to become his partner, and they opened what he envisioned as "the most elegant women's clothing store in Washington, D.C." The business flourished.

Builds a new career

In 1920, Frank White, an architect Howar knew, asked him to invest money in an apartment building he wanted to build. "I was already a partner in a very successful business, but the excitement of creating something wasn't there anymore," Howar recalled. "When White came to me with this proposition, I realized what I was missing. So I took him up on it." Howar wanted to be more actively involved in the project than just providing the money. He asked his partner to run the clothing store for him, and he started learning everything he could about constructing buildings.

"While White was drawing up the plans, every day I would go out to some construction site to see how they did things," Howar explained. When their own building got started, Howar watched its construction carefully. "By the time we were finished with that first building, I knew what I wanted to do. I wanted to be a builder." At the age of forty-one, he started a completely new career.

Howar built another apartment building with his friend, then another one with a different architect. On each project, Howar planned and supervised the building process. As he had with the peddling business, he tried new techniques. He had noticed that other builders used a different foreman for each task (such as carpentry, bricklaying, and cement mixing); the foremen often disagreed with each other on how to do something, and they wasted a lot of time arguing about it. Howar hired only one foreman to supervise and coordinate all the tasks. The strategy worked. "We began completing buildings in three or four months that it was taking other builders nine months to do," Howar recalled.

Goes home

Twenty-five years after leaving Tur, Howar decided it was time to visit his family. He came home with ten trunks full of gifts and treated the entire village to a feast. His father had died, but he had a joyful reunion with his mother, brother, and sisters. He donated money to build a school for the village. "When you have a heart and a little money, and you see poor people, you decide to help them," he recalled in his biography. He had a new house built for his mother, and provided money for her and his brother to make pilgrimages to the Muslim holy city of Mecca.

When it was time for him to return to America, he said good-bye to his mother. She accepted the fact that he would leave, but she asked him for a promise. "She wanted me to take a wife who was a Palestinian," he remembered. "She was concerned that if I married an American, I might get a woman who wouldn't understand me or our ways, or that I might not marry at all." Howar agreed to return in a few years to find a wife.

Chooses a wife

By 1927, Howar had built eight more apartment buildings and was planning the construction of two more. As a forty-eight-year-old millionaire, he headed home to Palestine to find a bride. Tradition called for him to accept a marriage arranged by his family, but he insisted on doing things differently. He accepted the fact that he and his bride could not communicate with each other before they were engaged, but he insisted on seeing what she looked like first. A friend told him that the mayor of the city of Acre had four beautiful, cultured daughters. Howar and his friend went to Acre and sat in a sidewalk cafe near the mayor's home. When three young ladies walked by, the friend told Howar they were the mayor's daughters. He watched them and decided he wanted to marry one of them, eighteen-year-old Badria "Bader" Haki.

Howar's friend met with the mayor to discuss Howar's proposal. As a dowry (gift for the bride's family), Howar offered a generous sum of money and a new house. He also swore that he would "honor the young woman with the utmost respect and affection." The mayor accepted, and the wedding took place within weeks. After a two-week honeymoon in Jerusalem, Howar and his wife left for the United States, stopping along the way in Egypt and France, where Howar bought her a new wardrobe. Despite the difference in their ages and the decision to marry without knowing each other first, Howar and his wife had a very happy marriage.

Poor again

The couple eventually had five children. Although the Great Depression (1929–39; a period in U.S. history in which the economy declined sharply and many people could not find jobs) began in 1929, Howar's business remained strong until 1931. Howar had entrusted his good friend, Ed Rheem, with managing his financial affairs, even giving Rheem a power of attorney that allowed him to make decisions without consulting Howar. In early 1931, Howar learned that Rheem had been stealing money from him and cheating other people too. Rheem was sent to prison, and Howar lost practically everything he owned.

According to Howar's biographer, he was very depressed for a few months: "I didn't know if I was going to live or die, things happened so rapidly. The worst was the day that we moved from our luxury apartment.... I waited in the downstairs hall for a man to come and buy the Pierce Arrow limousine that the chauffeur used to drive me around in. I sat down and I cried."

Howar eventually realized something. "I came to this country with $65 and I made good.... 'If I did it all once,' I said to myself, 'I can do it again. Only this time, bigger and better....' So I started again." Following his original pattern, Howar began by opening a carry-out restaurant, selling sandwiches and hot dogs. After months of long, hard work, the business became profitable. As soon as he saved enough money, he used it to open a fashionable women's clothing store. When that business became profitable enough, he bought his partner's share and hired a capable assistant to help him run the store.

Building again

Eventually he rebuilt his business reputation and saved enough money to begin constructing an apartment building. Letting his assistant run the clothing store during the week (Howar worked the weekends), Howar finished the building in 1934 with a sizeable profit. During the next six years, he built eight more apartment buildings, including the first one with central air conditioning in Washington, D.C. He also built an elegant home as a gift for his wife in appreciation of her devotion to him even during years of struggle.

Crowning achievement

In 1940, Howar decided to retire. World War II (1939–45; when the United States and certain European countries went

to war against Nazi Germany and Japan to stop their aggressions) was making construction materials scarce. Besides, he was sixty-one years old, and he had five children. Now that he was a millionaire again, he wanted to enjoy his family. He and his wife continued their role as prominent socialites, hosting parties for Middle Eastern dignitaries who visited Washington, D.C. In 1944, Howar was asked to finance an apartment complex, and he decided to come out of retirement to build it. During the next three years, he built five more apartment buildings.

During the mid-1940s, Howar joined with other prominent Muslims to plan the construction of a mosque in the capital city. They raised money from American Muslims and from the governments of Islamic countries, whose diplomats lived in Washington, D.C. Howar served as the builder of the Islamic Center, which included a Muslim studies complex in addition to the mosque. The elaborate structure took five years to build and was completed in 1954. The king of Jordan and the president of Egypt presented Howar with medals in recognition of his work.

Gradually, Howar turned over the operation of his construction company to his sons. He and his wife continued to be social leaders in Washington for many more years. Howar died at the age of 103 in 1982, seven months after the death of his beloved wife.

FURTHER READING

Orfalea, Gregory. *Before the Flames: A Quest for the History of Arab Americans*. Austin: University of Texas Press, 1988, pp. 122, pp. 189–91.

Sweeney, Harry A., Jr. *Joseph Howar: The Life of Mohammed Issa Abu Al-Hawa*. Washington, D.C.: The Howar Family, 1987.

Abdeen Jabara

Lebanese-American attorney, civil rights activist, and former president of the American-Arab Anti-Discrimination Committee (ADC)

Born September 14, 1940
Mancelona, Michigan

Reproduced by permission of AP/Wide World Photos.

An attorney and a passionate civil rights activist, Abdeen Jabara has used his legal skills to defend the rights of Arab Americans. He has filed suits against several government agencies, including the Federal Bureau of Investigation (FBI) and the Federal Election Commission (FEC), asking that both agencies treat Arab and Israeli-Americans the same as they would any other Americans. While he feels that Arab Americans still face challenges in the United States, Jabara believes there is "strength in numbers." Organization and unity, he told the American-Arab Anti-Discrimination Committee (ADC), "is the only winning strategy for Arab Americans."

The old way of life

Abdeen Jabara was born in 1940 in Mancelona, Michigan, to Lebanese immigrants Sam and Mymonie Jabara. His mother was born in Lebanon in 1906 and migrated with her family to the United States when she was three. Mymonie's family settled in North Dakota, where they struggled to raise crops and animals in the bitter northern winters.

Jabara's father emigrated from Lebanon in 1920 and arrived in New York City with a piece of paper that read, "Boyne City, Michigan." He had been told he could find work in that town. Shortly after arriving, Sam Jabara got a job at a tannery, where animal hides were soaked in tannic acid to turn them into leather. After the acidic chemicals took their toll on Sam Jabara's lungs, he quit his job and went in search of a Lebanese wife. He heard of Mymonie and a marriage was arranged in 1924. "That is a way of life that doesn't exist anymore," Abdeen Jabara mused in an interview with a Michigan newspaper.

Sam and Mymonie Jabara settled in Mancelona, Michigan, where they opened a grocery store. The couple had seven children. "I was very close to my father," Jabara told an interviewer for *Cafe Arabica*. "He had a very strong sense of ethnic identity of which he was proud and he was not afraid to tell people. In the store, he spoke Arabic to my older brothers and sisters, even if it sometimes embarrassed them." In an interview with a Michigan newspaper, Jabara described his parents as pioneers. "After that generation passes, they break the mold. There aren't likely to be any more people with that kind of stamina and grit."

Lends a hand in the civil rights movement

Although Jabara learned from and admired his parents' fortitude, he did not learn their Arabic dialect. In 1958, he enrolled in pre-law at the University of Michigan, partly because the school had many Arab students and offered Arabic language courses. After studying the language for two years, however, Jabara decided that the best way for him to learn Arabic was to live in the Middle East for awhile, where he would have to speak Arabic. He spent five months in Cairo, Egypt, before tracking down his father's mountain village in Lebanon. He returned to the United States and finished up his undergraduate degree in 1962.

Continuing on to law school at Wayne State University in Detroit, Michigan, Jabara began his legal studies as the Civil Rights movement (a movement in which black Americans fought to challenge segregation and achieve racial equality) was erupting in the South. Some northern law firms, including the one Jabara worked for, sent lawyers to the South to defend civil rights activists. At Wayne State, Jabara founded a local chapter of the Civil Rights Research Council, a group that studied racial and legal issues. He received his law degree in 1965.

After finishing law school, he returned to Lebanon for a year to improve his Arabic. He took several months of classes before finding a job with the Palestine Research Center, where he contributed to written reports. In the fall of 1966, he returned to Detroit, where he opened his law practice.

"Operation Boulder" gets rolling

Jabara became involved in Arab American causes the following year, after the 1967 Six Day War (a six-day battle during which Israel defeated Egypt, Syria, and Jordan, taking territory that had been controlled by Egypt) touched off a period of intense anti-Arab prejudice in America. "It was as if someone opened a huge floodgate of anti-Arab sentiment in the media," he told *Cafe Arabica*. "The American media trumpeted Israel's victory as if it were our own." In response to the rise in anti-Arab prejudice, a group of Arab American professors, students, and graduates met at the University of Michigan in 1967, eventually forming the Association of Arab American University Graduates (AAUG). In 1972 Jabara was elected president of the organization.

In the 1970s, President Richard M. Nixon's (1913–1994) administration started "Operation Boulder," a pooling of the Federal Bureau of Investigation (FBI) and several other agencies' resources to combat Middle Eastern terrorism. As part of the operation, the government closely watched the activities of Arab sympathizers like Jabara. It collected a 400-page file detailing many of Jabara's activities, which included writing articles, giving speeches, and defending clients. "[The operation] was used to create the pall of fear around [Arab Americans]," Jabara said in a 1998 interview. "They wanted to create informers in the Arab American community, they wanted to create the sense that the FBI was watching everybody."

Jabara launched a two-step attack on "Operation Boulder": he drew media attention to the operation by running informative ads in newspapers like the *New York Times*. He also sued the FBI for harassing him and illegally recording his discussions while he was simply exercising his First Amendment right to freedom of speech (given to every American citizen by the Constitution of the United States). With the aid of

"OPERATION BOULDER" GETS ROLLING

After the 1972 Olympic games in Munich, Germany, in which Palestinian terrorists killed eleven Israeli athletes, the Federal Bureau of Investigation (FBI) launched a program called "Operation Boulder." Its purpose was to monitor the activities of "ethnic Arabs"—anyone descended from Middle Eastern parentage—in order to root out any sources of Arab terrorism. To do this, the FBI closely examined all Arab applications for visa (permission to reside in a foreign country) and compiled information on the activities of Arab American activists. Thousands of Arab Americans were interrogated (questioned) and hundreds of Arabs were denied entry into the United States or were prematurely deported (expelled), according to information provided by the American-Arab Anti-Discrimination Committee (ADC).

Other cases of anti-Arab activity included an FBI interrogation of an Arab American engineer who lived in Kansas City, Missouri in 1972. The FBI told him that the bureau had information that he was a member of a terrorist group. The engineer complained to the local FBI office about the unfounded claim, and was told that the FBI uses such questions to obtain information. When an Arab exchange student living in College Station, Texas, was called into his college advisor's office, he found an FBI agent there to ask him "numerous personal questions."

Perhaps the best documented "Operation Boulder" case is that of lawyer Abdeen Jabara, who later sued the FBI for violating his First Amendment rights of free association and speech. According to accounts in the *New York Times,* the FBI started watching Jabara in 1967, five years before "Operation Boulder" started, and it stepped up its investigation of him once the operation was under way. FBI agents and informers watched and followed Jabara, studied his bank records, tapped his phone, and questioned his neighbors, family, and friends. All of this was done because Jabara's association with several Arab American groups made him politically suspect, not because there was any real evidence that Jabara was involved in criminal activities.

"Operation Boulder" stopped when President Richard M. Nixon's (1913–1994) administration ended in 1974. In 1984, Jabara won his lawsuit against the FBI. The Supreme Court ruled that the FBI violated his First Amendment rights to exercise free speech and free political association by watching Jabara when they had no real evidence to support their claims.

the American Civil Liberties Union (ACLU), Jabara finally won his suit against the FBI in 1984. The bureau was ordered to concede that Jabara's activities were constitutionally protected and to shred most of his file.

Challenges Israeli organization

A member of the executive committee of the ADC since its 1980 founding by former Senator James Abourezk (1931–; see entry), Jabara became the committee's president in 1986. His next target: the American Israel Public Affairs Committee

(AIPAC). Jabara complained that although AIPAC was acting like a political action committee (PAC) by giving contributions to candidates, AIPAC was not following PAC regulations. The government requires any PAC that contributes at least $1,000 a year to candidates to register with the Federal Elections Commission (FEC). The group must file forms with the FEC, listing the sources of its income and the size of donations given to each candidate.

Jabara said that AIPAC controlled a number of PACs, telling the PACs which candidates they should support. Contributions from all of the PACs under AIPAC's umbrella exceeded the maximum campaign contribution limits allowed by law, he said. Because it was not an official political action committee, AIPAC could accept money from corporations and not pay taxes on it—something that PACs could not do. Worst of all, Jabara said, AIPAC was able to influence elected officials without many Americans knowing it. "The fact that [AIPAC is] the strongest special interest lobby and [is] unknown to the overwhelming majority of Americans indicates how effectively they were able to hide their role from public scrutiny," he told *Cafe Arabica*.

First Jabara filed complaints with the FEC, requesting that AIPAC be held to the same rules as other political groups. However, the commission said that AIPAC was not a political action committee because its main activity was educating public officials, not contributing to their campaigns.

Still, Jabara said that because AIPAC used a good deal of its $14-million budget to aid candidates, it was acting as a political group and should have to follow PAC rules. Jabara led a lawsuit against the FEC (*Akins v. Federal Election Commission*). In 1995, the U.S. Court of Appeals ruled that AIPAC was acting as a political action committee and should therefore be held to PAC rules. In 1998, the Supreme Court set aside the lower court's ruling and ordered the FEC to reevaluate the status of AIPAC. "We've been at it for ten years, and we may be at it for another ten years," Jabara said in a 1998 interview. "We're up against some very powerful forces."

From Rahman to RAWI

Jabara's term as ADC president ended in 1990. He has continued practicing law, and in 1993 he defended Abdel

Rahman, who was convicted on charges stemming from the World Trade Center bombing. He has also remained active with the ADC, contributing to the creation of the Radius of Arab-American Writers (RAWI), a network of writers that put on workshops for youth and help authors get their work published. "RAWI's emergence as a serious organizing effort of Arab Americans who are professionally or non-professionally involved in writing and the arts comes at a time of greater national awareness of Arab Americans as an emergent community within the American quilt of many colors—one whose experiences, traditions, and culture provided a very distinct hue that was neither black nor white," Jabara wrote in the *Washington Report.*

FURTHER READING

"Abdeen Jabara: A Champion from and of the Heartland." *Cafe Arabica.* www.cafearabica.com/people/peojabara1.html

Burnham, David. "Court Says U.S. Spy Agency Can Tap A Overseas Messages." *New York Times* (November 7, 1982): 28.

Burnham, David. "Judge Rules F.B.I. Violated the Privacy of a Lawyer." *New York Times* (July 8, 1979): A-15.

Jabara, Abdeen. "RAWI (Radius of Arab-American Writers) Provides Creative Matrix for Writers Across America." *Washington Report* (January-February 1998): 34. Available online: http://washington-report.org/backissues/0198/9801034.htm.

James Jabara

Lebanese-American fighter pilot

Born October 10, 1923
Muskogee, Oklahoma

Died November 17, 1966
Delray Beach, Florida

"ALL OF A SUDDEN I HEARD A NOISE THAT SOUNDED LIKE A POPCORN MACHINE RIGHT IN MY COCKPIT. I LOOKED BACK AND SAW TWO MIGS FIRING AT ME, AND I COULD SEE BLACK PUFFS FROM THEIR CANNON EXPLODING ALL AROUND ME."

Fighter pilot James Jabara was the world's first jet-to-jet ace. Pilots must have at least five confirmed victories over enemy airplanes to receive the title of ace. His combat career spanned three wars—World War II (1939–45; when the United States and certain European countries went to war against Nazi Germany and Japan to stop their aggressions), the Korean War (1950–53; when the United States sent troops into Korea to help South Korea fight off its communist neighbor North Korea), and the Vietnam War (1965–73; when the United States sent troops into South Vietnam to help them fight off their aggressive communist neighbor, North Vietnam). In addition to his personal combat accomplishments (more than twenty enemy aircraft destroyed), Jabara helped develop air war tactics and techniques for the U.S. Air Force, was involved with development and testing of a new fighter plane, and taught other military pilots. He continued to volunteer for combat service, not just for the excitement, but because of a deep sense of patriotism. His service to his country was cut short when he was killed in an automobile accident.

Sprouting wings

James Jabara was born in Muskogee, Oklahoma, but he grew up in Wichita, Kansas, along with his two brothers. His parents, Lebanese immigrants, owned a grocery store, and Jabara started working at the store when he was eight years old. He earned the Boy Scout's highest rank of Eagle Scout, an achievement that eventually allowed him to enter the air force officer's school without having gone to college. He was fascinated with books and movies about World War I air combat. World War I (1914–18) started as a conflict between Austria-Hungary and Serbia and escalated into a global war involving thirty-two nations. He read everything he could find about Eddie Rickenbacker (1890–1973) and Baron von Richthofen (1892–1918), the war's most famous American and German aces, and he watched *Dawn Patrol,* an exciting war movie about a British pilot, over and over.

By the time Jabara was in the sixth grade, he had decided he wanted to be a fighter pilot. Historian Craig Miner wrote that when Jabara was in high school, he had to start wearing glasses. Realizing that his poor vision would keep him from becoming a military pilot, he ate "twenty carrots a day for a considerable time." Whether the carrots helped or not, his vision did eventually improve enough so he could stop wearing glasses. The day Jabara finished high school in 1942, he enlisted in the U.S. Air Force. After attending four flying schools in Texas, he became a pilot in 1943.

First combat missions

In January 1944, Second Lieutenant Jabara began the first of his two tours of duty in World War II. Stationed in Europe for both tours, he flew a P-51 fighter in 108 combat missions. By the end of his second tour in December 1945, he had destroyed three-and-a-half enemy planes in air-to-air combat (he received half-credit for sharing one triumph with another pilot) and wrecked six more that were sitting on the ground.

According to historian Craig Miner, in one air battle, Jabara and a German pilot fought each other so aggressively that their planes collided and they both had to parachute out. Upon reaching the ground, they approached each other for a handshake out of respect for each other's bravery and skill. In a 1960 oral history interview conducted by Kenneth

Jabara was the first pilot to achieve ace status during the Korean War, flying the new F-86 Sabrejet. Reproduced by permission of AP/Wide World Photos.

Leish, Jabara described a battle in which "I just about hit a German pilot with my propeller; in fact, I probably did, because there was blood all over my airplane when I landed. Of course, I didn't mean to. There were airplanes and parachutes all over the place." He added, "You really don't think of him [an enemy pilot] as an individual until he jumps out of his airplane."

Jabara was twenty-two years old when he came home from World War II in January 1946. He decided to go to college. But just before his military discharge became official, the air force offered him a promotion, which he accepted. In the peacetime service, he became a civilian personnel officer, supervising the hiring of nonmilitary employees in the air force. While he was stationed in Texas, he got married. He and his wife Nina eventually had three daughters and a son.

Jet pilot

Bored and frustrated with his new noncombat role in the air force, Jabara applied for an overseas assignment and was sent to Okinawa, a Japanese island the United States had captured during World War II. In 1948, he had his first chance to fly a jet airplane. (The jet engine was invented in England in 1937; Germany developed the jet aircraft in 1942, but the United States military did not have jet airplanes until the end of World War II.) "I was at 10,000 feet before I remembered to raise my landing gear. It was so quiet and so fast," Jabara told Leish, describing his first jet flight. "I guess that was probably the happiest moment of my life."

Korea, scene I

It wasn't long before Jabara had a chance to take the jet fighter into combat. At the end of World War II, the country of Korea had been divided in half; the north was controlled by the communist Soviet Union, while the south was occupied by the democratic United States. In 1950, the communist government of North Korea tried to take over South Korea. In cooperation with United Nations' forces, the U.S. military pushed the northern invaders back out of South Korea. The communist government of China came to the aid of North Korea, and fighting continued until 1953 when a truce agreement was signed.

Jabara went to Korea at the end of 1950. Jabara downed his first plane on April 3, 1951. A week later he downed another one. The war had been under way for nearly a year at that point, and the F-86 Sabrejets had been in action for four months. The air force decided it would be good for military morale and for publicity at home for someone to achieve ace status in the jet age. Jabara's commanding officer was instructed to select one of his pilots as the leading candidate. "I decided on Jabara as the most likely candidate," the officer told *Airman* magazine. "Anything that was a milk run [a routine mission not expected to involve combat], he didn't go, and anything up on the Yalu, he did go and we saw that he was in the flight-leader position." (The Yalu River was the dividing line between the opposing forces.)

Jabara got "kills" number three and four on April 12 and 22. (Destroying an enemy plane is called a "kill" even if its pilot escapes unharmed.) On the verge of becoming an ace, Jabara hit a month-long dry spell. On May 7 his squadron was sent to Japan for a rest, but Jabara stayed behind to continue flying missions. "He wanted [ace status] very badly," his commanding officer recalled. "Nobody gets to be an ace by accident.... You've got to be more aggressive and that means more risk. So it's got to mean a lot to you."

Finally an ace

On May 20 Jabara and fifteen other Sabrejet pilots flew to the assistance of another group of Sabres that were being attacked by fifty Russian-built MiG-15 jet fighters. As the Sabre pilots prepared to enter battle, they had to discard their under-wing fuel tanks to make their planes more maneuverable. When Jabara tried to drop his tanks, one of them failed to release. Flying with only one tank left his plane unbalanced as well as unstreamlined. Gripping the control stick with both hands, Jabara wrestled to control the awkward aircraft.

According to air force policy, Jabara should have headed for his home base immediately when his tank failed to fall. But his aggressiveness took over, and he chased after the MiGs. He shot one down, then turned to look for more targets. As the fight continued, Jabara's wingman was diverted, leaving Jabara essentially blind. "Fighting in pairs was essential in jet fighter battles, as the speed and g-forces (a force equal to the pull of gravity that normally acts on an object) in aerial maneuver were so great that the attacker had to concentrate fully on the target and rely on the wing man to cover him and warn of other planes approaching," Miner explained. "The rule was that if you were separated from your wing man you disengaged and returned to base."

Jabara's aggressiveness prevailed again. He attacked and shot down another plane, scoring his first combat double (two kills in one mission). "All of a sudden I heard a noise that sounded like a popcorn machine right in my cockpit," Jabara recalled in "James Jabara: Hero." "I looked back and saw two MiGs firing at me, and I could see black puffs from their cannon exploding all around me." After a couple of minutes of pursuit and some help from a couple of his fellow pilots, Jabara broke free and headed for home. "On the way back I was so low on fuel that I had to shut my engine off and glide," he told Leish. "Then before I got back to our base, I started the engine back up and landed."

Quiet confidence

When Jabara had first arrived in Korea, his commanding officer noticed him immediately. "He was a 'Hot-Shot-Charlie' type," the officer told *Airman*. "He sang the loudest in the club, made more noise than others, dressed on the extreme side for the military—those sorts of things.... The thing that really impressed me was the maturing effect that the experience of becoming an ace had on [Jabara]. It settled him down. You could see a tremendous growth in him as a man. Once he got recognition and admiration from his peers, for his real achievement, those negative characteristics disappeared, just totally. And he became a very modest, almost classically modest hero type."

Both Jabara and his commanding officer warned the other pilots not to take the kinds of chances he had taken, but to follow the rules about unreleased fuel tanks and separation from the wingman. But because Jabara had just become the world's first jet-to-jet ace, his commanding officer told *Airman,* "I didn't take any disciplinary action as I might have otherwise. I sort of remember talking to him about it, sort of patting him on the back with one hand and chastising [scolding] him with the other."

On tour

The air force sent Jabara back home to America for a well-deserved rest and a national celebration of his accomplishment. Wichita welcomed him back with a big parade. He and his father, John Jabara, appeared on local and national radio and television programs. The presentation of his Distinguished Service Cross (the nation's second highest medal) was reenacted at a baseball game in Boston, Massachusetts. Jabara even appeared as the hero in an adventure comic book.

The publicity tour went international too. The U.S. government sent Jabara on a goodwill trip to Lebanon. He gave a speech in Merjayoun, the town where his father had been born. Miner reported that Jabara began his speech by saying, "I am an American. You are Lebanese. Yet the same blood runs in our veins."

Korea, scene II

Once again growing restless with stateside assignments, Jabara requested another tour of duty in Korea. He returned to the war at the beginning of 1953. By the war's end seven months later, Jabara had increased his total MiG kills to fifteen, becoming a "triple ace." This time, he insisted on a quiet return home, slipping into Wichita in civilian clothes so he wouldn't be noticed.

In between wars

Back in the States, Jabara received training on the newest version of the F-86 fighter plane, which shot rockets rather than bullets. For three years, he headed a squadron of the new aircraft based at Yuma, Arizona. Other fighter pilots from around the country would go there to train on the new equipment because there was plenty of open space for practicing. In 1958, Jabara took his squadron to southeast Asia during a period of tension between the communist Chinese government on the mainland and the democratic Chinese government that was in exile on the island of Taiwan. "We used to fly up and down the Straits of Formosa at Mach II, twice the speed of sound, and had the Chinese Communists take a look at us on their radar," he told Leish. "I'm sure it shook them up a little bit."

During the next several years, Jabara had several assignments as an instructor and as a commanding officer. For over a year he worked on the development of the F-104 star fighter. By 1966, Jabara was the youngest colonel in the air force; he was commanding a fighter unit based in southern Florida and was rumored to be nearing promotion to general. That year, at the age of forty-three, he flew a combat mission in Vietnam while he was there to deliver an airplane. Restless to return to action after seven years in the United States, Jabara volunteered for a 100-mission tour of duty in the Vietnam War.

As he prepared to head overseas, Jabara moved his family to a new home in South Carolina. The family drove up from Florida in two cars, Jabara riding in one driven by his sixteen-year-old daughter. She lost control of the car and it overturned, killing him instantly and fatally injuring her. They were buried together in Arlington National Cemetery in Washington, D.C.

FURTHER READING

Manning, Stephen O., III. "A Race for an Ace." U.S. Air Force *Airman* (November 1975). Available online at http://www2.southwind.net/~afakans/special.html (June 18, 1998).

Miner, Craig. "James Jabara: Hero." http://www2.dtc.net/~mthesket/jabara.html (June 18, 1998).

Joseph J. Jacobs

Lebanese-American engineer,
business man, and philanthropist

Born June 13, 1916
Brooklyn, New York

As a chemical engineer, Joseph J. Jacobs developed processes for mass-producing penicillin, B and C vitamins, and fertilizers. As an entrepreneur (an independent businessman), he developed a one-man business into a $1.7-billion-a-year company with more than 15,000 employees. As a philanthropist (a person who gives financial help to others out of goodwill), he is working on giving away most of his wealth in ways that will truly help others. As a patriot with two heritages, he gives his time, energy, and knowledge to organizations dedicated to strengthening the political and economic bases of both Lebanon and the United States.

New country, new name

Although his family name was Nacouzi, when Jacobs's father came to the United States, the sixteen-year-old boy told the immigration officer he was Yussef Ibn Yakoob. In his homeland of Syria (now Lebanon), it was customary for a boy to identify himself by his first name and the first name of his father (for example, "Joseph, son of Jacob") because many families had the same last name. Upon entering the United States in 1886, then, the young man became "Joseph Jacobs" as the immigration officer translated his name into English. He had come to America alone, but a friend of his family had immigrated earlier and was willing to help him get started in business as a peddler. The friend gave him (on credit) a suitcase full of sewing supplies, which the boy sold door-to-door. Eventually, he married Affifie Forzley, another Lebanese immigrant who had come to America at the age of nine. Their first six children were born in various eastern towns as the peddler traveled with his wares. By the time the seventh child, Joseph John Jacobs, was born, the family had opened a store and settled in Brooklyn, New York.

Proud of two cultures

The Jacobs family lived in a Lebanese community in Brooklyn. The parents continued to speak Arabic at home and with their friends. The children, however, spoke English, even with their Lebanese friends. Jacobs later wrote in *The American Enterprise* magazine, "Lebanon was a wonderful country of nostalgic memory, but the United States was our home, our future, and especially our opportunity.... None of us has had his pride in his Lebanese culture diminished by becoming an enthusiastic, loyal American."

Jacobs's father was a successful businessman. He had the good fortune to be the distributor for a straight-razor factory in Geneva, New York. This factory and a factory in Germany were the main sources of shaving razors for the United States. When World War I (1914–18; a war that started in Europe and eventually involved many other countries from all around the world) began, the German supply was cut off, and everyone had to get their razors from Jacobs's father—everyone including the U.S. Army. The family's good fortune ended after the war, when the safety razor was invented and people stopped buying straight razors. Jacobs's father started another business, which supported the family until his health failed. His illness developed during the Great Depression (1929–39; a period in America when the economy suffered after the Stock Market crashed. Banks and businesses closed and many people lost their jobs and homes and lived in extreme poverty), making it even more difficult for the Jacobs family finances.

Long days

When he was twelve, Jacobs got his first job, selling sodas and snacks at a stand in Prospect Park in Brooklyn. During the summer, he worked twelve hours a day to help support his family. Although he understood that the family needed the money he earned, he resented having to turn over his earnings. In his autobiography, he recalls, "I was not above stealing the odd quarter from Mom's cash box to spend on myself. To this day I remember the constant fear that I would be caught."

Jacobs's fear of being caught taking change from his mother was strong because his family stressed honesty and integrity. Still, there were several memorable instances when Jacobs faced the problem of balancing honesty and ambition. For example, he was surprised and troubled when his boss showed him how to use a scoop to shave curls of ice cream, forming attractive balls that were hollow in the center. He later wrote, "I was embarrassed enough to take a much thicker slice when he wasn't looking and therefore to leave practically no air in it." In another instance, Jacobs watched his best friend win a high-school election by stealing blank ballots and "stuffing the ballot box." Although this bothered Jacobs, he said nothing about it, being torn between telling on a friend and telling the truth.

Frustration

By the time he was thirteen, Jacobs knew he wanted to be an engineer, so he attended Brooklyn Technical High School. His father died, after a long illness, when Jacobs was sixteen. Although the family was poor, Jacobs's mother insisted that he attend college after graduating from high school. He enrolled at Brooklyn Polytechnic Institute. Because he worked at a soda fountain from six in the evening until midnight after attending classes all day, he was tired and frustrated. His grades were only average, and he had little social life.

When it was time to start his second year of college, Jacobs did an unusual thing and acted on his rebellious feelings. He took his tuition money and ran away from home. Without telling his mother first, he left New York and enrolled at the University of Iowa, where a friend had gone to school. He had to work at least as hard as he had the previous year in order to support himself. Neither his grades nor his social life improved significantly. At the end of the year, he returned home. "The humiliation of defeat burned inside me," he later wrote in his autobiography. Eventually, he realized that "Defeat cannot be avoided. That is the price of daring."

Confidence

Jacobs returned to Brooklyn Polytechnic Institute and graduated with a degree in chemical engineering in 1937. He then began taking graduate courses, earning a master's degree in 1939 and a Ph.D. (a "doctor of philosophy" degree—the highest academic degree in most fields of science, social science, and humanities) in 1942. While he was a graduate student, he taught classes and found he loved doing it. Through sharing his knowledge with others, he finally began to feel confident in his own abilities. He also enjoyed the research work in the laboratory. His grades steadily improved.

While in graduate school, Jacobs began dating Violet (Vi) Jabara. It was unusual for Lebanese women to attend college let alone graduate school in those days, but Jabara had graduated from Wellesley College. They married four days after Jacobs received his Ph.D. degree. After many years of marriage, he wrote in his autobiography, "One characteristic Vi helped me to crystallize was integrity. My various jobs had exposed me to all sorts of small-time chicanery [deception], exaggeration, and outright misrepresentation—the law of the street. I had been raised to respect pride, honor, and integrity, but it would have been easy for me to be persuaded that in the real world one needed to present a 'hollow' ice-cream cone or practice other deceptions in order to survive—especially during those hard days of the depression." Jacobs credited his success in business to "those values, ethical standards, moral fiber, courage, and the need to reach for seemingly unattainable goals," which he learned from his family and his community.

Lifesaving breakthrough

Although he was happy and comfortable teaching, Jacobs felt he needed to try something different after having received his Ph.D. "Should I settle for the security of something I loved doing and did well?" he asked himself. "For me, a measure of success was reasonably assured, but my father had found new worlds to explore. Should I do less?" So he left teaching to take a job with Merck and Company, a medicine manufacturer.

The United States had entered World War II (1939–45; when the United States and certain European countries went to war against Nazi Germany and Japan to stop their aggressions) seven months earlier. Because of his poor eyesight, Jacobs could not serve in the armed forces. It turned out that his work at Merck would be even more valuable to the war effort.

Penicillin, a powerful new antibiotic, had been discovered recently, and Merck had begun producing small quantities of it. Large quantities were desperately needed for treating wounded soldiers. Jacobs was given the task of figuring out how to mass-produce penicillin. The process he developed boosted the monthly production of penicillin from 80 million units to 650 *billion* units.

Shortly after completing work on the penicillin project, Jacobs became deathly ill. He was hospitalized for a week with alternating chills and fever that reached nearly 107°F (42°C, normal temperature is 98.6°F or 37°C). Sulfa drugs, the best medicine available at that time, did nothing against the bacteria that attacked his body. Because penicillin was classified as a military secret, his doctor didn't know it existed. Finally, a doctor associated with the Merck project broke the government's rule that limited penicillin for military use only and gave Jacobs a series of penicillin shots. In three days, his fever was down to 99°F (37°C). In his autobiography, Jacobs wrote, "I often wonder what compelled Dr. Richards to think I was worth saving and sometimes think that some of the decent things I've done during my life have been prompted by a need to justify his faith in me."

His own business

It was traditional for a Lebanese man to operate his own business. It was so important, in fact, that when a close friend of Jacobs who had worked for Mobil Oil Company for many years finally bought a Montgomery Ward store, his mother was actually disappointed. She said to Jacob's friend, "It's not the same thing, I meant [you should have] your *own* store!" Jacobs gained valuable experience himself working at Merck and later at Chemurgic Corporation near San Francisco, California, but he felt he wouldn't be satisfied until he started his own business. He's not sure how much of this desire was "in his blood" and how much came from his response to the expectations of his mother and his community. As soon as he thought he had enough experience, he quit working for someone else's company.

In 1947, Jacobs opened Jacobs Engineering Company to design chemical processes for manufacturing companies. At first, he had to earn extra money by selling equipment, but eventually the consulting business became profitable. In the early 1960s, Jacobs sold the equipment sales branch of his company.

Jacobs Engineering Group, Inc., as his company is now known, has become an enormously successful company. In 1997, it had 15,870 employees and sales of $1.8 billion. It has completed very successful projects, like the plant it built in Jordan to recover potash (potassium or a potassium compound) from the Dead Sea. Using technology developed by Jacobs and his staff, the plant has forty square miles of evaporation ponds that produce more than a million tons of potash a year at the lowest cost of any plant in the world. Jacobs found personal satisfaction in designing and building this plant in the Middle East. While working on the project, he traveled to Lebanon, met relatives, and explored his cultural heritage.

The company has also had its share of failures. For example, in the early 1960s, a potassium nitrate factory the company designed and built in Mississippi failed to operate properly when it opened. Jacobs spent six months at the site, figuring out how to solve its problems. Even managing his own company proved to be difficult. When profits were dwindling in the mid-1980s, Jacobs had to reduce the number of administrative employees from 1,800 to 1,200 and cut back on company spending, even for employee benefits like retirement funds. It was a painful experience, but it turned the company around and made it profitable again, eventually allowing it to hire many more people.

Giving it away

Jacobs and his wife raised their three daughters in a comfortable but simple lifestyle. During his early married life, he and his wife had little money to spend, and they felt no need

PHILANTHROPY

"Because we love you very much, we have decided that we are not going to leave you a lot of money," Joseph Jacobs told his daughters. He and his wife didn't want them to be spoiled by having too much money, or to worry that someone wanted to marry them for their wealth, or not to have the fun and pride of earning their own success. One of the greatest joys of his life was that they were neither surprised nor disappointed, and that they wanted to help him decide to whom he should give the money.

Some of the other wealthiest Americans have made similar decisions:

Bill Gates, founder of Microsoft: "I won't leave a lot of money to my heirs because I don't think it would be good for them."

Bernard Marcus, chairman of Home Depot: "If my kids want to be rich, they'll have to work for it."

Herbert A. Allen, investment banker: "If you're the child of a wealthy person and your first paycheck is totally meaningless, you've had something taken away from you."

Gavin O'Reilly, son of the chairman of the H.J. Heinz Company, speaking of his father's wealth: "It's his money, his estate. I have no claim on it. I'll have my own estate someday."

to act rich when they could afford it. When the Jacobs Engineering Company began to sell stock in 1970, the Jacobs' daughters (then in their twenties) read descriptions of the company's worth. They were surprised, and one of them said, "Gee, Dad, you're rich!" Jacobs and his wife hadn't given much thought to their fortune, and they decided they should figure out how to handle it.

Because they didn't want to deprive their daughters of the chance to make their own success (and learn from their own failures), they decided to start giving the money to worthy causes. They formed the Jacobs Family Foundation and, with the help of their daughters, are choosing which applicants to help. In his autobiography, Jacobs described its purpose: "By its charter, the foundation is to support engineering education and education in general. It specifically refers to humanitarian help and education for young Lebanese people. It also is to be used to provide help to the disadvantaged, not as charity, but as support for self-help and training with particular concern about preserving the self-esteem of those being helped." Like other business ventures, the foundation has had successes and failures. The family continues to learn how to make it work better; one of its goals is to figure out how to measure the effectiveness of philanthropic donations.

Jacobs is a member of the advisory board for the Progress and Freedom Foundation's (PFF) Center for Effective Compassion. He wrote in an essay published by PFF, "It is from my lifelong engineering training that I have learned to revere the 'freedom to fail.' For from 'failure' comes knowledge and from knowledge comes success." He also has a favorite cartoon mounted on his office wall. It shows Babe Ruth, the most famous home-run hitter in major-league baseball, with the caption, "Babe Ruth Struck Out 1,330 Times."

FURTHER READING

Brandt, Ellen. "The Existential Entrepreneur." *Chemical Engineering* (August 1992): 65-68.

"Fresh Honor for Two Distinguished Engineers." *Chemical Engineering* (December 1992): 109-10.

Jacobs, Joseph J. *The Anatomy of an Entrepreneur: Family, Culture, and Ethics.* San Francisco, CA: ICS Press, 1991.

Jacobs, Joseph J. "The Sane Multiculturalism of Brooklyn," in the "In Real Life" Department of *The American Enterprise* (September 1, 1996): 74.

Jacobs, Joseph J. "Why 'Social Engineering' is an Oxymoron." *Progress and Freedom Foundation.* http://www.pff.org/pff/jaco0125.html (April 1998).

Joseph Jamail, Jr.

Lebanese-American trial lawyer

Born October 19, 1925
Houston, Texas

By any measure, Joseph Jamail, Jr., is one of the most successful trial lawyers in the United States. As a plaintiff's lawyer, he represents people or companies who sue other people or companies, claiming physical, emotional, or economic damages from some wrongful action. He has been listed twice in the *Guinness Book of World Records,* once for winning the largest tort (personal injury) cash settlement to date and once for winning the largest civil damages award to date. Between the mid-1950s and the mid-1990s, he became the first lawyer to win a damage award of $250,000 and later became the first to win a damage award of $1 billion. During that period, he was the lead attorney on more than 200 cases that resulted in awards of $1 million or more. He has accumulated judgments and settlements totaling $13 billion for all of his clients combined.

From lettuce to law

Joseph Dahr Jamail, Jr., was the second of the five children of Marie (Anton) and Joseph Dahr Jamail. His father had emigrated from Lebanon with his parents when he was twelve. When they entered the United States and told an immigration officer the family name was "Gemayel," the officer spelled it phonetically as "Jamail." The family opened a produce stand in the downtown Houston, Texas, farmers' market and eventually developed the business into a chain of twenty-eight grocery stores. "My father was a very stern man, self-disciplined till you cannot believe, but kind, warm, a good daddy," Jamail told a *Washington Post* reporter. "He'd knock the bleep out of you if you needed it, but he'd love you, too.... He never really spoiled us rotten with material goods because he had a sense of values." Jamail's mother, whom he described to the reporter as a strong woman who influenced him greatly, was also a Lebanese immigrant.

With his mother's encouragement, Jamail started thinking about becoming a lawyer. One day, when two of Texas's most famous lawyers were going to face each other in a criminal trial, Jamail skipped school in Houston to go to Austin and watch the proceedings. "I knew right then and there, this is where the action and drama is," he told Donald Vinson, author of *America's Top Trial Lawyers: Who They Are & Why They Win.*

By the time Jamail graduated from high school, World War II (1939–45; when the United States and certain European countries went to war against Nazi Germany and Japan to stop their aggressions) was raging. He joined the U.S. Marines and was assigned to duty in the Pacific Ocean region. After being discharged in 1946, he attended the University of Texas (UT) at Austin, graduating in 1950 with a bachelor's degree in history. In 1949, he married another UT student, Lillie Mae "Lee" Hage.

Off on the wrong foot

Jamail stayed at UT Austin for law school, but he was an "undisciplined and unexceptional student," according to a *Los Angeles Times* article. He failed his tort law class, which deals with injuries suffered from the commission of a wrongful act. One teacher became so annoyed with Jamail's poor performance that he scolded him for taking up a seat in the class and suggested that he quit law school and go to work in his family's grocery stores. That got Jamail's attention; the *Los*

Angeles Times reported that the insult "inspired his passionate pursuit of a legal career and helped forge some of his best-known traits: determination, persistence, discipline and astute use of verbal abuse to throw opponents off stride."

While he was still in law school, Jamail won his first personal injury suit. A waitress he knew had cut her thumb opening a bottle of beer at work, so he and some of his classmates helped her sue the company that made and bottled the beer. "The beer company's lawyer knew none of us knew what we were doing," he told *People*. "The judge knew we didn't know what we were doing, so when the beer company offered a settlement of $750, we took it."

After he graduated from law school in 1953, he took a job with a private law firm. On his first day, he realized he would be working behind the scenes and wouldn't have a chance to try a case in court for several years, so he quit immediately. Instead, he became an assistant district attorney for Harris County, which includes Houston. "We tried sometimes two cases a week," Jamail told Vinson. In the year he worked for the county, "I know I tried sixty to seventy-five felony cases. That was the greatest learning experience of my young career." Interestingly, his boss was the prosecuting attorney Jamail had skipped school to watch as a boy.

King of torts

With a full year of courtroom experience behind him, Jamail opened his own private law firm in 1955 and began specializing in personal injury lawsuits. The *Washington Post* reported that his first "big" win was a traffic accident case. His client had lost control of his car and hit a tree. Jamail claimed that although his client had been driving drunk when the accident happened, it was the city's fault for the tree being there and causing his injury.

Over the years, Jamail became so successful at representing injured parties in lawsuits that other lawyers gave him the nickname "King of Torts." His parents, however, never quite agreed with his decision to focus on suing for damages. "[My father] really didn't like this ... suing businesses, being a sore-back lawyer [legal slang for a personal injury lawyer], and he was oriented the other way. So was my mother," he told the *Washington Post*. Jamail looks at it differently. After more than thirty years in the practice, he told *Forbes* magazine that personal injury law is still his "first love ... because [he's] helping people."

Making a difference

Each time Jamail files a lawsuit, it is to help his client, but sometimes it accomplishes more than that. For example, one of his most famous victories was a 1978 case involving the Remington Arms company, a gun manufacturer. A fourteen-year-old boy accidentally shot and paralyzed his father when they were hunting deer. The boy said the gun went off accidentally when he slid the safety (a device that keeps the gun from firing even if the trigger is pulled) into position. The manufacturer said this was impossible. Jamail told Vinson that while preparing for trial, "I put a guy from the [Remington Arms] company in front of a camera for a videotape, pointed the gun at him. I had it on safety. I nudged the safety button. The thing exploded, guy dove for cover. They didn't go to trial, wrote us a check for six million, eight-hundred thousand." That was the largest individual cash settlement in a tort case up to that time. But there was another, more important result: Remington Arms recalled 200,000 rifles to fix their safety devices. "A lot of my cases have social ramifications like those recalls," Jamail told Vinson. "I take a lot of pride in something like that."

Jamail's most famous case involved a contract dispute, rather than a personal injury. Pennzoil Oil Company had made a verbal agreement to buy Getty Oil company. Before the sale was completed, Texaco, Inc. made Getty Oil a better offer and Getty sold to them despite the fact that they had already agreed to sell to Pennzoil. Jamail filed suit for damages on behalf of Pennzoil.

During the trial, he reduced a complicated case involving intricate contract negotiations to terms a jury could easily understand. With his questioning, he got one witness to admit that Pennzoil and Getty Oil had made a valid deal before Texaco got involved. He also got another witness to admit that he thought it would be all right to break the agreement with Pennzoil simply because there was so much money involved. The case ended with a jury awarding Pennzoil damages of $10.53 billion, more than five times as large as any previous civil judgement in U.S. history. Although some observers credited the victory to Jamail's skillful questioning and the relationship of trust he established with the jury, he told *People* that it was just a matter of having the facts on his side. "Our evidence was as strong as an acre of garlic," he said.

Jamail is highly successful, but not unbeatable. Between 1967 and 1997, he lost one case. In the suit, he represented an airline company that accused another one of trying to force it out of business with unfair pricing. "[The loss] isn't going to do me in," he told the *American Bar Association Journal*. "If I can only fight for people who have straight flushes, lay-down cinches, then I wouldn't be much of a lawyer."

Because Jamail loses so rarely, defense attorneys would rather negotiate a settlement with him without going to trial. He told Vinson that in the previous twenty years, only 5 percent of his cases had ended up in court.

Unique style

When Vinson wrote his book *America's Top Trial Lawyers: Who They Are & Why They Win,* he interviewed and analyzed Jamail and thirteen other civil (not criminal) lawyers who were generally considered the best in the country. "Jamail's courtroom style is flamboyant and truly his own," Vinson wrote. "He considers himself enough of a 'ham' to enjoy the spotlight." On the other hand, Jamail told him, "When a lawyer decides that he wants that spotlight in the courtroom on himself, that he wants to be the star of the show, he is going to fall on his [rear] every time.... The great trial lawyer knows where in the courtroom to move that spotlight around. It ought to be on whomever is important. [The jurors] want to hear the story."

Knowing how to relate to jurors is one of Jamail's strengths. *Forbes* quoted prominent Texas criminal defense attorney Richard "Racehorse" Haynes as saying, "Joe talks to jurors just like they were neighbors, so that each of them feels they could go out to dinner that night and become lifelong friends. The law is an unquestionable bore sometimes, [but] Joe can make it all come to life." The *Los Angeles Times* quoted an assistant dean at Houston's South Texas Law School as saying, "[Jamail] is tremendously persuasive, easy to listen to and easy to believe."

TRIAL LAWYERS WHO WIN

Joseph Jamail was one of fourteen highly successful civil trial lawyers Donald E. Vinson selected to study when he was writing his book *America's Top Trial Lawyers: Who They Are & Why They Win*. Vinson is a consultant who helps lawyers select and analyze juries; in fact, he invented the concept of jury consultation in 1976. Vinson found that the best lawyers rated high in the qualities of intelligence, communication skills, judgment, self-monitoring (a person's ability to control emotions and behavior so as to be most effective), charisma (a personal magnetism that makes someone attractive or influential to others), honesty, competitiveness, drive, emotional maturity, self-discipline, objectivity, and a belief in luck.

Although many people think lawyers will do or say anything that would help them win their case, Vinson found that the best lawyers are unusually honest. Eleven of the fourteen listed honesty as the most important quality of a lawyer. Successful lawyers are also constantly aware of the jury and how jurors will react to courtroom events and the personalities of witnesses and lawyers. The best lawyers plan their cases carefully to present the most important aspects of the case as clearly and quickly as possible.

Successful lawyers also select their cases carefully and prepare them thoroughly before presenting them to a judge or jury. In addition, Jamail told Vinson that it is very important for him to like his client because the jury would be able to tell if he didn't.

Besides having a good instinct about selecting jurors and presenting himself (and his client) to them as likable and believable, Jamail also takes great care to present cases as efficiently as possible. He believes that jurors dislike feeling like their time is being wasted. He breaks cases down to their simplest elements and questions witnesses as briefly as possible.

All that money

Jamail is often the highest-paid trial lawyer in the United States; *Forbes* reported that his 1991 income was $60 million. His fee in the Pennzoil-Texaco case was more than $400 million. But he doesn't think other people should resent the fact that he is paid so highly. "We're supposed to applaud achievement," he told *Forbes*. "It isn't like I robbed a bank or something, or I accidentally lucked into this [money]. If I didn't win, I wouldn't get paid."

Like other plaintiff's attorneys, Jamail gets paid on a contingency basis—that is, if he wins he gets paid a portion (usually one-third) of the damage award. Some people think that such a fee is outrageously high. For example, he told Vinson about one defense attorney who tried to turn a jury against

Jamail by emphasizing how much he would be paid if he won. "The jury kept looking over at me in astonishment, because it was a lot of money," Jamail said. "Finally, the other lawyer asked, 'What do you think Mr. Jamail's going to do with that money.' Well, that invited me: 'Your Honor, he's now invited me to tell you and this jury what I'm going to do with my fee. Most of it I am going to give to Galveston [Texas] charities for underprivileged children,' and I sat down. My client won."

Jamail's offer to donate most of his fee was neither a phony gesture nor an unusual event. In 1996 he was ranked among the top twenty-five philanthropists (a person who gives financial help to others out of goodwill) in the United States. He and his wife have donated tens of millions of dollars to educational and medical institutions in Texas.

Doing what he loves

Jamail told Vinson there is nothing he dislikes about being a trial lawyer. He enjoys helping people, and he likes being famous. In spite of his incredible success, though, he still gets nervous before each trial. He told *Forbes,* "Until I start talking, I'm almost ready to puke. But then it goes away, and it's just like my mama has got me in her lap again. Here I am, and it's where I need to be, and it's where I belong."

FURTHER READING

Brower, Montgomery. "Houston Lawyer Joe Jamail Sued the $10.5-Billion Pants off Texaco and Stands to Pocket a Record Fee." *People* (January 6, 1986): 45-46.

Coll, Steve. "Down Home with Texas' $10.5 Billion Barrister." *Washington Post* (July 31, 1986): B1, B2

Mack, Toni. "Triumph of the Sore-Back Lawyer." *Forbes* (May 4, 1987): 33-34.

Sachs, Andrea. "A Rare Loss for Joe Jamail." *ABA Journal* (November 1993): 166.

Vinson, Donald E. *America's Top Trial Lawyers: Who They Are and Why They Win.* Englewood Cliffs, NJ: Prentice Hall Law & Business, 1994.

Whitefield, Debra. "3 Texas Lawyers Share Spotlight in Texaco Case." *Los Angeles Times* (December 13, 1985): Section IV, 1-2.

Ralph Johns

Syrian-American civil rights activist

Born 1916
New Castle, Pennsylvania

Died October 2, 1997
Los Angeles, California

On February 1, 1960, four black students walked into the Woolworth's drug store in Greensboro, North Carolina. They bought some toothpaste, combs, and a few other items at one counter, then stepped over to the lunch counter—the one place in the store where only whites were served. They sat down and asked for a cup of coffee, knowing that the waitress would refuse to serve them. It was the beginning of the first sit-in to peacefully protest the system of racial segregation in the South. Segregation was a practice that mandated the use of separate facilities—from drinking fountains to school buildings—by white and black people. The Greensboro sit-in lasted 175 days and sparked hundreds more throughout the South, making heroes of the four black students during the Civil Rights movement. The architect of the sit-in, Ralph Johns, is rarely credited for his role in designing the protest. He had persuaded the students to launch such a protest and made other contributions to the Civil Rights movement. Disappointed that his sacrifices remained largely unknown to most people, Johns told the *Los*

"SELDOM DO PEOPLE GET UP AND SAY RALPH JOHNS WAS A STALWART IN THE CIVIL RIGHTS MOVEMENT. I PERSONALLY DON'T FEEL HE'S BEEN FULLY APPRECIATED."

—*John Kilimanjaro, editor of* The Carolina Peacemaker

Reproduced by permission of AP/Wide World Photos.

Angeles Times in 1989, "I just want somebody to say, 'Hey, Ralph, thanks a hell of a lot for what you've done.'"

"Ruffles" crashes the boxing ring

Ralph Johns was born in 1916, the second son in a family of nine. Both of his parents were Syrian immigrants who settled in New Castle, Pennsylvania. Johns's father arrived at the age of fourteen to begin working at the town's steel mills. Growing up, Johns had an undying thirst for adventure: at age twelve, he began "crashing" boxing events, rushing into the ring after the matches to have his picture taken with the champion. He got to these events any way he could—hitchhiking, hiding in railroad cars, convincing pilots to take him on their planes—and by age twenty, he had been through forty-eight states, Canada, and Mexico. By this point he had crashed six Rose Bowl games, the 1932 Olympics, and every heavyweight championship since the Dempsey-Tunney fight in 1927, earning the "world's greatest gate crasher" title bestowed on him by the *Pittsburgh Post Gazette.*

Johns's crashing strategy varied. The night before the 1936 Louis-Schmeling fight, he slept under the ring in order to evade security. For another match, he spent the night at Yankee Stadium in New York to get past the guards. Only once was he unsuccessful: at a middleweight fight in California. Local police who anticipated his arrival handcuffed Johns to a fence outside the building. Calling himself "Ruffles" Johns, he wrote letters to sportswriters across the country, bragging about his crashing adventures. "I have carried more heavyweight champions to their corners than any man alive," he boasted to reporters.

In 1936, Johns announced he was going to crash the boxing events at the 1936 Olympics in Germany and then tour the world on $5 that boxing promoter Mike Jacobs gave him. On the ship to Europe, he was discovered as an unpaying passenger and was refused the right to land in London, England. Instead, he had to take the next boat back to the United States, and with that defeat, he gave up the crashing hobby. He enrolled at Duquesne (doo-KANE) University in Pittsburgh, Pennsylvania, but dropped out in 1937 to go to Hollywood, California, and pursue an acting career. Johns landed a few bit parts, usually in gangster movies, but after he failed to get the lead role in *The Life of Valentino,* he left Hollywood and returned to the East.

Gripes about Greensboro segregation

Johns joined the Army Air Corps in 1940, and he was stationed in the Caribbean—a logical assignment, because he was fluent in Spanish. He was later transferred to the army's Overseas Replacement Depot in Greensboro, North Carolina, where he was discharged at the end of his service in 1944. He married a local woman whose father helped Johns set up a clothing store on the 200 block of East Market Street. His interaction with blacks (who were the majority of his customers) as well as several earlier incidents—such as the time when a mob of whites in Mobile, Alabama, attacked him for riding on a freight car with a black hobo (a person who moves from place to place)—made Johns very passionate about the status of blacks in the South. In the late 1940s, he joined the local chapter of the National Association for the Advancement of Colored People (NAACP), and he posted small signs outside his store, reading "Special This Week: Love Thy Neighbor," and "God Hates Segregation." The city council—filled with whites who wanted to maintain segregation—banned Johns's signs, saying they blocked the public sidewalk.

As the dark-skinned son of immigrants, Johns felt he could identify with how blacks felt as outsiders of a white society. During a time in which blacks and whites could not even share a seat on a bus, Johns befriended many blacks and openly criticized segregation. He even wrote a column called "Buzzin' with Cuzzin'" in the local black newspaper. His actions made him a target of Southern whites who wanted the system of segregation to endure: Johns was the victim of several beatings and the recipient of numerous bomb threats. Fearful of further endangering his wife and two daughters, Johns took a more behind-the-scenes role in opposing segregation. His family's safety aside, he also knew that he could do nothing directly—it had to be blacks who would present the challenge to segregation by appearing in areas designated for whites.

Spurs the sit-in

In 1950, Johns asked black students from the nearby North Carolina Agriculture & Technical College (A&T) if they "had any guts." The students asked what Johns meant, and he explained: "Well, at the Woolworth five-and ten-cent store and at Kress [another similar store] you can walk in and buy pencils at one counter, you can buy all kinds of items at other counters but right across, five feet away, there's a lunch counter [where] you can't sit down and buy yourself something to eat. You have to buy [at the take-out window] but walk out. You can't eat there, you're not allowed to sit down and eat. And I says this is supposed to be a public place, it's not a private club. They're taking your money at all the counters but you can't go to the lunch counter like a decent citizen." Johns proposed that the store might be forced to change its policy if a group of blacks sat at the counter and asked for service. If nothing else, he said, a Woolworth's sit-in would draw public attention to the unfairness of segregation. However, most students replied that there was little they could do about the social institution of segregation—they just wanted to stay out of trouble and graduate from school.

In December 1959, Johns finally met a student who was willing to stage a sit-in at Woolworth's. At first, Joe McNeil was hesitant to stir up any trouble. After he was refused service at the lunchroom of the Greensboro bus station, he decided it was time to do something about segregation, even if it was only at the local level. He recruited three of his friends—Ezell Blair, Jr., Franklin McCain, and David Richmond—and they went to see Johns, who gave them tips on what to do and say. "I'll give you the money and you go to different counters and buy items but make sure you get a receipt and go to the lunch counter," he told them. "And when you go sit down they'll tell you, 'I'm sorry but we don't wait on colored or Negroes.' Then you call her a liar and say you do wait on us because here's the receipt to prove it. You waited on us five feet from here."

Johns handled all the plans for the sit-in. He set aside bond money to bail the students out of jail if they got arrested (they were arrested the following April for trespassing). Once the sit-in was under way, he tipped off local reporters, and during the 175-day sit-in, he wrote weekly newspaper columns under the name "Ricardo Raffles" supporting the students. Support also came from black leaders who took charge of the students' campaign for equality.

The forgotten rebel

The Greensboro Woolworth's sit-in did many things: it desegregated the lunch counters at Woolworth's and Kress, effective July 25, 1960. It demonstrated the power of student activism, showing that a few people could achieve substantial gains. It inspired others throughout the South to use the same peaceful sit-in to protest segregation. It helped give form and movement to the massive unrest that would grow into the Civil Rights movement of the 1960s. But it did not make Ralph Johns famous, within the movement or on a national scale. "Seldom do people get up and say Ralph Johns was a stalwart (a person supporting a cause) in the civil rights movement," said John Kilimanjaro, editor of Greensboro's weekly black newspaper *The Carolina Peacemaker*, in an inter-

The lunch counter sit-in became a popular tactic among students in the South during the civil rights movement. Reproduced by permission of AP/Wide World Photos.

CIVIL RIGHTS MOVEMENT

The Civil Rights movement was a massive campaign, starting in the late 1950s, that used peaceful means to protest the system of racial segregation in the South. Although legislation after the Civil War (1861-1865; when the states of the North [the Union] and South [the Confederacy] went to war against each other over the issue of slavery) gave freedom and equal rights to blacks in theory, many Southern states instituted the practice of requiring blacks to use separate public facilities from whites. Restaurants, trains, schools, and other public facilities—if they served blacks at all—required blacks to use different facilities. The 1896 Supreme Court ruling in *Plessy v. Ferguson* gave the federal government's stamp of approval on segregation practices that provided "separate but equal" facilities for blacks and whites.

The federal government's first steps toward racial integration came from World War II (1940–45; when the United States and certain European countries went to war against Nazi Germany and Japan to stop their aggressions), with the 1941 ban on discrimination in the defense industry and the 1948 desegregation of the armed services. After the war, the National Association for the Advancement of Colored People (NAACP) brought a series of cases challenging segregation to the Supreme Court. In 1954, the NAACP saw a victory with the ruling in *Brown v. Board of Education*. The court overturned the *Plessy* ruling and stated that separate facilities are, by nature of their separateness, unequal and therefore unconstitutional.

The Supreme Court decision gave blacks the backing of federal law to challenge the segregation practices of the South. One of the first people to issue such a challenge was Rosa Parks (1913–), a black woman who was arrested in 1955 for refusing to move to the black section of a Montgomery, Alabama bus. Parks's cause was picked up by a local Baptist minister named Mar-

view with the *Los Angeles Times*. "I personally don't feel he's been fully appreciated."

Tired of living in fear, Johns's wife left him in 1963, and took their two daughters with her. For more than thirteen years, his daughters were too bitter at their father—his views made them the outcasts of Greensboro society—to even speak to him. In an ironic twist, Johns's store had to close; as formerly segregated stores began serving blacks, Johns lost many of his patrons, mostly blacks who before could not shop anywhere else.

In the late 1960s, Johns started a Vietnam prisoner exchange, in which he offered himself in exchange for any American being held prisoner in North Vietnam. He recruited about 1,200 volunteers who agreed to participate in the exchange, but the State Department declined to pursue Johns's idea. Johns moved to Los Angeles, California, in 1970, and he took a job as the associate publisher of a weekly newspaper in tin Luther King, Jr. (1929–1968; African American preacher and civil rights leader), who organized a lengthy bus boycott that forced the bus company to desegregate and inspired similar boycotts throughout the South. The sit-in movement came five years later, when a group of black college students sat at the lunch counter of a Woolworth's store in Greensboro, North Carolina, and insisted on being served. This technique also inspired similar protests that forced the racial integration of stores and theaters.

In 1961, groups of black and white students called "Freedom Riders" began road trips throughout the South to challenge the segregation of transportation facilities. That year, more than 70,000 students (3,600 of whom were arrested) made "Freedom Rides" through twenty states. The Civil Rights movement culminated two years later, when blacks embarked on a massive march on Washington, D.C., to show support for the pending civil rights legislation. In 1964, Congress passed the Civil Rights Act, officially banning racial discrimination in public facilities. It was followed in 1965 by the Voting Rights Act, which outlawed tactics that some Southern states had used to stop black citizens from voting.

The movement began splintering in 1966, as more militant blacks who were dissatisfied with the rate of progress pushed for more violent means of protest, setting off riots in several major cities. The 1968 assassination of King touched off more rioting, further separating the militant and peaceful resistance divisions of the movement. Since then, the push for racial equality has taken such varied forms (from laws creating affirmative action programs to the April 1992 Los Angeles riots) that the efforts are not seen as part of a single, coherent Civil Rights movement.

Beverly Hills, California. He lived out the rest of his years feeling disappointed—and at times even bitter—that the Civil Rights movement failed to recognize him for his contributions and sacrifices. He died in October 1997 of heart failure.

Only a handful of people recognize Johns's importance in the Civil Rights Movement, and some of them are working to make sure that history recognizes him too. John F. Reid, who directs two mentoring programs at California State University at Fullerton, has been trying to find a publisher for Johns's autobiography, *The Forgotten Rebel*. "He was very wise, courageous and very loving servant who just wanted to help us," Reid told the *Los Angeles Times*. "I'm going to make sure everybody knows what he did, the sacrifices he made to help us." George Simkins, who served as president of the Greensboro chapter of the NAACP for twenty-five years, summed up Johns's contribution in a 1989 interview with the *Times*. "He was the sit-in. There's no question about it, it was his idea."

FURTHER READING

Abrams, Garry. "Forgotten Rebel." *Los Angeles Times* (May 5, 1989): V1.

Wolff, Miles. *Lunch at the 5 & 10*. Chicago: Elephant Paperbacks, 1990.

Index

Italic type indicates volume numbers. **Boldface** type indicates biographies and their page numbers. Illustrations are marked by (ill.).

A

Abboud, Joseph *1:* **1–5**, 1 (ill.), 3 (ill.)

Abdul, Paula *1:* **6–11**, 6 (ill.)

Abinader, Elmaz *1:* **12–17**

Abourezk, James *1:* **18–25**, 18 (ill.)

Abraham, F. Murray *1:* **26–32**, 26 (ill.), 31 (ill.)

Abraham, Spencer *1:* **33-38**, 33 (ill.), 34 (ill.)

Abscam scandal *1:* 24

Abu-Lughod, Ibrahim *1:* 207

Academy Awards *1:* 29, 79, *2:* 489

ACLU (American Civil Liberties Union) *1:* 231

ADC (American-Arab Anti-Discrimination Committee) *1:* 24, *2:* 333, 345

Addes, George *1:* **39–47**, 39 (ill.), 44 (ill.)

Administration for Children and Families *2:* 435

AFL (American Football League) *2:* 384, 387

AFS (American Field Service) *1:* 85

AIPAC (American Israel Public Affairs Committee) *1:* 231–232

Air Force, U.S. *1:* 77, 144, 206–207, 235–237, *2:* 505

Air National Guard *1:* 207

al-Khwarizmi, Mohammed ibn-Musa *1:* 122

Albert Schweitzer Award *1:* 29

Amadeus 1: 29

AMA (American Medical Association) *1:* 62

American Beverage Institute *2:* 288

American Civil Liberties Union (ACLU) *1:* 231

American Federation of Labor *1:* 43

American Field Service *1:* 85

American Football League (AFL) *2:* 384, 387

American Israel Public Affairs Committee (AIPAC) *1:* 231–232

American Lebanese Syrian Associated Charities (ALSAC) *2:* 384, 470

American Medical Association (AMA) *1:* 62

American Middle East Peace Research Institute *2:* 345

American Music Awards *1:* 9

American Top 40 2: 273, 275

American-Arab Anti-Discrimination Committee (ADC) *1:* 18, 24–25, 132, 228, *2:* 276, 330, 333, 345

And Not Surrender: American Poets on Lebanon 2: 346

Anka, Paul *1:* **48–54**, 48 (ill.), 50 (ill.)

Apollo Space Program *1:* 120 (ill.), 121

Appalachia *2:* 364

Arab American Institute *1:* 210

Arab-Israeli Conflict *1:* 23, 195, 205, *2:* 275, 402, 404

Arab storytelling *2:* 272

Arab-American Congress for Palestine *1:* 207

Arabic language *1:* 120, 208, *2:* 339, 376

Arabic music *1:* 49, 104–105

Arabs *1:* 23, *2:* 447–448

Arafat, Yasir *1:* 207, *2:* 405

Army, U.S. *1:* 113, 115, 144, 147, 172, 205, *2:* 272, 292, 312

Army Air Corps, U.S. *1:* 259

Assali, Nicholas S. *1:* **55–62**

Association of Arab American University Graduates (AAUG) *1:* 230

Astro Dynamics *2:* 452

Atiyeh Brothers *1:* 67

Atiyeh, Victor *1:* **63–67**, 63 (ill.), 65 (ill.)

Autism *1:* 160

Auto racing *2:* 355–60

B

Baalbek International Festival *1:* 91, 93–94

Baccarat *2:* 281

Barber, Samuel *1:* 137–138

Basic Instinct 2: 281

Basques *2:* 267

Baylor College of Medicine *1:* 114–115

The Beach Boys *1:* 106–107

Before the Flames 1: 13, 68, *2:* 342, 344–345

Begin, Menachem *1:* 89, 171, 175, 206

Bernstein, Leonard *1:* 91

Bible *1:* 70–71, 74

Big Night 2: 440–441

Bipolar disorder *2:* 306, 309

Bishallany, Antonio *1:* **68–74**, 68 (ill.)

Blatty, William *1:* **75–81**, 75 (ill.)

Blossom 2: 488

Bobby Rahal Foundation, The *2:* 361

Bonfire of the Vanities 1: 30

The Book of Khalid 1: 167, *2:* 371

Boston College Eagles *1:* 154–157

Bourjaily, Vance *1:* **82–89**, 82 (ill.)

Brian's Song 2: 487

Brill Among the Ruins 1: 88

British Columbia Lions *1:* 158

Brown, Jerry (Governor of California) *2:* 286

Buffalo Bills *1:* 159–160

Bulimia *1:* 10

Bush, George *1:* 35, *2:* 451, 454

C

Calgary Stampeders *1:* 158

Camp David Accords *1:* 171, 174-175

Canadian Football League (CFL) *1:* 152, 158

Capital of Solitude 2: 346

Car racing *2:* 355–60

Caring Program for Children *2:* 509

Carolco Pictures, Inc. *2:* 277–283

Carr, Bob *1:* 36

Carter, Jimmy *1:* 14, 174–175

Casey's Top 40 2: 275

Catholic *1:* 13, 40, 69, 70, 78, 163, *2:* 312, 343, 370, 382, 452, 465, 479

CDC (Centers for Disease Control and Prevention) *2:* 435

Center for Study of Responsive Law *2:* 320

Centers for Disease Control and Prevention (CDC) *2:* 435

Central Intelligence Agency (CIA) *1:* 191, *2:* 393–394

Chaib, Elie *1:* 90–94

Challenger Space Shuttle *2:* 299-303

Chamoun, Camille *2:* 392

Championship Auto Racing Teams (CART) *2:* 355, 357–358

Chess *2:* 419, 421-423

Chicago Bears *1:* 157

Chief of Protocol *2:* 396

Children of the Roojme 1: 15

Christianity *1:* 49, 68, *2:* 425

CIA (Central Intelligence Agency) *1:* 191, *2:* 393–394

CIO (Committee for Industrial Organization) *1:* 43–45

Circus, Hamid-Morton *1:* 198–199

Civil Rights Movement *1:* 262

Cliffhanger 2: 282

Clinton, Hillary Rodham *2:* 314

Clinton, William Jefferson *2:* 314, 321, 433, 438

Co-operative Health Federation of America (CHFA) *2:* 432

Cold War *1:* 46, 138

Committee for Industrial Organization (CIO) *1:* 43–45

Communism *1:* 45–46

Community Caring Program *2:* 509

Congressional Medal *2:* 470

Conrad, Joseph *2:* 401

Consumer Product Safety Act *2:* 320

Coppola, Francis Ford *1:* 27

Coptic *1:* 130, *2:* 411

Corey, Elias *1:* 95–101, 95 (ill.)

Cotton Bowl *1:* 157

Crossfire 2: 456

Cutthroat Island 2: 282

D

Dacron arteries *1:* 114

Dale, Dick *1:* 102–109, 102 (ill.), 104 (ill.), 107 (ill.)

The Danny Thomas Show 2: 469, 486

Darwish, Tiffany *2:* 491–497

Day, Fred Holland *1:* 165

Dead Poets Society 2: 488 (ill.), 489

DeBakey, Michael Ellis *1:* 110–116, 110 (ill.)

The Del-Tones *1:* 105

Department of Health and Human Services *2:* 433, 435, 438–439

Department of Housing and Urban Development (HUD) *2:* 435–436

"Diana" *1:* 48, 50

Discrimination *1:* 13, 23-25, 163, 257, 259-263, *2:* 275, 339, 342, 391, 402, 425, 430–431

Dole, Bob *2:* 321

Domingo, Placido *1:* 138

"Don't Eat the Yellow Snow" *2:* 514

Donahue, Phil *2:* 482

Doug Flutie Jr. Foundation for Autism *1:* 160

Drunk Driving *2:* 286–287

Druse *1:* 69

Dyslexia *2:* 348-350, 353

E

Easter Seal Society *2:* 361

Eastern Orthodox *1:* 40, *2:* 343

Eban, Abba *1:* 207

Egypt *1:* 117, 121, 127–128, 175, 206, *2:* 343

El-Baz, Farouk *1:* 117–125, 117 (ill.)

El Guindi, Fadwa *1:* 126–133, 126 (ill.), 131 (ill.)

Elias, Rosalind *1:* 134–140, 134 (ill.), 136 (ill.)

Emmy Awards *1:* 90, 94, 134, *2:* 307, 461, 469, 471, 483, 487, 489

Empty Nest 2: 309, 488

Engler, John *1:* 35–36

Erika 1: 138

Estevez, Emilio *1:* 10

Exorcism *1:* 76, 78

The Exorcist 1: 75, 79–80

F

FAA (Federal Aviation Administration) *1:* 189, 192–194

Family 2: 306

Farah, James *1:* 142–144

Farah, Mansour *1:* 141–145

Farah, William *1:* 142–144

Faris and Yamna Naff Arab American Collection *2:* 327

Farouk, King *1:* 118, *2:* 343

Farr, Jamie *1:* 146–151, 146 (ill.), 149 (ill.)

FBI (Federal Bureau of Investigation) *1:* 24, 77, 208–209, 228, 230–231

FDA (Food and Drug Administration) *2:* 435

FEC (Federal Elections Commission) *1:* 228, 232

Federal Aviation Administration (FAA) *1:* 189, 192–194

Federal Bureau of Investigation (FBI) *1:* 24, 77, 208–209, 228, 230–231

Federal Elections Commission (FEC) *1:* 228, 232

Feld, Irvin *1:* 51

First Blood 2: 279

Flutie, Darren *1:* 160

Flutie, Doug *1:* 152–161, 152 (ill.), 156 (ill.), 159 (ill.)

Food and Drug Administration (FDA) *2:* 435

Football *1:* 152–161, *2:* 384–389

Forever Your Girl 1: 9

Forman, Milos *1:* 29

Foster, Simone *1:* 187

Fox Broadcasting *2:* 407, 409

Freedom Foundation *1:* 139

Freedom of Information Act *2:* 320

G

Gaffney, Maureen "Mo" *2:* 329, 331

Gandhi, Mahatma *1:* 208

General Motors *2:* 319

Getty Oil *1:* 253–254

Gibran, Kahlil *1:* 162–170, 162 (ill.), 164 (ill.)

Goldberg, Whoopie *2:* 332

Golden Girls *2:* 488–489

Golden Globe Awards *1:* 29, 80, *2:* 461

Gorbachev, Mikhail *2:* 397

Governors *1:* 65, *2:* 453

Grammy Awards *1:* 134

Grape Leaves: A Century of Arab American Poetry 1: 16, *2:* 346

Grey Cup *1:* 158

Guggenheim Fellowship *1:* 97

Guinness Book of World Records 1: 250

Gulf War *2:* 338

H

Habibi 336, 337 (ill.)

Habib, Philip *1:* 171–177, 171 (ill.), 176 (ill.)

Haggar, Edmond *1:* 180, 182, 202, *2:* 386

Haggar, J(oseph) M(arion) *1:* 178–183, 178 (ill.)

Haggar, Joseph *1:* 181, 202, *2:* 386

Haje, Khrystyne *1:* 184–188, 184 (ill.)

Halaby, Najeeb *1:* 189–196, 189 (ill.), 194 (ill.)

Hamid Circus Royale *1:* 200

Hamid, George A., Jr. *1:* 197–203

Hamid-Morton Circus *1:* 198

Hanania, Raymond G. *1:* 204–211, 204 (ill.)

Hanks, Tom *1:* 6

Hansel and Gretel 1: 139

Haskell, Mary *1:* 166

Havel, Vaclav *2:* 516

Hazo, Samuel *1:* 212–218, 212 (ill.)

Headlee, Richard *1:* 35

Health and Human Services, Department of *2:* 433, 435, 438–439

Health care reform *2:* 314–315, 424, 429-431, 439

Heisman Trophy *1:* 152, 156

Hill, Peggy *2:* 329, 333

Horatio Alger Award *1:* 115

Hot Rats 2: 512

House of Representatives, U.S. *1:* 21, *2:* 363, 365, 453

Howar, A. Joseph *1:* 219–227

HUD (Department of Housing and Urban Development) *2:* 435–436

Humphrey, Hubert H. *2:* 384

Hunter College *2:* 436

I

I'll See You in My Dreams 2: 467

I'm Glad I Look Like a Terrorist 1: 204, 206, 210

"I Think We're Alone Now" *2:* 494

IBM Deep Blue *2:* 422

Ibn Saoud of Arabia: His People and His Land 2: 371

Immigration *1:* 33, 36–37, 60

Immigration and Naturalization Service (INS) *1:* 36, 60

Indianapolis 500 *2:* 355, 358

International Poetry Forum *1:* 217

Intifada *2:* 340, 404

Iran hostage crisis *1:* 14

Iran-Contra affair *2:* 314

Irving, Washington *2:* 369

Islam *1:* 130–131, *2:* 369, 403

Islamic Center *1:* 226 (ill.), 227

Israel *1:* 22, 175, 204–206, 209, 211, *2:* 336, 343, 366, 444–447, 449–450

J

Jabara, Abdeen *1:* 228–233, 228 (ill.)

Jabara, James *1:* 234–241, 234 (ill.), 236 (ill.)

Jackson Five *1:* 8

Jackson, Janet *1:* 6, 8

Jackson, Reggie *2:* 420

Jacobs, Amos; see Danny Thomas

Jacobs, Joseph J. *1:* 242–249

Jamail, Joseph, Jr. *1:* 250–256, 250 (ill.)

Jan & Dean *1:* 106

Jesus *1:* 73, 169

Jesus, The Son of Man 1: 169

Jews *1:* 23, 89, *2:* 425, 447, 448

JHS Engineering Company *2:* 453

Johns, Ralph *1:* 257–264, 257 (ill.), 261 (ill.)

Johnson, Lyndon B. *1:* 62, 173

Just the Way You Are 2: 308

K

Kamali, Norma *2:* 265–270, 265 (ill.)

Karpov, Anatoly *2:* 421

Kasem, Casey *2:* **271–276**, 271 (ill.)

Kasem, Kemal Amen; see Casey Kasem

Kasparov, Garry *2:* 422

Kassar, Mario *2:* **277–283**, 277 (ill.)

The Kathy & Mo Show 2: 329, 332

Kennedy, Jackie *2:* 394, 474

Kennedy, John F. *1:* 62, 88, *2:* 297, 474

Khaury, Herbert Buckingham; see Tiny Tim

Khomeini, Ayatollah Ruhollah *1:* 14

King of the Hill 2: 329, 333

King, Martin Luther, Jr. *1:* 208, 262

Kinko's *2:* 348, 352–353

Klinger, Corporal Maxwell Q. *1:* 146

Korean War *1:* 77, 113, 146, 150, 237–240, *2:* 505

Ku Klux Klan *1:* 41, *2:* 431

L

Labor unions *1:* 39, 42–43, 46, 142, *2:* 505–507, 509

Laker Girls *1:* 7

Last Action Hero 1: 30

Lauren, Ralph *1:* 1–2

Laurents, Arthur *1:* 91

Learning disabilities *2:* 348–350

Lebanon *1:* 22, 56, 89, 91, 111, *2:* 345, 366

Lebanon travel ban *1:* 33, *2:* 363, 366

Legion 1: 80

Lewine, Frances *2:* 474

Lewis, Carl *2:* 423

Lewis, John L. *1:* 43

LHASA (Logic and Heuristics Applied to Synthetic Analysis) *1:* 99

Liberty Bowl *1:* 155

Lightner, Candy *2:* **284–289**, 284 (ill.)

Little Darlings 2: 307

"Lonely Boy" *1:* 51

Los Angeles Film Critics Award *1:* 29

Los Angeles Lakers *1:* 6, 8

Lumpy Gravy 2: 512

M

Maari, Abu al-Ala al- *2:* 370

*M*A*S*H 1:* 146, 148–150

MADD (Mothers Against Drunk Driving) *2:* 284, 286–287

The Madman 1: 167

Make Room for Daddy 2: 463, 469

Maloof, Sam *2:* **290–295**, 290 (ill.)

Manic-depressive illness *2:* 306, 309

The Man Who Knew Kennedy 1: 87

Marines, U.S. *1:* 214, 251

Martin, Homer *1:* 45

McAuliffe, Christa *2:* **296–304**, 296 (ill.), 301 (ill.)

McGovern, George *1:* 21, *2:* 384

McNeil, Joe *1:* 260

McNichol, Kristy *2:* **305–310**, 305 (ill.)

Menotti, Gian-Carlo *1:* 137

Messengers of the Lost Batallion 2: 347

The Met *1:* 135, 137

Miami Dolphins *1:* 202, *2:* 382, 387

Michigan Republican Party *1:* 35

Middle East conflict *1:* 22–23, 171, 174–175, 189, 195, *2:* 275, 402, 404

Mighty Aphrodite 1: 30

Military *1:* 19–20, 64, 77, 85, 113, 115, 144, 147, 172, 191, 199, 206, 214, 234–241, 251, 259, *2:* 272, 292, 312, 383, 459, 505

"Misirlou" *1:* 105, 108

Missionary *1:* 68

Mr. Magoo 2: 275

Mitchell, George John *2:* **311–316**, 311 (ill.)

Mitchell, John *2:* 475

Mitchell, Martha *2:* 475

Modeling *1:* 185

Monsour, Richard; see Dick Dale

Moors *2:* 369

Mosque *1:* 220, 227

Mothers Against Drunk Driving (MADD) *2:* 284, 286–287

Mothers of Invention *2:* 512–515

Mountains of the Moon 2: 281

Mozart, Wolfgang Amadeus *1:* 29

MTV Video Music Awards *1:* 9

Mundt, Karl *1:* 21

Municiple Assistance Corporation (MAC) *2:* 435

Murdoch, Rupert *2:* 409

Music Box 2: 281

Muskie, Edmund *2:* 312

Muslim *1:* 130–131, 163, 220, 224, 227, *2:* 369, 403

Mussorgsk, Modest *2:* 346

The Myth of Ritual 1: 129

N

Nader, Ralph *2:* **317–323**, 317 (ill.)

Naff Arab American Collection *2:* 327–328

Naff, Alixa *2:* **324–328**, 324 (ill.)

Najimy, Kathy *2:* **329–333**, 329 (ill.), 331 (ill.)

The Name of the Rose 1: 30

NASA (National Aeronautics and Space Administration) *1:* 121, *2:* 299–300, 303

NASCAR (National Association for Stock Car Auto Racing) *2:* 359

Nasser, Gamal Abdel *1:* 118, *2:* 343–344, 412

National Aeronautics and Space Administration (NASA) *1:* 121, *2:* 299–300, 303

National Association for Stock Car Auto Racing (NASCAR) *2:* 359

National Association of Arab Americans *2:* 345

National Charities Information Bureau *2:* 287

National Endowment for the Humanities *2:* 326

National Football League (NFL) *1:* 157–159, *2:* 382, 384, 387

National Institutes of Health (NIH) *2:* 435

National Library of Medicine *1:* 115

National Medal of Science *1:* 115

National Museum of American History *2:* 327

National Organization for Women (NOW) *2:* 480

National Press Club *2:* 476

National Traffic and Motor Vehicle Safety Act *2:* 318

Navy, U.S. *1:* 19–20, 191, 199, *2:* 383, 459

Never in a Hurry: Essays on People and Places 2: 338–339

New England Patriots *1:* 157

New Jersey Generals *1:* 157

New York Metropolitan Opera *1:* 135, 137

NFL (National Football League) *1:* 157, 159

NIH (National Institutes of Health) *2:* 435

The Ninth Configuration 1: 80

Nixon, Richard *1:* 67, 231, *2:* 476

Nobel Prize *1:* 95, 98, 100, *2:* 405

North Atlantic Free Trade Agreement (NAFTA) *2:* 321

North Atlantic Treaty *1:* 192

North, Oliver *2:* 314

NOW (National Organization for Women) *2:* 480

Now Playing at Canterbury 1: 88

Nye, Naomi Shihab 2: 334–341, 334 (ill.)

O

O'Neil, John *2:* 386

Obie Awards *1:* 28, *2:* 332

Occupational Safety and Health Act *2:* 320

Olympics *2:* 421

OMO Norma Kamali *2:* 267

Only When I Laugh 2: 307

Orfalea, Gregory 2: 342–347

Orfalea, Paul 2: 348–354

Organic Chemistry *1:* 98, 100, 101

Orientalism 2: 402

Ottoman Empire *1:* 56, 69, 71, 96, *2:* 371, 425

P

Pahlavi, Mohammed Reza *1:* 14

Palestine *1:* 22, 23, 89, 111, 209, *2:* 336, 400, 405, 444–447, 449, 450

Palestine Aid Society *1:* 132

Palestine Liberation Organization (PLO) *1:* 206–207, *2:* 405

Palestine National Council (PNC) *2:* 403–405

Palestinian American Congress *1:* 210

Palestinian American Institute for Non-Violence *1:* 208

Pan Am (Pan American World Airways) *1:* 189, 194–195

Paramount Television *2:* 407

Parents Music Resource Center (PMRC) *2:* 510, 515

Parks, Rosa *1:* 262

A Parrot's Tale 2: 442

Patrick, Sister Mary *2:* 332

Patriotism *2:* 380

Paul Taylor Dance Company *1:* 90, 93

Peddlers *1:* 40, 204, 213, 222, 243, *2:* 324, 427

Penicillin *1:* 246

Penzoil Oil Company *1:* 253, 254

Perkins, Frances *1:* 42

Perkins, Maxwell *1:* 85, 87

PFLP (Popular Front for the Liberation of Palestine) *1:* 195

Phelan, Gerard *1:* 155

Pictures at an Exhibition 2: 346

The Pirate Movie 2: 308

PLO (Palestine Liberation Organization) *1:* 206–207, *2:* 405

PMRC (Parents Music Resource Center) *2:* 510, 515

PNC (Palestine National Council) *2:* 403–405

Poetry *1:* 162, 216–217, *2:* 338, 346, 370, 446–447

Popular Front for the Liberation of Palestine (PFLP) *1:* 195

Porter, J. A. *1:* 144

Post, George *2:* 426

Presidential Medal of Freedom *1:* 115

Presley, Elvis *1:* 203

The Prophet 1: 162, 168–169

Protestant Reformation *1:* 70

Public Citizen 2: 320

Pulitzer Prize *1:* 137, 204, 210

Pulp Fiction 1: 102

"Puppy Love" *1:* 51

"Put Your Head on My Shoulder" *1:* 51

Pyramids *1:* 117, 123–124

Q

Quayle, Dan *1:* 33, 35

The Question of Palestine 2: 404

R

Rabin, Yitzhak *2:* 405

Racial prejudice *1:* 13, 23–25, 230, 257, 259–262, *2:* 275, 333, 335, 339, 342, 391, 402, 425, 430, 431, 455, 473

Radius of Arab-American Writers (RAWI)*1:* 233

Rahal, Bobby 2: 355–362, 355 (ill.), 358 (ill.)

Rahall, Nick Joe II 2: 363–367, 363 (ill.)

Rambo: First Blood 2: 277, 279

Rambo: First Blood Part II 2: 279

RAWI (Radius of Arab-American Writers *1:* 233

Reagan, Ronald *1:* 35, 174, *2:* 299, 314, 390, 395–396

The Red Skelton Show 1: 147

Religious discrimination *1:* 163, 167

Remington Arms Company *1:* 253

Remote Sensing *1:* 122–123

Reuther, Walter *1:* 43, 45–46

Rihani, Ameen Ferris 2: 368–373, 368 (ill.)

The Ritz 1: 29

Rizk, Salom 2: 374–381

Robbie, Joseph *2:* 382–389, 382 (ill.), 385 (ill.)

Robbins, Jerome *1:* 91

Roosevelt, Selwa *2:* 390–398, 390 (ill.), 395 (ill.)

Rugs, Iranian *1:* 4, 64

S

S&P 500 Index *2:* 414

Sadat, Anwar *1:* 171, 175

Said, Edward *2:* 399–406, 399 (ill.)

St. Jude Children's Research Hospital *1:* 183, *2:* 384, 463, 469 470–471, 489

Salhany, Lucie *2:* 407–410, 407 (ill.)

Salieri, Antonio *1:* 29

Sarofim, Fayez Shalaby *2:* 411–416

Scarpacci, Antonio *2:* 440–441

Schwarzenegger, Arnold *2:* 279

Scooby Doo 2: 275

Seirawan, Yasser *2:* 417–423, 417 (ill.)

Senate, U.S. *1:* 21, 33, 35, *2:* 313, 315, 453

Shadid, Michael *2:* 424–432

Shah of Iran *1:* 14

Shakespeare, William *1:* 91

Shalala, Donna *2:* 433–439, 433 (ill.), 437 (ill.)

Shalhoub, Tony *2:* 440–443, 440 (ill.)

Shammas, Anton *2:* 444–450, 444 (ill.)

Sharples, Mel *2:* 458, 461

Sheik Yerbouti 2: 514

Shriners *1:* 199

Shula, Don *2:* 389

The Siege 2: 442

Sister Act 2: 329, 332

Sister Mary Patrick *2:* 332

Sit-in *1:* 257, 259–261

Sitti's Secrets 2: 338

Six Day War *1:* 13, 205, 206, 230, *2:* 336, 402

Smithsonian Institution *1:* 122, 130, *2:* 327

Soap 2: 488

Sondheim, Stephen *1:* 91

Speaking in Tongues 1: 94

Spellbound 1: 10

Sphinx *1:* 123

Stallone, Sylvester *2:* 279

Star Trek: Deep Space Nine 1: 132

Star Trek Voyager 2: 410

Stargate 2: 282

Steel Pier *1:* 200-202, 201 (ill.)

Stills 1: 215

Strikes *1:* 43, 44, 142

Sununu, John Henry *2:* 451–457, 451 (ill.)

Super Bowl *2:* 389

Superfriends 2: 275

Surf music *1:* 103, 104

Surfer's Choice 1: 105

Sweatshop Law *2:* 269

Synthetic Organic Chemistry *1:* 98–101

Syria *1:* 206, *2:* 343, 345, 366

Syrian Yankee 2: 374

T

Taft-Hartley Act *1:* 46,

Tangerine Bowl *1:* 155

Tayback, Vic *2:* 458–462, 458 (ill.), 460 (ill.)

Taylor, Paul *1:* 90, 93

Terminator 2 2: 277, 281, 282 (ill.)

Terrell, Ernie *1:* 202

Terrorism *1:* 194–195, 206, 208, 230, 231

That Girl 2: 481

Thermal Research *2:* 453

Thomas, Danny *2:* 463–471, 463 (ill.), 468 (ill.)

Thomas, Helen *2:* 472–477, 472 (ill.)

Thomas, Marlo *2:* 478–484, 478 (ill.), 482 (ill.)

Thomas, R. J. *1:* 45

Thomas, Tony *2:* 485–490, 485 (ill.)

Tiffany *2:* 491–497, 491 (ill.), 495 (ill.)

Tiny Tim *2:* 498–503, 498 (ill.), 500 (ill.)

Tiny Tim's Second Album 2: 501

"Tiptoe Through the Tulips" *2:* 498

Tobin, George *2:* 492–494, 496

The Tonight Show with Johnny Carson 2: 501

Tony Awards *1:* 135

Toronto Argonauts *1:* 159

Total Recall 2: 277

Travel ban; Lebanon *1:* 33, *2:* 363, 366

Tribal Thunder 1: 108

Trilateral Treaty in the Animal Kingdom 2: 370

Twelfth Night 1: 30

Tyson, Mike *2:* 423

U

UAW (United Automobile Workers) *1:* 39, 43–46, *2:* 504-509

Until I'm Not Here Anymore 1: 215

United Automobile Workers (UAW) *1:* 39, 43–46, *2:* 504–509

United Mine Workers *1:* 43

United Paramount Network (UPN) *2:* 410

United Press International (UPI) *2:* 472, 474

United States Football League (USFL) *1:* 157

United States House of Representatives *1:* 21 *2:* 363, 365, 453

United States Information Agency *2:* 339, 435

United States Senate *1:* 21, 33, 35, *2:* 313, 315, 453

University of Wisconsin at Madison *2:* 436

Unsafe at Any Speed 2: 317–318

Unser, Al, Jr. *2:* 360

UPI (United Press International) *2:* 472, 474

UPN (United Paramount Network) *2:* 410

USFL (United States Football League) *1:* 157

V

Vajna, Andrew *2:* 278, 280, 283

Vanessa 1: 137–139

Verdi, Giuseppe *1:* 138

Veronica's Closet 2: 329, 333

The Very Fall of the Sun 1: 215

Veterans Administration Medical Center System *1:* 113

Vietnam War *1:* 62, 113, 173, 241

The Violated 1: 87–88

W

Walt Disney Studios *2:* 488

Watergate *1:* 67, *2:* 475

We're Only in It for the Money 2: 512

West Side Story 1: 91

Whitehead, Charles *1:* 69–71

Wholesome Meat Act *2:* 320

Wings 2: 440–441

Witt/Thomas/Harris Productions *2:* 488–489

Women's Movement *2:* 480

World War I *1:* 42, 55–56, 235, *2:* 372, 400

World War II *1:* 85, 110, 113, 144, 172, 191, 199–200, 205, 235–236, 246, 251, *2:* 292, 346, 383, 467

X

The X Files 2: 441

Y

Yakhoob, Muzyad; see Danny Thomas

Yemen *2:* 343

Yokich, Stephen *2:* 504–509, 504 (ill.)

You Are What You Eat 2: 500

Yunus, Ibn *1:* 122

Z

Zappa, Frank *2:* 510–517, 510 (ill.), 513 (ill.)